Wellington's Commander of Cavalry

Wellington's Commander of Cavalry

The Early Life and Military Career of
Stapleton Cotton

ILLUSTRATED

The Right Hon. Mary, Viscountess Combermere
and
W. W. Knollys

With a Short Biography of Lord Combermere
by Alexander Innes Shand

LEONAUR

Wellington's Commander of Cavalry
The Early Life and Military Career of Stapleton Cotton,
by The Right Hon. Mary, Viscountess Combermere and W. W. Knollys
With a Short Biography of Lord Combermere
by Alexander Innes Shand

ILLUSTRATED

First published under the title
Memoirs and Correspondence of Field-Marshal Viscount Combermere

Leonaur is an imprint of Oakpast Ltd

Copyright in this form © 2018 Oakpast Ltd

ISBN: 978-1-78282-760-3 (hardcover)
ISBN: 978-1-78282-761-0 (softcover)

http://www.leonaur.com

Publisher's Notes

Contents

Preface to the Original Complete Edition   9

Origin of the Family   11

Prepares for the Army   23

Capture of Seringpatam   34

Colonel Cotton's Marriage   64

The Peninsular War, 1808, 1809, and 1810   80

Combat of the Coa   108

Battle of Fuentes d'Onor   130

Fall of Ciudad Rodrigo   151

Wellington's Advance Against Marmont   174

Cotton Recovers, and Rejoins the Army   190

Escape of Napoleon from Elba and Renewal of the War   207

Lord Combermere: A Short Military Biography   221

Who is the happy warrior, who is he,
That every man in arms should wish to be?
It is the generous spirit who, when brought
Among the tasks of real life, hath wrought
Upon the plan that pleased his boyish thought;
Whose high endeavours are an inward light
That makes the path of duty always bright.
He who, though thus endowed, as with a sense
And faculty for storm and turbulence,
Is yet a soul whose master being leans
To home-felt pleasure and to gentle scenes. ,
Who, not content that former worth stands fast,
Looks forward, persevering, to the last.
This is the happy warrior, this is he,
That every man in arms should wish to be.

Wordsworth.

COMBERMERE ABBEY

Preface to the Original Complete Edition

In offering these *Memoirs* to the public, the authors wish to take the opportunity of expressing their thanks to the various individuals by whose assistance they have been enabled to bring to a conclusion a work upon which for many months past they have been constantly engaged. To General Sir Thomas Brotherton, K.C.B., Lieutenant-General Lord de Ros, Lieutenant-General the Hon. Sir Edward Oust, K.H., Colonel Boyd, Colonel Tompkinson. Colonel Luard, Colonel and Captain Tonnochy, to whom they are indebted for much valuable information, they particularly desire to render their grateful acknowledgments. With such assistance, in addition to that derived from the private papers of the deceased general, and other sources of information to which they had access, the authors trust that the volumes which they now submit to the judgment of their readers will be found to contain a comprehensive view of the public and private life of one of England's most distinguished soldiers.

CHAPTER 1

Origin of the Family

Stapleton Cotton, the second son of Sir Robert Salusbury Cotton, Bart., M.P. for Cheshire, was born on the 14th November, 1773, at Llewenny Hall, in Denbighshire, where Sir Robert resided till, on the death of his father, he took possession of Combermere Abbey. The Llewenny estates had become the property of the family in 1684, by the marriage of an ancestor with Hester, the only child and heiress of Sir John Salusbury; but the Cotton possessions were in Cheshire, and the Cotton race was essentially Saxon. Their seat, previous to the Conquest, was at Coton, in Shropshire, where Sir Hugh Cotton, in the reign of King John, married Elizabeth Hammond, of Titley, county Chester.

After several intermediate successors, George Cotton married Mary Ongley in 1530. He was Esquire of the Body to King Henry VIII., Privy Councillor, Steward of Bromfield Gate, Chirk, and Chirkland, and Vice-Chamberlain to Prince Edward, afterwards Edward VI. This Sir George Cotton had an only son, and four daughters, one of whom, Mary, married, first, Edward Stanley, Earl of Derby, and afterwards Henry Grey, Earl of Kent.

Sir George Cotton's youngest brother, Richard, of Bedlehampton, Hants, and Warblington, Sussex, attendant at Court in the reign of Edward VI., outlived that monarch, and was ancestor to a Richard Cotton, born in Hampshire, and educated at the Free School of Guilford, who became a commoner of Magdalen College in 1566, or thereabout. He married, about 1571, a lady named Patience, by whom he had nineteen children. On the 12th November, 1598, he was consecrated Bishop of Salisbury. He was godson to Queen Elizabeth when she was the Lady Elizabeth, who, as it is reported, usually said that she had blessed many godsons, but that now this godson should bless her.

11

He gave way to fate 16th May, 1615, and is buried at Salisbury. (*Athenae Oxonienses*).

To Sir George Cotton was granted the abbey and lands of Combermere by Henry VIII., at the abolition of monastic orders in 1533; and the deed of endowment, with the appended great seal, is still in good preservation at the abbey. The first grant of the land, and endowment of the abbey, was made in 1133, by Hugh Malbank, Earl of Nantwich, and Petronel his wife. The objects of their religious zeal were a brotherhood of Benedictine monks, who thus obtained an endowment of very considerable value and importance. The Abbot of Combermere at once became an influential personage, ruling over a large community, and, with the Abbot of Vale Royal, sat in the Parliament of the county palatine of Cheshire. Amongst the documents extant in Cheshire connected with the Abbey of Combermere, few are of great interest. We shall only give one, which is a decree of William Wilkesey, Archbishop of Canterbury, empowering the Abbot of Combermere to rescind a sentence of excommunication on a certain Richard Donne:—

Commission from William Wilkesey, Archbishop of Canterbury, to the Abbots of Combermere and Vale Royal, *a.d.* 1369, to the venerable and discreet men the Abbots of the Monastery of Combermere and Vale Royal, of the Cistercian order, in the diocese of Lichfield. Health, &c. &c. &c.

Whereas, Richard Donne, of the parish of Athenton, in the aforesaid diocese, now dead, was lately, by the authority of our predecessor the Lord John De Stratford, of good memory, formerly Archbishop of Canterbury, involved in a sentence of the greater excommunication, on account, as we have heard, of the carrying off by him, together with others his accomplices, of the Lady De Beche; under which sentence of excommunication the same Richard, overtaken by death, departed without absolution; we, therefore, by the tenor of these presents, grant full power to you, conjointly and separately, provided his penitence whilst living was manifested to you by evident signs, to absolve his body in due form, and to do whatever may be necessary and proper with respect to the foregoing. Given at Lambeth, the twenty-second day of February, in the above year.

William Wilkesey.

A curious fact relating to Combermere is thus recorded by Camden:—

> A mile from the abbey in time of mind sunk a piece of a hill, having trees on it, and after in that part sprang out water, and the abbot there began to make salt, but the men of the Wyches composed with the abbey that there should be no salt made there. The pit yet hath salt water, but much filth has fallen into it.

This pit still exists near the lake of Combermere, and the neighbouring peasants persist in declaring that it is fathomless.

Although the exterior of the abbey has been much altered since its construction in 1133, some parts of the interior remain in their original state, and the large rafters which cross the ceilings of many rooms, as well as some walls five feet thick, attest the solidity of the original structure. The refectory, converted into a library, is adorned with old oak carvings, and at one end of it remains a balustrade, which formerly enclosed a space on the floor above, from whence the monks could be seen at their meals. In the centre of this gallery a reading-desk shows where one of their number read aloud during the times of refection. The high pointed walnut roof, resembling that of Westminster Abbey, still in perfect preservation, is above a ceiling added by the Cottons to render the room more habitable. The refectory has also been reduced in length, and an apartment made of the excluded part. In it William III. once slept on his way to Ireland, a circumstance to which Mrs. Savage alludes in her *Life*, published at the time:—

> The year 1690 is memorable for King William's expedition against Ireland, and the battle he gained at the Boyne. Friday, June 6th, King William came to Whitchurch, in his way to Ireland. He lay that night at Combermere; thence, next day to Peel, to Colonel Whelleys; thence to Hoylate, to take ship. I have earnestly prayed God that His blessing may go with him.

In 1795, when Sir Robert Cotton was making some additions in the abbey, he found a stone tablet, on which was this inscription:—

> Master Richard Cotton and his sons three,
> Both for their pleasure and commoditie,
> This building did edifie,
> In fifteen hundred and sixty-three.

Richard Cotton had, apparently, only made some additions to the original structure.

This Richard Cotton, the son and successor of Sir George, the grantee of the abbey, married Mary Mainwaring, and was in his turn succeeded by his son George, who married Mary, daughter of Sir George Bromley, chief justice of Chester. His successor was a son, Thomas, who married, first, Elizabeth, daughter of Sir Hugh Calveley; second, Frances, daughter of Lord Kilmoray. By the latter lady he had a son. Sir Robert was created a baronet in 1677, and represented Cheshire in Parliament for thirty-six years. He added largely to the wealth and importance of the family by his marriage with Hester, daughter and heiress of Sir John Salusbury, of Llewenny, in Denbighshire. She brought with her considerable estates, and the name of Salusbury was prefixed to the name of Cotton from this time until the sale of the Welsh property by Lord Combermere's father in 1794. In 1685 Sir Robert was committed to the Tower on a charge of treasonable correspondence with the Electress Sophia. The following is a copy of the warrant for his committal:—

Robert Earl of Sunderland,
Baron Spencer, &c. &c.

These are in His Majesty's name to authorise and require you to receive into your custodie the bodie of Sir Robert Cotton, of Cheshire, herewith sent to you, for dangerous and treasonable practices. Keep him safe and close, till he be discharged by due course of law, for which this shall be your warrant. Given at the Court at Windsor, the 23rd daye of September, 1685,

Sunderland.

To the Lieutenant of the Tower.

By an act of kindness, unusual on the part of James II., Sir Robert was allowed the society of one of his family within the Tower. He chose his fourth son, Thomas, a boy of eleven years old, and beguiled the tedium of captivity by teaching him to read. Lady Cotton, not being allowed to share her husband's imprisonment, used to walk every day at a certain hour on Tower Hill, till she learnt by an agreed signal hung out from a window, that her husband was well. After a short delay Sir Robert was released, the charge made against him having been found to be groundless. That there were, however, letters—although, perhaps, not treasonable—from the Electress Sophia, we learn from Mrs. Piozzi, who, when a child, saw some of this correspondence. She was too young to recollect anything about the contents, but was afterwards told that they were full of Latin quotations. In accordance with

14

what seems to have been a family mania for the destruction of papers. Lord Combermere's father burnt the letters in question.

When Thomas Cotton reached the age of seventeen his father received a most extraordinary proposal from Admiral Sir George Herbert, afterwards Lord Torrington, which he seems to have accepted without the slightest misgiving as to its morality. Sir George was uncle and guardian to Philadelphia, daughter and heiress of Sir Thomas Lynch, twice Governor and Captain-General of Jamaica, who had died possessed of large estates in the West Indies, a share in which Sir George coveted. He, therefore, agreed to marry his ward, though only thirteen years old, to young Thomas Cotton, on condition that his consent was purchased by a portion of the property. The marriage actually took place, and the terms were duly carried out. Eventually Thomas, though only a fourth son, succeeded, through the death of his elder brothers, to the title and estates, but did not enjoy them long, dying in 1715, after only a three years' tenure. His widow shortly afterwards married a Mr. King, on whom she bestowed the whole of her large fortune, to the entire exclusion of her nine sons and six daughters.

In the parish register of Wrenbury Church, near Combermere, the birth of a young King is recorded, who soon after was christened there by the name of Cotton; a novel compliment to the memory of the lady's first husband. Sir Thomas. Lady Cotton survived her second partner for some years, and lived at East Hyde, a fine place in Hertfordshire, where her four magnificent horses were the objects of great attention to her little niece, Hester Salusbury, afterwards Mrs. Piozzi. The stately old lady was in the habit of driving about in the neighbourhood of her country place in a ponderous antiquated coach drawn by four black horses, as solemnly grand as herself. The animals were the delight of her little niece, who, in her autobiography, thus fondly alludes to them:—

At East Hyde I learned to love horses; and when my mother hoped I was gaining health by the fresh air, I was kicking my heels in a corn-bin, and learning to drive of the old coachman, who, like everybody else, small and great, delighted in taking me for a pupil. Grandmamma kept four great ramping war horses, *chevaux entiers*, for her carriage, with immense long manes and tails, which we buckled and combed; and when, after long practice, I showed her and my mother how two of them, poor Colonel and Peacock, would lick my hand for a lump of sugar or fine white bread, much were they amazed; and more, when my skill in guiding them round the court-yard on the break could no longer be doubted or denied, though strictly prohibited for the future.

Sir Thomas was succeeded by his son, Sir Robert, who married Lady Betty Tollemache, daughter of the Earl of Dysart, and dying in 1748 without issue, was succeeded by his brother, Lynch. He married his cousin. Miss Cotton, of Ethwall, and died in 1775, leaving behind him, besides other issue, Robert, who succeeded him, and was the father of Lord Combermere; Roland, an Admiral in the Royal Navy, and father of General Sir Willoughby Cotton, G.C.B., at one time Commander-in-Chief at Bombay; Lynch; George, Dean of Chester; Thomas; William; Richard, an officer in the army, killed in action; Henry; and Calveley, Captain 1st Life Guards, who married Miss Lockwood, by whom he had Major-General Sir Sidney Cotton, K.C.B., Admiral Frank Cotton, and Major-General Sir Arthur Cotton, Kt., Madras Engineers, celebrated for his irrigation labours in India.

As Lord Combermere was the representative of the Salusburys as well as of the Cottons, a few particulars concerning the former may not be considered out of place here. The general interest, moreover, which the ordinary reader cannot fail to feel in a sketch of this once powerful house, will in many cases assume a more individual character, for in Wales and on its borders the families which claim descent from the Salusburys are very numerous. For many of the details we shall here give we are indebted to Mrs. Piozzi, who, proud of her maiden name, and her consequent connection with the Cottons, makes constant allusions to both families in her autobiography.

The Salusburys claimed to have sprung from Adam de Saltzburg, a son of Alexander, Sovereign Duke of Bavaria. Adam came to England with William the Conqueror, and in 1070 obtained, as the reward of his valour, an estate in Lancashire, afterwards called Salusbury Court. When Mrs. Piozzi went to Saltzburg, she satisfied the heralds there of her descent from the above-named worthy, and was treated by them with great honour in consequence. After several intervening successors came Henry Salusbury, who was knighted on the field of battle by Richard Coeur de Lion, for having with his own hand taken three noble Saracens in the Holy Land. The king, as a lasting testimony of his valour, allowed him to carry three crescents in addition to the old

Bavarian lion, as coat armour.

On his return home, he married a Welsh lady and settled in Denbighshire, where he built a house which he called Llewenny Hall; from *llew*, a lion, and *ny*, for us. Upon the highest tower of this house he set up a brazen lion. This worthy is the hero of a popular Welsh ballad, and is still known to the harpers of the principality by the name of "Black Sir Harry." During the Wars of the Roses, a descendant and namesake fought on the side of the Yorkists at the Battle of Barnet. Sparing a vanquished enemy on that occasion, the latter, looking on Sir Henry's device, threw himself at his feet and exclaimed, "*Sat est prostrâsse leoni!*" These words were at once adopted by the Salusburys as a motto, and have been retained as such ever since. It is curious to find Sir Henry fighting in the ranks of the Yorkist party, for most Welshmen were Lancastrians.

Some hundred years later we find a Sir John Salusbury of Llewenny Hall marrying a ward of Queen Elizabeth's, Katherine of Berayne, then only fourteen years old. She was an heiress, and a descendant in the fifth generation from Owen Tudor and the Princess Katherine of France. On Sir John's death, in 1567, his widow followed him to the grave, and in going to church was escorted by Sir Richard Clough, the owner of property in the neighbourhood, formerly in the service of Sir Thomas Ghresham, and at that time a very eminent merchant. In returning home after the burial, she was attended by a young gentleman of property, named Morris Wynn. He perceiving the widow to be not very inconsolable, and fired by her charms, profited by the opportunity to whisper a tale of love into her ears, and finally asked her to be his wife. She, by no means startled at this oddly-timed proposal, civilly declined his offer, saying that she had accepted a similar one from Clough on her way to church; but, probably observing young Wynn to be much cast down at her refusal, and being a large-hearted, compassionate woman, she sought to console the rejected lover by the assurance that if she survived Clough, Wynn should be her third husband.

This promise she duly kept, when three years later she was a second time left a widow. Again, a third time, did she outlive her husband, and a fourth time became a wife, marrying a Mr. Edward Thelwall, also a Denbighshire man. This husband survived her. So numerous and influential were the descendants of this Katherine of Berayne, that she was long known by the title of *Mam Cymry*, or Mother of Wales. By her first husband. Sir John Salusbury, Katherine had a son, who was

17

called Sir John the Strong, and who married Ursula Stanley, a natural daughter of Henry, Earl of Derby. Many letters from the latter to his son-in-law are preserved, to insert them here would retard the progress of the narrative. Sir John the Strong was succeeded by Sir Henry, whose son and successor, Sir Thomas, is mentioned in *Athen. Oxon.* as "being distinguished by his natural genius" for poetry. Sir Thomas was followed by Sir John, with whose daughter Hester, who married Sir Robert Cotton, the main line of the Salusbury family terminated.

Sir Robert Salusbury Cotton, Lord Combermere's father, took his degree at Cambridge, and married, in 1767, Frances, daughter and heiress of Colonel Stapleton, uncle to Sir Thomas Stapleton, afterwards Lord Le Despencer. Sir Robert represented the county of Cheshire, in the Tory interest, for thirty years. His eldest son Robert, born in 1768, died in 1799, of an inflammatory attack, brought on by exposure in an open boat at Weymouth. Four daughters and three sons were his juniors; the eldest of the former, Penelope, married Viscount Kilmorey, whose estate in Shropshire, Shavington, joined that of Combermere. There was a disparity of twenty years between Frances Cotton and her husband, but they were buried the same day, as, overcome by grief at her loss, he survived her death but a week, and was thus quickly reunited in death to her from whom in life he could not bear separation.

William Cotton, the third son of this large family, educated at Oxford, took orders and held the family living of Audlem, in Cheshire, and that of Adderley, in Shropshire, together with the private chaplaincy of Burlydam, where a place of worship for the Cotton family had been built and endowed by one of their ancestors.

The second daughter, Penelope, expired suddenly at an early age, and the third, Hester, lived till 1845, and died unmarried. Sir Robert's youngest son, Lynch, entered the army, and while serving in the 23rd Welsh Fusiliers during the Flemish campaign, was taken prisoner at Ostend. He subsequently commanded the 17th Light Dragoons, and having gone with them to India, died at Calcutta. His widow, Mrs. Cotton, married General, afterwards the Honourable, Sir William Lumley, son to the Earl of Scarborough.

The youngest of Sir Robert Cotton's children, Sophia, married Sir Harry Mainwaring, of Peover Hall, Cheshire, father of the present baronet.

Soon after the birth of Stapleton, who was Sir Robert's second son and fifth child, his father removed, on succeeding to the title, from the old Salusbury seat, Llewenny, to Combermere. At the former place the heir-apparent mostly resided; and it was not till his father Sir Lynch's death that Sir Robert established himself in Cheshire. Although passionately devoted to hunting and rural pursuits, he had, besides, other tastes, of a military character; and the disturbances in France a few years later inspired him with the patriotic spirit which caused at that time so many country gentlemen to leave their comfortable homes and train themselves to arms. On settling at Combermere Abbey, Sir Bobber Cotton, with that hospitality which is proverbially Cheshire, opened his house to his neighbours and constituents, receiving them at all times in the frank, unceremonious manner which was characteristic of the man. His table was daily surrounded by old friends of the family, who thronged the house and partook of its good cheer on the plea of political support and neighbourly attachment. In these days, we can scarcely realise the requirements of electioneering partisans ambitious of the social attentions which formerly condemned the resident county member to an incessant reception of guests.

Perhaps, also, when the difficulties of transit rendered county intercourse a matter of trouble and time, people were willing to suffer the encroachments of inferior neighbours rather than live entirely without any society. Sir Robert Cotton's hospitality was by no means grudgingly dispensed, however much it might exceed the limits that his family considered desirable. They, on their parts, were always at liberty to invite any chosen companions of their own age. Even the domestics were permitted to receive their guests; and as the establishment was very large, and the servants' connections lived on the estate, as farmers or labourers, it may readily be inferred that their department was not the least crowded in the house. Sir Robert likewise kept a large hunting establishment, and, of course, held open house for his companions "in the field," for whose horses stable accommodation was always liberally provided.

There seems to have been but little ambition in the Cotton family: a deficiency arising perhaps from the love of rural pursuits, field sports, and country sociability. Their even course of life was only occasionally interrupted by a periodical sojourn in London during the sitting of Parliament. Indeed, so thoroughly did the entire family at Combermere devote themselves to acts of hospitality and works of charity, that many who benefited by both did so as a matter of course, until the poor on the estate at last came to consider the gifts received as a right, openly expressing their conviction that some deed, by which the property was held, enforced the periodical distribution of alms and food.

When Lord Combermere's father succeeded to the title and estates, he found the latter much encumbered. His uncle, Sir Robert, had been very extravagant, and his father, blessed with a patriarchal family of fifteen children, had considerably added to the burdens of the estate. Sir Robert, being a bad man of business, and shrinking from the trouble of investigating his affairs, determined to release himself from his difficulties by a sacrifice of the Salusbury estates in Denbighshire. Without apprising his family of this intention, he sold the Welsh property to Mr. Fitzmaurice, a brother of Lord Shelburne's, at the very inadequate price of £110,000. Llewenny and Beraine were some years afterwards transferred to Lord Dinorben, for the sum of £280,000.

Indeed, there is no doubt that Sir Robert's easy disposition, and his anxiety to conclude the bargain before it came to the knowledge of his relatives, conduced to the sacrifice of a fine house and estate for an amount very inferior to their real value. His desire to hear no more on the subject, even prevented the removal of some fine old portraits of the Salusburys, by first-rate artists, which, with a collection of rare coins, books, and armour, long in possession of the family, passed with the property into the hands of Mr. Fitzmaurice. It appears that Sir Robert, after all, did not escape the trouble which he so much dreaded, for it was a long time before he received the purchase money of the property. Mr. Fitzmaurice referred him to his brother, Lord Shelburne, the late Lord Lansdowne's father, to whom he had lent a large sum, which he now required to discharge his debt to Sir Robert. It was not till Lord Shelburne became minister that the money was paid. Lord Shelburne, it is well known, realised a large fortune by speculations which his knowledge of government secrets rendered successful. After one of these transactions Sir Robert Cotton received the amount of his sale.

It is somewhat significant that about this time Sir Robert was offered a peerage by Lord Shelburne, which he without hesitation declined, declaring that he preferred being a county member to taking his place at the bottom of the peerage. This honour had been refused, in the reign of Queen Anne, by Sir Robert Salusbury Cotton, when the head of the family represented Cheshire and returned the eldest son for Denbigh. The same feeling then prompted a similar rejection. Soon after the family had departed for London, in 1774, Mrs. Thrale came into the neighbourhood of Llewenny, and in Lady Cotton's absence visited the children, bringing with her Queeny, her eldest daughter, afterwards Lady Keith. The following letter was written by her to Lady Cotton on the subject of this interview.

Gwaynynnog, 1st Sept., 1774.

Dear Madam,—I am this moment returned from a drive to Llewenny, where I saw your children, with emotions not unlike those I expect to experience at the sight of my own. They are all perfectly well, and have never had a complaint, as the servants told me, since you left them, I asked the eldest if he wished for your return. 'Not much,' says he; 'for if she should not come back at all, till I am grown up, I shall then set out on my travels, and go to see her.' Guess if I could help giving him a kiss for such an answer.

The girls were running on the lawn with Rathbone, but Bob was getting his lesson upstairs, nor could any inclination to play with his cousin induce him to quit it for a moment. Hetty, in whom you know I take a particular interest, looks not only well but blooming, and Stapleton has come on visibly since we parted; his stays grow tight over the breast, I see, and I advised his maid to put in a gore, as nothing can be more against your liking than such confinement, I am sure. Fanny clung to me so kindly and kissed my Queeny so often, that I gave leave she should dine with them, and accordingly they all sat down in great felicity to a shoulder of mutton and potatoes, with bread pudding for the little ones.

I must add that the nursery was nicely clean, and everything just as you would have had it, if you had been there. Mrs. Rathbone has heard that the smallpox is somewhere across the river, but I believe there is no danger; nothing can be more healthy, or more lively, or more lovely than they are, and there is not a heavy eye amongst them.

And now let me beg pardon for this tiresome letter, though I think the subject will excuse me, too, as one always wishes not only for a good report of one's children, but a particular one; and I shall add nothing from myself, but that I have the honour to be, with great affection. Madam,

Your most obedient servant,

Hester S. Thrale.

In the earlier years of her life, Mrs. Piozzi, then Hester Salusbury, lived much at Combermere Abbey, and continued on intimate terms with the family till her second marriage with Piozzi. This imprudent union offended all her relations, and none more than the Cottons, who from that day declined her acquaintance. She brought Dr. Johnson with her into Cheshire in 1774, and Mr. Hay ward tells us that Mrs. Cotton—for Lord Combermere's father had not yet inherited the baronetcy—"found Johnson, despite his rudeness, at times delightful, having a manner peculiar to himself in relating anecdotes that could not fail to attract both old and young. Her impression was that Mrs. Thrale was very vexatious in wishing to engross all his attention, which annoyed him much." (Hester Salusbury married first Mr. Thrale, and on his death Mr. Piozzi, an Italian singer).

In some letters of Lady Cotton to her sister. Miss Stapleton, her godson Stapleton's healthy and vigorous infancy is alluded to. He, as well as his brother and sisters, was nursed at home, although the practice of sending an infant out "to walks" in the cottage of a peasant nurse was still prevalent in the country districts of England. Stapleton's uncles had been thus reared "from the month," but the custom had somewhat gone out of fashion, and he was therefore exempted from a similar destination.

Chapter 2

Prepares for the Army

Stapleton, in his eighth year, was sent to Audlem, a small market town within five miles of Combermere Abbey, to attend a grammar-school endowed by a benevolent individual one hundred years ago. Some of the neighbouring gentry used to place their younger sons there, either for the sake of cheap education, or with the mistaken notion of keeping them at an early age near home. Stapleton was consigned to the inefficient tuition of the Rev. William Salmon, head-master of this establishment. (He was also chaplain of Sir Robert's private chapel beyond the park gates). Stapleton being the favourite child of his father, a pony was sent every Saturday to bring him home, where he remained till the following Monday, when the ride back encroached on the morning studies and unsettled him for the afternoon lessons. Vernon, afterwards Archbishop of York, was his schoolfellow at this insignificant place.

Persons who recollected Stapleton in childhood retained a lively impression of his good looks and pleasant manners, of his attention to old and kindness to young people, and of his universal popularity. Full of fun and frolic, lie constantly got into scrapes from courting risks and attempting exploits which more often terrified than amused his female relations, whose fears acting on his kind disposition frequently terminated the rash performances. Otherwise ardent and impatient in character, there was never any delay in carrying out his boyish projects, always so quickly conceived and accomplished that he was called "Young Rapid" by the family.

Stapleton always expressed much regret at having been sent to such a school as that of Audlem, where he was neither taught judiciously nor trained to those habits of application which are the most valuable of all acquirements in early life. During the holidays, French and drawing were alone thought of at Combermere, there being no time for other studies; for the mornings were occupied by hunting and shooting, into which pursuits Sir Robert delighted to initiate his young sons. Stapleton justified his father's preference by being the foremost in these pastimes, and always the most eager and untiring of the party.

After remaining at the Audlem school for three years, Stapleton was sent to Westminster, where he was placed in the fourth form under Dr. Dodd. Robert Cotton, his eldest brother, had at that time just commenced his college course at Cambridge, after leaving Westminster, where he had Sir Francis Burdett and Lord Titchfield, afterwards Duke of Bedford, for schoolfellows. The late Marquis of Lansdowne was still at Westminster when Stapleton commenced his studies there, and, as Lord Henry Petty, was remarkable for the reserve and coldness of his manner. The late Field-Marshal Lord Strafford, then known as Jack Byng, the poet Southey, and Sir Robert Wilson, were also his contemporaries. Some of these boys used to assemble in a shed occupied by an old pensioner, turned cobbler, who was a great favourite amongst them. This odd fellow entertained them with recounting his adventures, real or imaginary, while they regaled themselves and him with a beverage called hot-pot, made of porter and apples, procured from a neighbouring public-house. Another of their pleasures during play hours was to hire hackney coaches and to drive them about, seated beside "Jarvey," who found it necessary to superintend closely the wild proceedings of the boy charioteers.

Amongst the cleverest of Stapleton Cotton's companions was Charles Bunbury, son of Colonel Bunbury, the famous caricaturist, pre-eminent for fun and frolic. Young Bunbury consumed a great amount of hot-pot and other drinks; even at that early age evincing the unfortunate propensity which afterwards shortened his life. A most entertaining companion, his convivial qualities extenuated his failing in some degree to the jovial companions who listened with pleasure to his wit, or laughed at the ludicrous productions of his ready pencil. Even as a boy, his taste for politics and his radical opinions were very freely expressed, while the speeches of Fox and of Burke were correctly repeated by him, with a fluency of utterance and precision of memory which surprised his young companions. He also recited admirably.

When Colonel Cotton commanded the 25th Dragoons, or Gwynn's Hussars, as they were then called, this Charles Bunbury joined

24

the regiment at Weymouth, where it was stationed more than two months for the purpose of attending on George III., who was there with his family.

Bunbury afterwards went with the regiment to India, was engaged in the Battle of Mallavelly and the siege of Seringapatam, and died at the Cape, where he landed on his passage home. He had not attained his thirtieth year when, full of hope, enjoyment, and talent, he was cut off in the flower of his age.

Charles Wynn, afterwards Speaker of the House of Commons, was another of Stapleton's schoolfellows, and the boyish friendship contracted at Westminster never flagged through life, and only terminated at the death of Wynn.

Sir Robert Cotton at this time had a house in Berkeley Square, to which he accompanied his family for the parliamentary session. The session and the season in those days terminated together, and after the birthday, on the 4th of June, country families departed for their homes. Sir Robert performed the journey, driving four greys, harnessed to a large coach, containing the ladies of the family. When his sons were of the party they followed on horseback, and the cavalcade always spent three days in accomplishing the distance between London and Combermere Abbey.

While his father was in London, Stapleton accompanied him every Sunday to spend the evening with the Marquis, afterwards Duke, of Buckingham, who was his godfather. This formal visit always bored the restless Stapleton, who, however, never objected to the annual call of his other godfather. Sir Watkin W. Wynn, at Westminster School on St. David's Day, when he presented all the Welsh boys whom he knew with a guinea, and young Cotton, as his godson, with two.

After remaining four years at Westminster, Stapleton had his ardent wish fulfilled, when Sir Robert consented to his preparing for the army. With this object, he was sent to a military school at Bayswater, called Norwood House, conducted by Major Reynolds, a Shropshire militiaman, who had been an early acquaintance of Sir Robert's. County associations prevailed here again, and although the young aspirant urged the propriety of being sent to a military college abroad, for the purpose of acquiring foreign languages Sir Robert persisted in placing him with the Shropshire major, from whom he learnt little more than the best method of cleaning firelocks and accoutrements: an accomplishment on which he did not at all pride himself.

On the 26th February, 1790, Sir Robert obtained a second lieutenancy without purchase, for his son, in the 23rd, or Royal Welsh Fusiliers, which regiment he joined at Dublin in 1791. It was then commanded by Major Gibbings, great uncle to Lord Combermere's third wife, and a veteran of the American and German wars. Sir Robert accompanied his son to Ireland, and presented him to his commanding officer, who was a fine, handsome, military-looking man, always talking of the Battle of Minden, in which he had been engaged. Stapleton, who became lieutenant 16th March, 1791, did duty with the regiment until the 28th February, 1793, when he was appointed captain by purchase in the 6th Dragoon Guards, which corps he accompanied to Flanders in August of that year.

Captain Cotton embarked at Cork, and landed at Ostend just after the siege of Dunkirk. On its arrival, the regiment proceeded to Ghent, where headquarters were established for the winter.

On the appointment of the young soldier to the 6th Dragoons, or Carabineers, his relatives became exceedingly alarmed, from having heard of the Irish habits of this regiment. Stapleton was the only Englishman amongst the officers, and the ladies of the Cotton family could not conceal their apprehensions that, if the young captain were not shortly killed in a duel, he might be spared to die more slowly of the daily potations which he would be obliged to swallow.

At this time the excesses in many regiments, and even those of the generals in command, were such as would not be credited by the sober members of the profession in our own time. In Flanders, General Erskine was never to be seen after a certain hour, however urgent the necessity for his presence; while at headquarters the officers of the staff were generally assisted to bed at night by attendants nearly as tipsy as themselves. Young Cotton, endowed with one of those iron constitutions more common in his time than in ours, withstood the evil effects of the occasional excesses which it might have been thought unmanly to evade; while, with a degree of moral courage unusual in early life, he still resisted the persuasion and example that would have induced him to persist in them.

The Irishmen who officered the regiment exemplified the national character by the wit and drollery which still belong to it, but which is now softened by the more refined habits of modem society. The conviviality of former days, to give it a mitigated epithet, enhanced the natural hilarity of the Hibernian character, and the young English captain, with his joyous temperament, entered into the jokes of his associates with so keen a relish that they could not understand how he should belong to the sober race which then, even far more than now, differed so much from their volatile neighbours. As frank and cordial as themselves, he had none of that sheepishness which the French wittily ascribe to the great consumption of mutton in England.

The *carabineers* were quartered at Bruges and Ghent, and with national conviviality did not spare the good wine which their vicinity to France rendered very, attainable at moderate prices. Young Cotton's power of self-restraint, which enabled him through life to resist the temptations of the table, already displayed itself in the sobriety which astonished his less cautious companions, who, from rash indulgences, prepared themselves for the early deaths which left Cotton their survivor even long before the period when they should naturally have preceded him. Arthur Ormsby, the colonel, was the most joyous and jovial of the party. His Irish fun had been fully appreciated in all circles in Ireland, and now furnished many amusing scenes. Young Cotton was an especial favourite of his, and in after-life often recalled the drollery of his commanding officer. Ormsby could not speak a word of French, and was unable to conceal his contempt for the *monsieurs*, who *would* not understand him. Nor did their religion satisfy him more than their conversation, and he frequently very freely and emphatically expressed his opinions upon both to a priest in whose house he was billeted. "Confound that fellow! Tell him, Little Cotton"—for "Little Cotton" spoke French—"tell the blackguard that, if he does not let my servant cook in his kitchen, it will be the worse for him."

"What does the rascal say. Little Cotton?"

"He says that he'll see you hanged first"—the priest having in reality only made a civil objection.

"Now, Little Cotton, I won't stand this. Tell the d——d scoundrel that if he objects to let my servants cook (they are of his own confounded religion, tell him)—if he won't let them cook, I'll have him hung up on his own steeple, and leave him there till I take his Royal Highness the Duke of York's pleasure about him."

It was a part of "Little Cotton's" fun to give some other message to the priest, and he thus caused many ridiculous scenes. One day, when Ormsby was suffering much pain from gout in his feet, and was seated with disabled limbs in an easy chair, the priest gave him some extra cause for anger. After desiring Little Cotton to translate the usual compliments, which were of course misinterpreted in the usual way, indeed, in some manner made agreeable to his reverence, who smiled, the colonel broke out with—"What is the devil grinning at?"

"He says, Colonel, that you are very brave in your gouty chair, abusing him; but that, if the French marched in at one end of the town, you and your men would run off at the other!"

"Oh, then, the infernal scoundrel!" roared Ormsby, brandishing his crutch, "Take him out of my sight. Get him away, Little Cotton, or, by all that's sacred, I'll break every bone in his Papist body. Turn him out, I say."

An unusual effort here increased the gouty torture, and Ormsby sank back in his chair, uttering curses on the priest, invectives against his own incapacity to move, and groans at the paroxysm which rendered it doubly unbearable.

The duties exacted by his patron's preference did not end here. Little Cotton was obliged to sleep in a closet adjoining the colonel's room, and he, being a bad sleeper, required conversation to beguile the tedious wakefulness of his nights; so whenever his companion, during a long sentence, fell off into a doze, the colonel bawled out, with stentorian lungs, "Little Cotton, why the deuce do you go to sleep?" and at all hours this question received the usual necessary answer, more good-humouredly spoken, however, than it mostly is under similar circumstances.

In the campaign of 1794, Captain Cotton was engaged in the affair of Fremont, and in the cavalry action of Cateau, when the British horse were led by General Mansell, who was killed at the head of the brigade. In this battle, the Carabineers distinguished themselves. It was by a mere chance that Stapleton was present on the occasion, for soon after the affair at Fremont he learnt that, through family interest, he had, at the early age of twenty-one, been promoted within a few days, first to the majority of the 59th Regiment, and secondly to the lieutenant-colonelcy of the 25th Light Dragoons. The latter regiment was then quartered in England, and he received orders to join it at once. His few preparations being completed, he left the officers' mess early on the morning of the 25th May, to commence his journey to the coast, being accompanied by Lieutenant Crosbie, afterwards Sir John Gustavus Crosbie, who had just sold out of the *carabineers*.

They had proceeded about a mile from the camp, when the sound of shots broke the morning stillness and announced a battle. The signal was eagerly responded to by the two young men, who galloped back to the lines, and, placing themselves at the head of their former troops,—their successors not having been yet appointed,—commanded them during the whole of the action. Nothing could equal young Cotton's satisfaction at taking part in this battle, so unexpected by him, and which he had so nearly missed; for even his promotion could scarcely reconcile him to leaving the seat of war.

The following is an account of the action, given almost literally in Lord Combermere's own words:—

On the evening of the 16th of April, 1794, the allied troops (about forty thousand men) encamped on the heights of Cateau; and on the morning of the 17th the 6th Dragoon Guards, or Carabineers, moved with a division of Hessian and Austrian infantry, about three leagues, or nine English miles, to a small town called Fremont, which was attacked and carried. The enemy ran into the plantations, and by that means escaped our cavalry—(Here it was that Stapleton Cotton first smelt powder.)—On the 26th the allied camp was nearly surrounded by a very strong force of the enemy, who made his attack on (as he supposed) the most vulnerable part of the camp. In this day's action the brigade of cavalry composed of the 1st and 5th regiments of Dragoon Guards distinguished itself; the former corps commanded by Colonel Vyse, and the latter by Colonel the Honourable Robert Tayleur, late Colonel of the Carabineers. In a few hours, the allies gained a complete victory; but not cheaply, for their losses were considerable. General Mansell fell, whether fairly or not, it were hard to decide, for Captain Mansell; (his son and *aide-de-camp*) recognised him, after the battle, in a ditch, with his throat cut, and in a state of complete nudity. The *carabineers* had been engaged the previous day in some partial skirmishes, in small parties, on the outposts, and while returning to the neighbourhood of Tournay on one night (for we marched much by night) the sergeant (Mape) in rear of our centre squadron fell asleep on his horse; and the night being excessively dark, it was not perceived for some time that we had separated from the first and second squadrons.

The officer in command of the 3rd, or Light Squadron (Captain Trotter) was so much enraged on discovering the circumstance, that but for the interference of Captain Cotton, he would have cut the sergeant down. Having wandered about for some time, Captains Cotton and Trotter formed the squadron on an elevated spot, on which we lay until the morning, when, after daybreak, the enemy descried us from the next hill, and sent a swift-flying messenger from a field-piece, which passed over us and took the ground a few yards from our front. At break of day an *aide-de-camp* from the Austrian general. Otto, the general of the day, galloped up to our lines (not supposing the *carabineers* to be mounted) and exclaimed, 'The enemy has taken us by surprise, and surrounded us; I fear you'll be too late.'

But Sir Thomas Chapman instantly formed the regiment into close column of half troops to the left, and in a few minutes, we met the enemy and stemmed his progress. He had formed, on our approach, a solid square of from four to five thousand bayonets, with field-pieces, with the staff in the centre and the cannon placed at intervals. The *carabineers*, having formed line with intent to charge, the enemy fired a very uncourteous salute, and gave us some volleys right in the face.

Here we got orders to pause, until a light six-pounder, with sixty rounds of canister, sent by General Otto, with a detachment of the 14th Foot, could be brought to bear with effect upon the enemy. It was placed in front, and fired a signal for the *carabineers* to keep back, when Captain Craufurd, *aide-de-camp* to General Sir William Erskine, unfortunately, without deliberation, ordered the regiment to charge; but it was impossible for cavalry to break the enemy's square; and what rendered our situation worse was that he had formed his square close to the end of a field of rape, sown in ridges with very deep furrows between. Over these we had to pass; and many of the horses having fallen in consequence, the riders were either killed or made prisoners, and some of the horses (whose owners had been killed) fell into the ranks and manoeuvred with precision till picked up by men of all corps whose horses had been shot.—(Lord Combermere often alluded to the extraordinary sagacity of these animals, who seemed animated with human motives.)

When the *carabineers* rallied on a large plain, or flat of land (between the enemy's column and Lisle), we could muster only ten men of the lieut.-colonel's troop mounted. In that charge one officer (Lieut. Bond) was wounded in the upper arm, but did not leave the field until all was over. One sergeant and thirty rank and file killed, wounded, and missing, besides ninety-five horses killed; and one sergeant and several rank and file taken prisoners by the enemy, some of whom (the prisoners) joined us again. Sir Thomas Chapman's and Captain John French's horses were killed. The same column or square of infantry of the enemy was attempted to be broken by nine regiments of cavalry in succession that morning, but without effect. The *carabineers* and parts of some other regiments of cavalry were obliged to avoid (by manoeuvring quickly) as much as possible the enemy's long-shot (while on the plain), fired on them from a windmill on one side, and a temporary battery on the other. Here they were about three hours between two fires.

At length, a strong force of unbroken cavalry moved from the direction of Lisle, and formed a long line parallel to us. The French *carabineers* were on the right, and some Hussars or light regiments on the left, which extended towards Lisle, and the right towards Tournay. Our men, having seen some of the French *carabineers* before, knew them at once (by their large bearskin caps and *cuirasses*), and called on Sir Thomas Chapman to lead them to the charge. At that moment, our assistant-surgeon, Caldwell, rode up close to the front of the French *carabineers*, fired his pistols in their faces, and retired zigzag at speed, while the enemy fired several rounds after him. Having rejoined us, he said that the enemy's horses would never be able to stand a charge, they were so small and light.

Our men continued their solicitation for liberty to charge, crying out, 'This regiment beat us in the German war, capturing our standards and kettle-drums, and we will beat them now, if you only lead us on.' 'Patience, my brave boys,' was the major's answer. Sir William Erskine, the senior British general officer, happening to come up at this moment. Sir Thomas Chapman rode up to him, lowering the point of his sword, and saying, 'General, *my boys* are most anxious to charge their namesakes.' 'Sir Thomas,' answered Sir William, 'I fear you are not equal to do so; they are more than four to one of your men. However, if you are able, go on.' 'Thank you, General; I have a light troop of the Fifth Dragoon Guards with me,' replied Sir Thomas.

Turning to the regiment, the commanding officer cried to the officers and men, 'Now, my boys, mind the signals for movement, and when I raise my sword to the St. George, shout as loud as you are able, and into them, as quick and as close together as possible, and we'll have a glorious day yet, March, trot, canter, charge.' But the enemy did not wait to receive us, for the whole line wheeled in some way (perhaps by threes) to the left, and the Hussars got clear off, while we came into contact with the *carabineers*, nearly four squadrons of whom we unhorsed in a few moments, leaving many dead on the field. The other squadron got off after the Hussars. We, however, followed the fugitives close to Lisle, when an eighteen-gun battery opened a smart fire with grape upon us. Having reassembled, we observed the infantry that had given us so much trouble in the morning passing between two plantations.

The Oxford Blues (now Horse Guards, Blue) were ordered to charge them; but Sir William Erskine, finding that their *very heavy horses* sank to the knees in the tillage ground, owing to the continuous rain that had fallen in the morning, permitted us to take their place. Sir Thomas Chapman having said, 'General, our light Irish horses will do the work,' 'Ay, and the men, too,' added Sir William. We charged, and killed about eight hundred, and as many more laid down their arms and surrendered themselves prisoners of war. Having sent the captured guns with the prisoners to headquarters, the several regiments marched to their former ground. The *carabineers* were encamped again about three o'clock p.m., so that they lost no time, save while between the two fires on the plain.

The following letter, alluding to the action at Cateau, was written by the Countess of Chatham, wife of the second Lord Chatham, to Mrs. Stapleton, Stapleton Cotton's aunt and godmother:—

My dear Mrs. Stapleton,—Your good sister. Lady Cotton, need not have put herself in any fuss about asking me to present Miss Sophy. (Stapleton Cotton's sister, and afterwards Viscountess Kilmorey). I was very glad to do it, and she went through the ceremony remarkably well. She was in luck in her drawing-room, as it was as full as a birthday, which young ladies always like, and indeed it does make the presentation much less formidable. Lady Cotton's other more serious fuss, about her son, is over too now, I hope, for she told me that she believed he was only detained by the wind from coming over; she says he thinks himself very lucky in having by a mistake been kept so long in Flanders. I am quite of her mind, particularly as he is in the cavalry; it has been quite fortunate that he has stayed to see so much. There can be no doubt about his coming away for promotion; they all must do it at the same time. I think it is an amazing pity when a young man is obliged to do it so early in the campaign.

I speak this very sincerely, for I think it's going to be my brother's case: he will get his promotion immediately, and then his duty is at home, and I *really* do wish it may be some time before the other officer can go out to relieve him. I trust to Providence for taking care of him, and I cannot but wish him to have his share of service. Just now, is a very anxious moment, and the wind contrary for hearing from Flanders. This south-west and the pouring rain, which is at this moment accompanying it, is doing a great deal of good, but when one can think of nothing but the fleets and armies, one must pray for what is favourable for them, though odious to everything else—a good north-east wind. . . . . . Since I began this a mail came in; our army near Tournay, and all quiet as late as the 6th. I *admire* you for wishing yourself in the fleet, and you could certainly be nowhere better than in the *Royal George*, if you like such a *great house*. I am all for a smart frigate, and should like a cruise in one most amazingly.

Dear Mrs. Stapleton, with kind regards from me and Lord Chatham to his mother,

    Yours faithfully,

                        Mary Chatham.

CHAPTER 3

Capture of Seringpatam

On joining the 25th Light Dragoons, then called Gwynn's Hussars, he found the regiment quartered at Margate and Ramsgate. While at the former place he became enamoured of a very pretty Jewess, a Miss Barnett, afterwards Mrs. Rolls. She was a lively and fascinating girl, and at length influenced the young soldier's feelings so seriously as to render an abrupt retreat his only chance of safety. Very prudently, therefore, he obtained leave of absence, spent some time at Combermere Abbey, and did not return to his regiment till the danger was over.

Gwynn's Hussars were next ordered to Weymouth, to attend George III. during his stay there. Colonel Cotton was presented to the king and royal family soon after his arrival. The handsome young dragoon was received with much cordiality and kindness by the august party, the king especially seeming to take great pleasure in his society. The Princess Mary, afterwards Duchess of Gloucester, who was then a most lovely and engaging young woman, often selected Colonel Cotton for her partner in the dance.

He was well calculated to attract the attention of ladies, for, in addition to agreeable manners and lively, intelligent conversation, he was a decidedly handsome young man. About 5 feet 8 inches in height, slightly but strongly built, and possessing great activity, he was an indefatigable sportsman and an excellent pedestrian, even up to his eighty-seventh year. A swarthy complexion, a profusion of dark hair, thick eyebrows, and bright hazel eyes, shaded by long eyelashes, gave him somewhat of a foreign appearance. His glance was rapid, and the expression of his face good-humoured, though when excited by anger it could be fiery enough; but, to do him justice, this was seldom the case, and any ebullition of temper was generally very transient. The head was small and well proportioned, the nostril open, and the nose aquiline; while a massive Saxon chin indicated the firmness of character which distinguished him through life, and was indeed one of his principal characteristics.

Colonel Cotton used occasionally to accompany King George III. on his rides and visits of military inspection at Weymouth, and the good-natured monarch enjoyed the merry laugh which his jokes provoked when the young colonel was entertained with their readiness, and the joyous way in which they exploded. When the king visited Salisbury, a rash sailor, who had on other occasions exposed himself to the same risk, stood at the top of the steeple with a dangerous footing that excited wonder and fear in the admiring spectators, when His Majesty, being asked what should be his recompense, quickly answered, "Give him a patent!"

At this time Colonel Cotton occasionally visited Burton Pynsent, the residence of the Dowager Countess of Chatham, widow of the great Lord Chatham, and mother to Mr. Pitt. With this old lady generally resided Colonel Cotton's aunt, Miss Stapleton, a person as much valued by society in general as loved by her intimate friends. She watched over Lady Chatham's declining years, and, possessing a very large income, was enabled to serve, in pecuniary matters, some of the poorer members of the family. Her influential connections were numerous, and with many of these did Miss Stapleton keep up an active correspondence. Some of these letters have been found among the Cotton papers, and as they describe a good deal of the domestic life of George III. and his family in a very attractive manner.

These epistles were addressed, with others, that must have been of weekly repetition, to Miss Stapleton, by the Hon. Georgina Townshend, daughter of the first Lord Sydney, who, as well as her parents, held an appointment at Court. Her sister had married Lord Chatham, son to the Dowager Countess with whom Miss Stapleton resided.

The Court of George III. is so minutely described by three very communicative ladies of his time, that the letters in question might be considered superfluous, had not the writer's position placed her on a level, from which her view of the personages described was cleared by a more constant intercourse than that which the other ladies enjoyed.

Society offered with no niggard hand her varied pleasures to the handsome young Colonel of Hussars; but life at fashionable watering-places did not satisfy Stapleton Cotton's aspirations. He panted for more active service long after the disappointment of his unwished-for return from Flanders had been mitigated by the ill success of the army he had left there; and it was with a joyful heart that he received orders to hold his regiment in readiness to take the field. What, however, was to be its destination he did not learn for some time. While quartered on the coast, as well as at all times, he kept up a regular correspondence with his family, and wrote constantly to his aunt at Lady Chatham's. In the following letter, he informs her of his expected removal from England:

Exeter, May, 1795.

My Dear Aunt,—I intended myself the pleasure of seeing you last week, but an order from Lord G. Lennox, to prepare ourselves to take the field immediately, prevented my leaving Exeter. I afterwards received an order to augment the regiment to eighty men per troop, and have been, and shall still be, very busy till the end of the week, sending out recruiting parties, and making exertions to conform to both the orders. Towards the end of the week I hope to have the pleasure of paying another visit to Burton, which I fear will be but short. I am quite ashamed of having given you so much trouble about the hounds for my father. One lady is called *Fair Maid*, the other, *Fanny*. We are both grateful for your valuable help.

With best regards to Lady Chatham, My dear aunt,

Your very affectionate nephew,

Stapleton Cotton.

Soon after the date of this letter the regiment was ordered to Roborough Camp, where it remained three weeks.

Roborough Camp, 21st June, 1795.

My Dear Aunt,—We encamped upon this bleak common on Wednesday last, and had two shocking nights (that and Thursday) for our poor horses to stand out after coming out of comfortable stables.

General Grenville has promised to keep us here as short a time as possible, as far as his authority extends. I dined with him yesterday, and he desires to be kindly remembered to yourself and Lady Chatham. A letter from my father yesterday brings me intelligence of the death of our cousin Rowland Cotton, of Bellaport. The family estates devolve to Lord Ferrars and my father, I believe; I don't know in, for a wonder; he was present when the Oxford militia-men were shot. Lynch, I hear, is gazetted as second lieutenant in the Royal Welsh Fusiliers. Pray when does Mr. Meichill join us? General Greig informs me that he has approved of him as cornet in the 25th, and that the money is lodged.

The bad news of late has damped my spirits very much, but the expedition, I'm glad to find, is by no means at an end; that the troops here will shortly embark is pretty certain, but where destined very uncertain. The artillery and waggon horses are most of them already embarked, and are now still embarking. I find by this day's papers that the Spaniards have made peace with the Republic of France. I think we shall soon be left alone to oppose them. I have not heard from my brother since we left for Roborough Camp. My father writes that they are all well, and going this week to Knutsford races.

Kind compliments, &c., attend Lady Chatham.

> My dear aunt, believe me,
> > Your very affectionate nephew,
> > > Stapleton Cotton.

Some few weeks later Colonel Cotton learnt with great delight that his regiment was before long to proceed to India; a country which, to an adventurous mind like his, offered unusual attractions, and the accounts of which seemed fabulous to the then stationary inhabitants of Europe. His feelings on the subject may be gathered from the following letter:—

> Weymouth Camp, Aug. 31, '95.

My Dear Aunt,—You will be surprised at hearing from me from this place, and still more so at the news I have to tell you, which is, that we are to embark for the East Indies early in December. To be sure, the passage is tedious and unpleasant to me, as I hate being confined in a ship; but when we arrive it certainly will be a very advantageous thing for the regiment, particularly for me as lieutenant-colonel. We are most pleasantly situated here, about a mile from the town of Weymouth, where we see a great deal of the royal family. The prince and princess are expected about Thursday for a few days. I fancy we shall not remain long after the king; where we go, till we embark, is not yet known. I have not heard from home since my father has heard of our destination.

Best wishes attend Lady Chatham.

My dear aunt,
        Your very affectionate nephew,
                        Stapleton Cotton.

When in 1796 Colonel Cotton's regiment was at last definitely ordered to India, his mother and sisters used every effort to induce him
to exchange into some other corps, rather than encounter the risks
of an eastern climate and the inconveniences of a voyage so tedious
and uncertain in those days. Their entreaties could not overcome his
determination to accept even the most unpleasant duties of his profession, and he threatened to relinquish it entirely, rather than forego this
opportunity of seeing service.

Sir Robert Cotton, himself a captain in the Cheshire militia at the
time, secretly encouraged his son's military ardour, although, to please
the ladies of his family, he seemed to concur in their wishes that Stapleton should not proceed to India. The parting was mutually distress-
ing, for he was the favourite brother of his sisters, who deplored his
departure as if they were never to meet again.

He sailed in the *Nottingham*, Indiaman, in April, with two troops
of the 25th and one company of the 33rd; the rest of the regiment
proceeded in transports. Three hundred vessels started together, and
at the chops of the Channel parted company, some for the East, and
some for the West Indies, and others for various ports in different parts
of the world.

                        On board the *Nottingham*, Indiaman,
                                April 30th, 1796.
Lat. 20° N. My Dear Aunt,—I take the opportunity of writing to you afforded by the departure of the *Canton*, Indiaman,
about to part company. I met the homeward bound fleet at St.
Helena. I was sure that you would pardon me for not paying a
visit at Burton1 before I left England, when you heard of the
sudden order which I received when in London to embark. We
have had a most delightful passage hitherto, and as we are now
in the trade winds, there is no doubt of our having a speedy
one to the Cape. Thank God, I never was in better health. We
passed very near Madeira on Thursday last, and are now within
sight of the Canary Islands. (Burton Pynsent, where Mrs. Stapleton lived with the Dowager Countess of Chatham Mr. Pitt's
mother). I trust to be able to write to you from the Cape on the
20th of June. By the next fleet I hope to hear of the wellbeing

of yourself and Lady Chatham.

    Believe me, my dear aunt,
        Your very affectionate nephew,
                            Stapleton Cotton.

The *Nottingham* was becalmed for three weeks near the line, and during this interval the officers on board the *Asia* entertained the crews of the other ships with theatrical performances and balls. Some young ladies going out to India, on their preferment, enlivened these parties, where the deficiency of female dancers was supplied by young middies, who dressed in ladies' attire, and imitated the airs and graces of the most affected specimens of the gentler sex. These amusements promoted two marriages, arranged on the voyage: the commodore— Losack—espousing one of two sisters, and Major Shea, of the 33rd, the other. Colonel Wellesley, who commanded the 33rd Regiment, followed in another vessel.

The usual ceremonies on crossing the line were performed, to the great amusement of the soldiers. There is always a favourite victim on such occasions, and the cook of the *Nottingham*, by his airs and pretensions, had excited the animosity of the sailors. He had particularly offended them by lamenting the pecuniary difficulties which reduced him to the degradation of accepting a situation on board a merchant-man. This boast aggravated the grudge they had against him for feasting on luxuries while they were obliged to put up with biscuits and salt junk. Accordingly, the poor cook was subjected to the severest trials at the hands of Neptune, prompted by the spite of his malicious messmates.

The *Nottingham*, after encountering very severe gales, arrived at the Cape. On landing there, Colonel Cotton was informed by General Craig that the French and Dutch fleets were expected, and was ordered to have his men disembarked immediately for the purpose of marching to Saldanha Bay, where the two fleets had appointed to meet.

The untrained wild horses of the country were procured from the Boers to mount the Hussars, who proceeded directly to Saldanha. It was a ludicrous scene to witness the fully-accoutred dragoons mounted upon these sorry chargers, which, unaccustomed to such caparisoned riders, struggled to regain their independence; the contest between the soldier and his steed often ending in the ludicrous discomfiture of the former. From an elevation above the bay, the Dutch fleet was seen at anchor. One of the vessels had proceeded up a creek for water, where a patrol of the 25th Light Dragoons took eight men, who had just landed from her boat, prisoners.

The governor had sent a fast-sailing ship to bring back Vice-Admiral Sir George Keith Elphinstone, (afterwards Lord Keith), who was cruising about the coast, and on his arrival the Dutchmen struck their colours and surrendered to the English, greatly to the disappointment of Colonel Cotton and his officers, who had anticipated much enjoyment from witnessing a naval engagement so comfortably from the shore. While at the Cape he wrote the following letters home:—

On board the *Nottingham*,
Simons Bay, Cape of Good Hope,

August 5th, 1796.

My Dear Mother,—I have only time to say that I am well, and have been so ever since we left Portsmouth. The hot weather under the line agrees with me much better than I expected. The climate here is delightful; it is now the depth of winter; we have been here at least a fortnight, and not had a rainy day. The *America* sails for England in the course of an hour, therefore I must defer giving you an account of the Cape. If I have time, I will send you some Constantia wine, ostrich feathers, and seeds of different sorts.

Pray don't forget the newspapers, pamphlets, &c.

Duty and love, my dear mother,
Your very dutiful son,

S. Cotton.

On board the *Nottingham*,
Simons Bay, Cape of Good Hope,
August 5th, 1796.

Dear Father,—We arrived in this bay the 24th of last month, after a tedious passage of fifteen weeks. The second fleet, which sailed sometime after us, arrived the first of this month. Admiral Elphinstone is going in search of a Dutch fleet of nine sail, which was seen yesterday off the Cape; he is afraid that they heard of his force and have made off. Had they put into Saldanha Bay he must have taken the whole fleet. The *America*, of seventy-four, parts company from the admiral after the cruise, for England, of which I have but just been informed, so that my time for writing is very short. I shall, however, have plenty of leisure for that purpose before we leave here, as we cannot sail till Admiral Elphinstone returns. I have been twice at Cape Town, which is about twenty miles from here; it is large and well built, in the Dutch style, and remarkably clean. The inhabitants I cannot much admire; they do not seem very well affected to the English.

The Hottentots are more reconciled to their present masters, though the Dutch have tried as much as possible to prevent this. General Craig is raising a corps of Hottentots; he has already enlisted upwards of fifty very fine-looking men. I saw them about a week ago at Cape Town, at drill. The horses here are very small and short of bone; they put me in mind of the worst of the Hungarian hussar horses, remarkably sure-footed, but unpleasant to ride from their nasty ambling pace, which it is difficult to get them out of.

The general is making this place very strong, so much so that the Dutch will find it a difficult matter to reach it, should they ever effect a landing. The garrison consists of the following regiments:—78th, 84th, 80th, 95th, 98th Infantry, and 28th Light Dragoons. The 27th Dragoons came out in the last fleet; they go on with us to Bengal. Watkin Griffith, (young Welsh officer, afterwards killed at Waterloo), has just been with me. He brought me neither letters nor news of any sort. We hear that Parliament was certainly to be dissolved in July, therefore I fancy you have by this time got over the bustle of an election.

Our people have been very healthy, except in one ship, the *General Goddard*, where the ship fever prevailed. I have removed all the men from that vessel, and encamped them about a quarter of a mile from the beach; we are in hopes the fever is put a stop to. Since our embarkation we have lost one corporal and six privates, of which Johnson and Chesters are the only men you know. The 27th have lost one officer and seven men. Pray let me know if you received two letters which I wrote at sea: one in May, which went to St. Helena in the *Canton*, Indiaman; the other sent by a Portuguese brig, which we met in lat. 23°, bound to Oporto.

I am afraid you will hardly be able to read this scrawl, which I can with difficulty write, owing to a blow which I got on my hand last night when returning on a tired horse from Cape Town. I shall be very much obliged to you for the old newspapers whenever you have an opportunity of sending them, and all the military books and pamphlets you can pack up for me.

Duty and love from, dear father,

Your very affectionate son,

Stapleton Cotton.

Camp near Saldanha Bay, Cape of Good Hope.
August 19, 1796.

Dear Father,—You will be very much surprised at hearing from me at this place. As my time is short, as well as the history of the campaign, I write you but a few lines by the *Moselle* frigate, which sails this evening for England, with dispatches from Sir G. Elphinstone and General Craig. A few days after I wrote to you by the *America*, a battalion, with one hundred mounted men, was sent off from Cape Town, and arrived here a week after, since which time we have been a good deal employed in patrolling round the bay, and in preventing the Dutch from landing their troops. Sir George Elphinstone arrived here with fourteen sail two days ago, to whom the Dutch immediately surrendered. The sight was glorious. We are on a height about two miles from the shipping, and of course had a fine view of the whole affair. For a short time we were under the fire of one of the frigates about three days since, but lost no men. I suppose that we shall re-embark and proceed to India in about three weeks. The Dutch fleet numbers nine sail. The officer just going on board obliges me to conclude.

With duty and love,

Stapleton Cotton.

P. S. You will see Sir George Elphinstone's and General Craig's report before receiving this.

The following dispatches give an accurate account of the affair, and will be read with interest by those officers whose regiments were employed on the occasion:

Parliament-Street, Nov. 3.

The following dispatch was this day received by Mr. Dundas, from Major-Gen. Craig, commanding His Majesty's troops at the Cape of Good Hope, dated 'Camp on the shore of Saldanha Bay, August 19, 1796':—

Sir,—I have great satisfaction in reporting to you the event of an attempt which has been made by the enemy, and which was terminated to the honour of His Majesty's arms, in the entire capture of the squadron of Dutch ships of war, destined for the purpose of retaking this settlement. Having made every arrangement within my means, by the establishment of a small post, and the laying the road by a sufficient number of the few men which I had been able to mount, by watching Saldanha Bay, I received a report on the 3rd instant, transmitted in fourteen hours, that nine ships had appeared off the coast on the preceding afternoon, which I immediately communicated to Vice-Admiral Sir George Keith Elphinstone.

By the same report there appeared to be the strongest probability that His Majesty's brig, the *Hope*, had been captured by them; and as there was no further account of them the next day, I concluded that the information which they had received by that means of our strength here, had induced them to continue their route, and that they would stand far to the westward before they doubled the Cape, to avoid Sir George's fleet, which had put to sea as soon as possible after the receipt of the intelligence.

In order, however, to omit no precaution, I sent up Lieutenant M'Nab, with a few mounted men, to watch the bay more narrowly; and from him I received a report on Saturday night, the 6th instant, at twelve o'clock, that the same number of ships which had formerly been reported had anchored that morning in the bay, and that there was no doubt, of their being enemies. I lost not a moment in sending directions to Simon's Town, whence, by the general willingness and activity which prevailed amongst all ranks, five vessels were dispatched by nine o'clock in quest of the admiral, with the information.

As it fortunately happened that the 25th and 27th Light Dragoons, with part of the 19th, and the whole of the 33rd regiment, were in Simons Bay, I could be under no apprehension for the safety of the colony from any force which could be landed from nine ships of war. It became, however, an object of infinite importance to the welfare of the settlement to prevent any body of the enemy from throwing themselves into the country. At the same time, the security of the Cape Town became an object of peculiar attention, both from the reasonable expectation that the enemy would not have come with such a force without a prospect of a junction with some other armament, and from the possibility of the Admiral being prevented from doubling the Cape by the north-westerly winds which usually prevail at this season, and which would carry the enemy in six hours from Saldanha to Table Bay. It was, therefore, with peculiar satisfaction that I found myself possessed of a force adequate to both these objects. No time was lost in making the necessary arrangements in a country totally unused to a movement of this nature.

The troops began their march on Sunday morning, necessarily by divisions, on account of subsistence. The Burgher Senate was assembled, to whom I exposed my intentions, to which they expressed the most ready compliance. Waggons were everywhere demanded by them, and furnished with cheerfulness. Cavalry was necessary, but the appointments of the 28th were on board a ship which had sailed in quest of the admiral. Those of the 25th were also on board ships in Simons Bay. and we had not above fifty horses. The appointments were brought up, and I did not scruple, on such an occasion, to require all saddle-horses without exception to be brought in, which were valued by two members of the court of justice and two officers of the 28th Dragoons, and paid for on the spot, to the entire satisfaction of the owners. By these means. Sir, leaving Maj.-Gen. Doyle in the command of the troops at and about Cape Town, amounting to near 4000 men, and Brig.-Gen. Campbell, in the immediate command of the town, I, on the morning of the 16th, reached Saldanha Bay, at the head of the advanced guard, consisting of the Light Infantry, a body of Hottentots, and fifty of the 25th Light Dragoons, assisted by Brig.-Gen. M'Kenzie, the remainder of whose corps, consisting of the grenadiers, the 78th and 20th battalions, 50 more of the 25th, and 100 of the 18th Light Dragoons, in all about 2500 men, with two howitzers and nine field-pieces, arrived there also in an hour after. In the meantime, the admiral had returned to False Bay, and, on there receiving the first accounts of the enemy being in Saldanha Bay, had put to sea again with the utmost expedition; and we had the satisfaction, from the heights, whence we descended to the shores of the bay, to see him, with all his sails crowded, advancing with a fair wind directly to the mouth of the harbour, though still at some distance.

One of the enemy's frigates, which lay near the shore to cover their watering, cannonaded us very briskly as we descended the heights, though without effect; and we returned their fibre with as little, having at that time only three-pounders with us; but a howitzer being brought up, a few shells were thrown with great precision by Captain Robertson, who would probably soon have destroyed her; but, perceiving that our fleet was then entering the bay, and that there was no possibility of her escaping, I desisted from firing, thinking it more for His Majesty's interest that she should share the fate of the remainder of the squadron, the capture of which appeared to me to be inevitable, than that we should risk the destroying her, from a vain punctilio of obliging her to strike to us. We then employed ourselves in making the necessary dispositions for affording such assistance as might be in our power, in the event of the obstinacy of the enemy obliging the admiral to attack them, as well as such as would be expedient in case they should run their ships on shore, neither of which, however, I thought probable. I was accordingly informed, by a letter from Sir George the following morning, that the whole had surrendered themselves to him.

The means by which this event has been accomplished. Sir, has not afforded any opportunity to His Majesty's troops of displaying that bravery in his service which I am confident they would have shown had the occasion presented itself; but, if the utmost alacrity and cheerfulness, under almost every privation, except that of meat, during a march of ninety miles, through so barren a country that there exist but five houses in the whole line, have any merit, I can with truth present them to His Majesty's notice. This march, Sir, has never yet, I believe, been attempted by any body of troops, however small, and, permit me to assure you, has been attended with such uncommon difficulties, that it never could be accomplished but by the display of the qualities I have mentioned in the troops, and a union of extraordinary exertions in all the departments concerned.

In these all have equal claim to my acknowledgments; but I cannot dispense with particularising the intelligence and activity with which, regardless of the uncommon fatigue which attended it, Lieut. M'Nab, of the 98th Regiment, with about twenty of his mounted men, performed the service allotted to him of watching the enemy, and preventing any communication with them, from the first moment of their coming into the bay until our arrival. It is, Sir, with very particular satisfaction that I have further to report, that I have received on this occasion every possible assistance from His Majesty's subjects of the colony.

The Burgher Senate have discharged the duty imposed upon them with the greatest readiness, impartiality, and activity; whilst their requisitions and orders to the inhabitants for their waggons, cattle, and horses have been complied with a cheerfulness which could, I am satisfied, only proceed from a conviction of the preference to be given to His Majesty's mild and paternal government over the wild system of anarchy and confusion from which they were furnishing the means of being effectually defended. This will be delivered to you. Sir, by my *aide-de-camp*, Captain Baynes, who has been in this country since the first arrival of His Majesty's troops under my command, and to whose intelligent and active assistance I have been, on every occasion, highly indebted. I beg leave. Sir, most humbly to recommend him to His Majesty's notice.

J. H. Craig.

The following dispatches were this day received by Mr. Nepean from the Hon. Vice-Admiral Sir George Keith Elphinstone, K.B., dated *Monarch*, Saldanha Bay, August 19.

Sir,—I have the honour to enclose a list of a Dutch squadron under the command of Rear-Admiral Engelbertus Lucas, sent hither for the reduction of this colony, but which were compelled to surrender by capitulation, on the 17th instant, to the detachment of His Majesty's ships under my command. I hope the Lords Commissioners of the Admiralty will approve the measures I have taken, so essential to the British commercial interests in the East. The ships are all coppered, and in good condition, excepting the *Castor*, whose rudder is defective.

In justice to the officers and men I have the honour to command, it is my duty to observe that, in consequence of the most violent tempestuous weather I ever beheld, and the very unpleasant situations in which the squadron was at times placed, they cheerfully, and much to their credit, underwent a degree of fatigue hardly credible. Captain Aylmer will have the honour of presenting these dispatches. I beg leave to mention him to their Lordships as a respectable gentleman and an active officer.

G. K. Elphinstone.

Monarch, Saldanha Bay, August 19.

Sir,—I have the honour to inform you that intelligence was received at Cape Town, on the 3rd instant, of a number of ships having been seen in the offing at Saldanha Bay, which was confirmed on the 5th. In consequence of this, every preparation was made for putting to sea immediately with the squadron under my command; but, from the *Monarch's* mainmast being out and the tempestuous weather, I was not able to quit the anchorage in Simons Bay until the 6th, when we proceeded to sea. On getting under weigh, an officer from the shore came on board to inform us that a number of sails had been seen the preceding night in the offing, near False Bay. I then resolved to steer to the southward and west, in expectation of their having taken that course.

The squadron continued cruising in the most tempestuous weather I have ever experienced, which damaged many of the ships, and at one time the *Ruby* had five feet water in her hold. We were joined at sea by His Majesty's ships *Stately*, *Rattlesnake*, and *Echo*, sloops. On the 12th I returned, with a fresh breeze blowing from the southeast, and, upon anchoring in Simons Bay, the master-attendant came off with information that the ships seen, consisting of nine sail, had put into Saldanha Bay on the 6th, the same day on which I had proceeded to sea; that they remained there by the last advice, and that four ships had been dispatched in quest of me to communicate this welcome intelligence.

I immediately made the signal to sail, but the *Crescent* had got ashore. The wind blew strong, and increased on the following day to a perfect tempest, in which the *Tremendous* parted two cables, drove, and was in great danger of being lost; so that, notwithstanding every exertion, and the most anxious moments of my life, I could not get out till the 15th.

On the 16th, the squadron arrived off Saldanha Bay at sunset; and the *Crescent,* which had been ordered ahead to discover information, and to report, made the signal for the enemy, consisting of three ships of the line, three frigates, and other ships, being moored in the bay. The squadron stood on into the bay in the order of sailing, but the night coming on, and the rear being too far extended for action, I judged it expedient to come to an anchor within shot of the enemy's ships, and, perceiving their numbers very inconsiderable in comparison with the ships under my command, I considered it my duty, and an incumbent act of humanity, to address the Dutch officer in command, and consequently forwarded a letter to him demanding his surrender. To this I received a verbal return, that a positive reply should be sent in the morning at daybreak. I was fearful the enemy might attempt to injure the ships, and therefore ordered Lieutenant Coffin to return immediately with a letter, insisting that no damage should be done to the ships.

On the 17th, at nine in the morning, a Dutch officer came on board with a flag, and presented proposals of terms for capitulation; at five p.m. the terms were ultimately agreed upon, but it was impossible to take possession of the ships until the 18th, on account of the stormy weather. The consequent joy of this fortunate event is much augmented from the consolatory reflection on its accomplishment without effusion of human blood, or injury to either of the enemy's or British ships, not a single shot having been fired.

I must, however, beg leave to observe, that any resistance on the part of the enemy could only have occasioned the wanton sacrifice of a few lives; and I doubt not, that, had their numbers been adequate to contention, their conduct would have confirmed the acknowledged merit at all times accorded to the martial spirit of subjects of the United States; and I can, with similar confidence, assure you that the officers and men under my command would have exhibited a conduct equally creditable to themselves. The repeated advices communicated in your letters, respecting the enemy's forces destined to this quarter, agreed so correctly with the intelligence I obtained by other means, that I have long been expecting this arrival, and was thereby enabled to be perfectly prepared to receive them, and constantly to keep a vigilant look-out.

G. K. Elphinstone.

(Here follow the articles of capitulation, by which Rear-Admiral Lucas agrees to surrender his squadron, and Vice-Admiral Gr. K. Elphinstone states that he considers the surrender of the Dutch squadron as a matter of necessity, and not of choice, and agrees to it to prevent the effusion of human blood. Officers behaving with propriety shall be allowed to wear their swords and side-arms, and be treated with respect; private property is to be respected; the crews of the ships, and particularly the sick, shall be taken care of equally with British; and the Batavian colours are to be struck as soon as the British officers take possession of the ships.)

Ships late belonging to the United States, under the command of his Excellency Rear-Ad. Engelbertus Lucas, which surrendered Aug. 7, 1796, to a detachment of the squadron of His Majesty's ships under the command of the Hon. Sir Gr. Keith Elphinstone: *Dortrecht*, Rear-Ad. Lucas, 66 guns, 370 men; *Revolution*, Capt. Rhenbende, 66 guns, 400 men; *Admiral Tromp*, Capt. Valkenburg, 54 guns, 280 men; *Castor*, Capt. Clarisse, 44 guns, 240 men; *Braave*, Capt. Zoetmans, 40 guns, 234 men; *Bellona*, Capt. Valk, 28 guns, 130 men; *Sirene*, Capt. De Cerf, 26 guns, 130 men; *Havik*, Capt. Bezemer, 18 guns, 76 men; *Maria* (storeship), 112 men. Many of the guns are brass, besides which they are well furnished with carronades.

They have four field-pieces of land artillery on board. The troops are under the command of the Rear-Admiral; Lieut.-Col. Hunri is adjutant-general; and Mons. Grandecourt, *commandant* of artillery.

Ships of the detachment of the squadron to which the Dutch surrendered: *Monarch*, 74 guns, 612 men, Vice-Ad. the Hon. Sir George Keith Elphinstone, K.B., Capt. John Elphinstone; *Tremendous*, 74 guns, 590 men. Rear-Ad. Thomas Pringle, Capt. John Aylmer; *America*, 64 guns, 491 men, Commod. John Blanket; *Stately*, 64 guns, 481 men, Capt. Billy Douglas; *Ruby*, 64 guns, 491 men, Capt. Jacob Waller; *Sceptre*, 64 guns, 491 men, Capt. W. Effington; *Trident*, 64 guns, 491 men, Capt. E. G. Osborne; *Jupiter*, 40 guns, 343 men, Capt. Geo. Losack; *Crescent*, 36 guns, 264 men, Capt. Edw. Buller; *Sphinx*, 24 guns, 156 men, Capt. Andrew Tod; *Moselle*, 16 guns, 121 men, Capt. Ch. Brisbane; *Rattlesnake*, 16 guns, 121 men, Capt. Edw. Ramage; *Echo*, 16 guns, 121 men, Capt. John Turner; *Hope,* sloop, Capt. Alexander.

As soon as the safety of the colony had been assured. Colonel Cotton was allowed to proceed to his original destination. He arrived at Madras, after a very prosperous voyage, and was, with his regiment, quartered in the fort, from which he wrote to his mother, giving her several interesting details concerning Indian life at the close of the eighteenth century.

Fort St George, Jan. 20th, 1797.

My Dearest Mother—

It was generally understood that we were to have been sent to Bengal; but I fancy, owing to General St. Leger s interest with the prince and Duke of York, a private letter was sent by the overland despatches, desiring Lord Holland to place the 27th Dragoons (of which St. Leger's cousin is lieut.-col.) on the Bengal Establishment. In point of emolument this Presidency is certainly very far inferior, but being the seat of war, and the climate being more favourable to Europeans, it is upon the whole as well for me, and indeed the regiment at large. Owing to part of the regiment being gone on to Bengal (in a ship that parted company soon after we left the Cape), we have been kept in this fort.

I expect the people from Calcutta in the course of a week, when we shall march either to Pallamablu or the Mount (distant ten or fifteen miles), and receive about two hundred horses, which are to be drafted from the native cavalry. Our people have been healthy since we landed, but we have experienced the finest cool weather they ever have enjoyed; it is not *much warmer* in general than a *very hot* summer's day in England. In about six weeks or two months' time we shall, I fancy, have it pretty warm. We get up in general before sun-rising, and ride till the sun begins to be hot, which is about eight or nine o'clock. It is necessary to keep out of the sun till about four in the afternoon. The dinner hour is six, when it begins to be dark. We are very gay at present; balls, concerts, &c. &c., every night, now and then a play. As the command of a station is everything here (indeed without it a person can only live, *though very well,* here) I am very desirous of getting the rank of colonel, which would ensure me a command.

An officer commanding any station receives full *batta*, which, if colonel, is very considerable. I now receive only half *batta* of lieut.-colonel, and my king's pay. On the Bengal Establishment, every officer receives *full batta*, and the commanding officer *double full batta*. A command in Bengal is a certain fortune in the course of five years. General Floyd is now (including his king's pay as major-general on the staff, lieut.-colonel of the 19th, his Company's pay, and allowances from the Company and *Nabob* as Commander of the Southern District) in the receipt of about fourteen or sixteen thousand pounds a year. I rather think he will not stay here more than two years. The rank of colonel, even if it was only temporary, would be a great thing to me, as I am next King's cavalry officer to General Floyd; but there are many officers of native cavalry above me, although by only very few days. They have no full colonel; therefore, I should be above them all.

With most affectionate regard to my sisters, I am, dear mother,

Your dutiful and loving son,

S. Cotton.

From Fort St. George, Madras, Colonel Cotton was transferred to Trichinopoly. At this place, he remained for some time, under the command of General Floyd, who was in charge of the district. Mrs. Floyd, who had accompanied her husband to India, by her eccentricities tormented the general, a man as precise and formal as she was wild and impulsive. Many curious scenes were the result of this contrast, when the grave martinet was made the victim of her practical jokes. On one occasion she stood near him, with her baby in the nurse's arms, when, after an inspection, the troops were marching past. Shrieking as if the child was threatened with some unseen danger, she threw it on her husband's saddle, and running away with the nurse, who was privy to her purpose, left the general with a squeaking baby in his arms before all the troops.

At another time, Mrs. Floyd had a woman, dressed for the occasion, placed in a *palanquin* and carried to the general's tent. On arriving there she raised a great outcry, and seemed in intense agony, caused, as she said, by the attack of a tiger, from whose fangs she had been miraculously rescued, on a mount rising on the plains some distance off. The general was at that moment giving orders to his officers, but moved by the woman's cries and excited by the prospect of a successful hunt, all were eager for immediate action, and business was for the time forgotten. They proceeded forthwith with some *sepoys* to the spot, and in a short time saw an enormous tiger crouched behind some shrubs halfway up the rock.

The general ordered a volley to be fired at him, while some venturesome youth clambered up the side of the mount, to take a more active part in the capture of the prize. The volley was fired, but the tiger remained immovable. Another volley was now directed at him by the *sepoys*, and still he continued motionless, as if regardless of such unskilful assailants. At length, those who had advanced up the rock approached nearer and nearer, when one of them giving the animal a blow with the butt end of his gun, it rolled down the precipitous rock and fell at the feet of its astonished pursuers below—a stuffed skin! General Floyd went back to his tent, without an observation, and no one in his presence ever alluded to the morning's adventure.

Mrs. Floyd insisted against all precedent on giving a newly-born daughter two godfathers, who were to be Colonel Wellesley and Colonel Cotton, and on having the child named Flavia. Both officers officiated accordingly at a grand christening, which was followed by an evening party. When most of the guests had departed, Mrs. Floyd requested the two colonels to oblige the clergyman to christen the child again, as she declared he had not crossed its forehead properly in the morning. It was in vain that they expressed themselves quite satisfied with the ceremony, and urged the impropriety of having it repeated. The lady became so nervous and irritable, that to appease her the chaplain however crossed the child's forehead, without repeating any part of the baptismal service.

Mrs. Floyd was the mother of the beautiful Lady Peel and Lady Fuller. She died early, and General Floyd, when commanding in Ireland, married Lady Denny, a celebrated Dublin beauty, who long survived him.

Colonel Cotton at this time saw much of Colonel Wellesley, who was his senior by seven years. He found him cheerful and good-natured, but reserved, never even at that age indulging in the confidential intercourse of youth. Always anxious to dress well, he was never successful in his efforts, yet the scrupulous neatness of his attire was always remarkable.

From Trichinopoly, the 25th Light Dragoons were transferred to Arcot, where they continued till the 1st of January, 1799. On the breaking out of hostilities with Tippoo the regiment was ordered to join the force assembling at Vellore. The command of this army was temporarily held by Colonel Wellesley until the arrival of General Harris, when he was transferred to a brigade consisting of his own regiment, the 33rd, and two battalions of *sepoys*, to which, shortly after, was added the *nizam's* contingent, nearly twelve thousand strong.

In the interval Colonel Wellesley occupied himself by practising the regiments under his command in division movements, with which they possessed very little acquaintance.

In the campaign which followed Colonel Cotton took an active part, and was present at the Battle of Malavelly and the capture of Seringapatam. From the papers in the possession of the Combermere family we can find no mention of the military operations of that year, with the exception of a MS. journal (never before, we believe, published) kept by the late General Sir Patrick Ross, K.C.B., at that time a captain in Colonel Cotton's regiment. It is from this journal that we have principally compiled the following brief account of the campaign.

At the end of January, General Harris, and the rest of the troops destined for the expedition, arrived. The whole force ultimately employed in the campaign amounted, including the Bombay column,

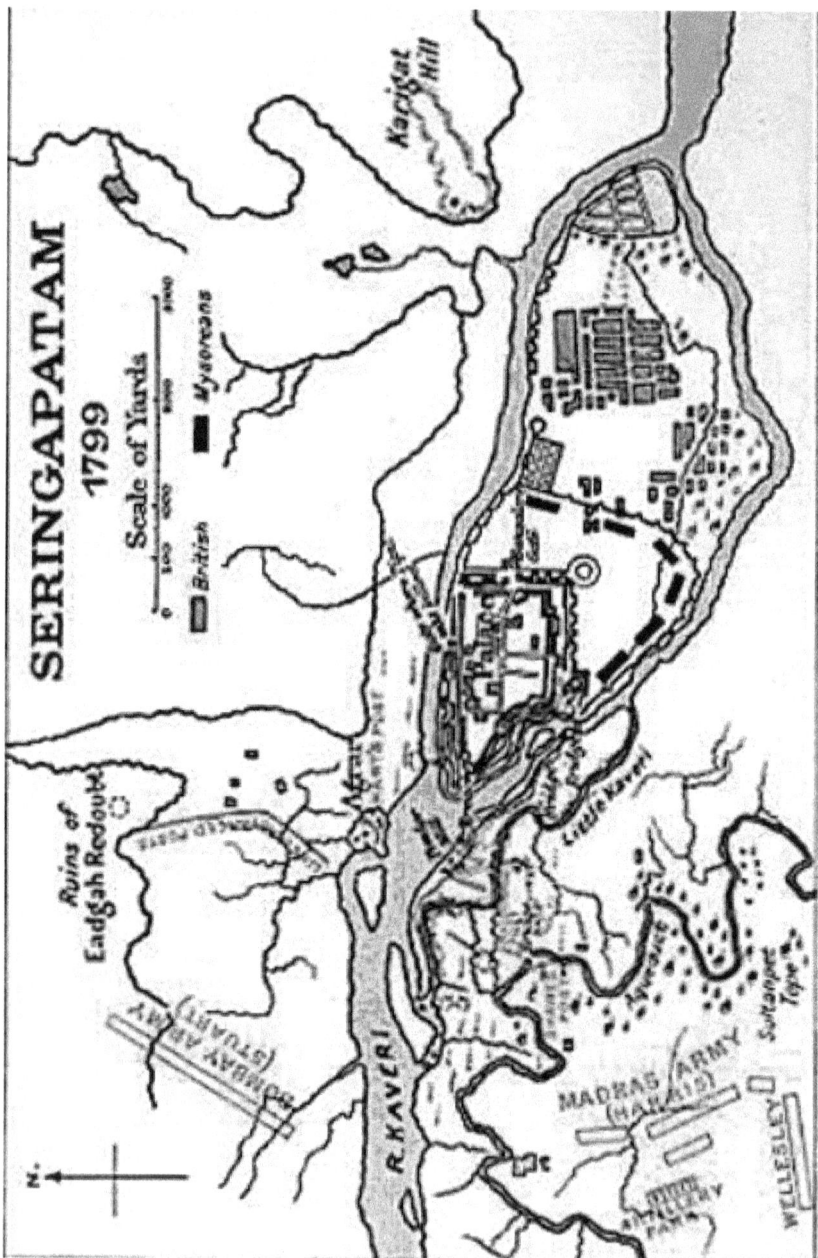

Storming of Seringapatam

the army, and the forces under Colonels Roberts and Read, to about forty-six thousand men; the army of Tippoo reaching to about the same number. The main British Army may be estimated, if we exclude Colonel Roberts' column and the *nizam's* army, in which latter was incorporated H. M's. 33rd regiment, the whole under Colonel Wellesley, at nearly nineteen thousand men, divided into six brigades of infantry and two of cavalry. Colonel Cotton's regiment was in the 2nd brigade, in which were also the 2nd and 3rd regiments of Native Cavalry, the brigadier being Colonel Prater. At the end of February, the *nizam's* army joined General Harris on the frontiers of Mysore.

On his arrival the *nizam's* son and general, Meer Alum, expressed a wish to review the British army, and it was accordingly drawn out to receive him. At four o'clock in the afternoon everything was ready, but no visitor appeared. Hour after hour passed away, still the glittering looked-for cavalcade came not. At length, at seven in the evening, when the sun had set and darkness was spreading rapidly over the plain, a group of horsemen could be faintly seen approaching. It was Meer Alum and his suite, who, to gratify their vanity, had thus kept the British Army waiting for three long hours.

The darkness was now so great that a man could scarcely be distinguished at the distance of five yards. Still, not wishing to affront his allies, General Harris caused torches to be lit, and by their flickering light the troops marched phantom-like past, and performed a few conjectural manoeuvres. On the 6th of March the army entered the Mysore territory and advanced on Seringapatam, though somewhat slowly, on account of the difficulty of moving the battering train and gun platforms. During the march, the army was continually harassed by parties of Tippoo's horsemen, but no serious affair took place until, on reaching Malavelly, early in the morning of the 26th March, General Harris found the enemy's army drawn up in two lines to receive him.

The British advance, consisting of cavalry, was at once halted, and the right wing of the infantry hurried to the front, the baggage and battering train being left under the escort of the left wing. At ten a.m. all was ready for the attack, when suddenly the enemy began apparently to move off to their left and to decline the combat. This, however, was only a ruse, for on the quartermaster-general proceeding to mark out the camping ground under escort of the 25th Light Dragoons, the 2nd Native Cavalry, and the picquets of the army commanded by Colonel Sherbrooke, the general of the day, a heavy fire of artillery was opened from the heights in front, and Tippoo's army again displayed itself. For three-quarters of an hour were the picquets and cavalry left unsupported, and exposed to the fire of the enemy's guns, which, however, were too badly served to inflict much loss.

This supineness was the reason that the results of the action were not equal to what might have been expected. Several Frenchmen, taken prisoners in the battle, declared that had the British cavalry at once attacked scarcely a gun could have been saved. At length, the picquets and cavalry were ordered to retire, their place being taken by the right wing. About half-past eleven the British line of battle was formed as follows: in the centre, the right wing of the infantry; on the right Colonel Sherbrooke's command; and on the left the remainder of the cavalry and Colonel Wellesley's force.

The army now advanced up the heights in its front in the most regular order, and had accomplished half the ascent when a large body of Mysorean cavalry formed in the shape of a wedge, and moving with great precision, charged General Baird's brigade. This brigade consisted of H. M.'s 12th and 74th regiments, and the Scotch brigade. (This corps had been in the service of Holland, till at the French Revolution it was recalled to England, and numbered the 94th Regiment, after Waterloo, it was disbanded). Nothing could exceed the steadiness of the British troops, who allowed Tippoo's furious horsemen to approach within fifteen yards of them, and then opened a fire of musketry which brought most of the Mysoreans to the ground.

At the same time a large body of infantry, supported by cavalry, attacked Colonel Wellesley's force on the left. The efforts of the enemy were chiefly directed against H.M.'s 33rd regiment. They allowed the foe to approach quite close and to deliver an almost harmless volley, and then coming to the "charge bayonets," rushed furiously upon their assailants, scattering them instantly in terrified rout. But flight availed the panic-stricken mob but little; for into the midst of them, with disciplined impetuosity, dashed General Floyd, at the head of the 19th Dragoons and two regiments of native cavalry, who in a few minutes sabred nearly the whole of the fugitives.

In the meantime, Tippoo, seeing so large a body of British cavalry brought into action on the left, concluded that the picquets, who formed the right, would be without any support from that arm. He therefore determined to try and turn the left flank, and with this view sent a considerable body of horse in that direction, who approached under cover of a large grove of trees. When, however, they began to form up in front of the grove, to their dismay they found the 25th Light Dragoons and the 2nd regiment of Native Cavalry, both under Lieut.-Colonel Cotton, drawn up and on the point of charging them. The enemy did not venture to await the shock, and rapidly retired on the main body, which by this time had withdrawn their guns and were giving way in every direction. The skill and promptitude with which Colonel Cotton handled the two regiments of cavalry under his command, when the right flank was threatened by the enemy's horsemen, obtained for him General Harris's thanks and honourable mention in dispatches. Here occurred the first of a long series of instances in which Stapleton Cotton proved that he was not only a brave dragoon, but also a cool and skilful cavalry leader. In fact, Malavelly may be said to have been his first essay as a commander.

The loss of the British in the action was but sixty killed, wounded, and missing; while that of the Mysoreans was, including the desertions which resulted from the battle, nearly four thousand. Yet Tippoo had made every exertion to encourage his troops and obtain victory. The day before the battle he had addressed his army, promising them success, and informing them that they had nothing to fear from the British, as the latter were raw soldiers, unused to fighting, and not those to whom they had been opposed in the former war. He called upon his men to behave themselves as became them, on the one hand threatening those who gave way with instant death, and on the other hand promising every man in the army a gratuity of one month's pay as a reward for victory. The sabres and bayonets of the British, however, prevailed over the gold and threats of Tippoo, and the Mysoreans were so thoroughly beaten that they made no further attempts to resist the invaders' progress in the open field.

The *sultan* had laid waste the country and erected many strong posts on the line which he thought General Harris would take in his advance from Malavelly or Seringapatam, namely, by Arakerry; but the British commander was too wary to adopt the route chosen for him by the enemy. The day after the battle the British Army moved to the southwest, and managed to cross the River Cauvery without the slightest molestation from the enemy.

During the remainder of the operations, which resulted in the capture of Seringapatam, the cavalry had little opportunity of distinguishing themselves. We find, however, that when, on the 6th of May, Colonel Wellesley attacked and captured a *tope*, or large grove, close under the walls of the fortress. Colonel Cotton, with the 25th

Light Dragoons, and Colonel Prater, with the 2nd Native Cavalry, supported.

Among the documents found at Seringapatam by the captors was the account of a republican club established, by the French officers of Tippoo's army, in that city. The building, surmounted by the cap of Liberty, fronted (curious anomaly) the palace of the greatest despot of the East. The members of this association had sworn eternal hatred to all sovereigns, "the citizen Tippoo alone excepted." And this took place in a city peopled by slaves! Truly liberty, like misery, makes people acquainted with strange bedfellows.

The day after the capture of the city, Colonel Cotton was breakfasting with Colonel Wellesley in the latter's tent when Tippoo's children were brought in. The youngest was only five years old, and looked very much terrified at his position. To comfort the little fellow, Colonel Cotton good-naturedly crammed a lump of sugar into his mouth. Sixty years afterward Gholam Mahomed, the boy in question, came to England, and dined at Lord Combermere's, where he recalled the incident to his host's recollection. He said that, having heard of the trial by rice, he had thought, when the sugar was first put into his mouth, that some punishment would follow, and had been greatly frightened at the idea.

CHAPTER 4

Colonel Cotton's Marriage

Shortly after the fall of Seringapatam, Colonel Cotton learnt that, owing to the death of his elder brother, he had become the heir to the baronetcy, and that his father, anxious for his return to England, had procured for him an exchange to the 16th Light Dragoons. He prepared at once for his departure, and while taking leave of some friends at Madras observed to one of them, a merchant there, that they should never meet again. That gentleman replied, "Not until you are our commander-in-chief." The casual and joking remark was prophetic; for thirty years afterwards, when filling that appointment. Lord Combermere shook hands with his old friend at Calcutta.

In January, 1800, Colonel Cotton landed at Cork, and proceeded to Waterford, where he embarked for Milford Haven, and from thence hastened to London, to deliver duplicates of the Seringapatam dispatches.

On his arrival, he found that on the 1st of the month he had been promoted to the rank of full colonel. His mother announces his return in the following letter to Mrs. Stapleton:—

Combermere Abbey, January 20th, 1800.
Dear Sister,—I am sure you will joyfully pay eightpence for the few lines I send you, as they announce the safe arrival of our dear colonel in Ireland. He is, before this, I conclude, in London. Three letters we received from him yesterday, first dated the 12th, the two others 13th. He landed at Cork on the 12th, wrote the 13th from Waterford, was going immediately to sail for Milford Haven, then to London, with duplicates of the dispatches that Mr. Wellesley had gone with, the day before, by Bristol. He should not stay a moment in town after delivering

them, but set out immediately for this place. He never was in better health in all his life (thank God for all his mercies); in a day or two we hope to be convinced of it. I am too much agitated to write. You will, I am sure, rejoice and *feel* with us. I wish that the meeting was over; it will be too much joy for

Your very affectionate Sister,

F. Cotton.

On arriving in town, he himself wrote to his aunt:

St. James's Hotel, Jermyn Street, 21st Jan., 1800.

My Dearest Aunt,—I have just time to let you know of my arrival with dispatches from Lord Mornington to Mr. Dundas and the Court of Directors. It will be some time, I am sorry to add, before I can set out for Cheshire, as I must appear at the levee. I shall be most happy to hear of the well-being of Lady Chatham and yourself; pray let me receive a letter by return of post. You cannot say too many kind things for me to Lady Chatham.

My dear aunt,

Your very affectionate nephew,

Stapleton Cotton.

To Mrs. Stapleton, at the Countess of Chatham's.

Colonel Cotton, as soon as it was possible, released himself from London engagements, in order to join his family at Combermere Abbey. All were truly rejoiced at the arrival of the favourite son and brother, safe and well, after so many perils. Returning to London from Combermere, after a short stay at home. Colonel Cotton wrote the following letter to Miss Stapleton:—

My Dear Aunt,—Many thanks for your kind letter. I have, upon inquiring, been given to understand that Mr. Pitt has no levees except for Parliament men. I will, however, leave my name there tomorrow, and at Lords Grenville, Temple, and Buckingham. My uncle H. has promised to speak to Mr. Rose (with whom he is intimate) upon the subject in question. I will let you know what steps he recommends being pursued. I was very much gratified, upon my arrival at Combermere, at finding my mother looking so well and in such good spirits. I think she looks younger than when I left England, and is certainly much fatter.

I beg you will make my kindest remembrances to Lady Chatham.

Believe me, my dear aunt,

Your very affectionate nephew,

Stapleton Cotton.

I have been so long out of England that I do not receive cards to all the gay places as formerly, but this may be managed by your having the goodness to give Lady Carysfort (whom I shall call upon tomorrow) a hint to introduce me to the Duchess of Gordon, Lady Chatham, &c.

St James's Hotel, Jermyn Street, March 13th, 1800.

Having indulged in a brief taste of London gaiety, Colonel Cotton proceeded to join his regiment at Ramsgate, having been appointed to command the cavalry on the Kentish coast. At Margate, he met Lady Anna Maria Clinton, who was staying there with her mother, widow of the third Duke of Newcastle. She was a beautiful girl of nineteen, brought up carefully by the dowager duchess, who, in the education of her children, even exceeded, in exaction of obedience and respect, the domestic discipline of the times.

Her son, the young duke, though of age, deferred to his mother's rule with the most affectionate submission. Colonel Cotton, after some intercourse with the family, fell in love with Lady Anna Maria, and before three months had expired since their first acquaintance was received as her accepted suitor. The entire family approved of the match, and indeed the duchess and her second husband, General Craufurd, not only then, but ever afterwards, evinced the warmest attachment for their new relative; while the young Duke of Newcastle became, not merely his brother in law, but in love, and to the end of his life manifested the same warm affection on every occasion.

The marriage took place in 1801. The ceremony was performed in the duke's private chapel at Clumber; and the newly-wedded pair proceeded to spend the honeymoon at Elvaston Park, the seat of the Earl of Harrington, uncle to the bride.

Colonel Cotton was for two years after his return to England stationed at Brighton, where he and Lady Anna Maria became frequent guests of the prince regent.

Mrs. Fitzherbert was at this time residing in her house on the Steyne, and the intimacy subsisting between her and the Prince of Wales became matter for universal comment and speculation. His visits were always private, and every expedient was used to keep the nature of their intercourse a secret. It was, however, one day whispered that a sprained leg, from which the prince suffered, and which confined him to the house, had been the result of a fall at Mrs. Fitzherbert's door after a nocturnal visit. General Cotton, hearing the accident discussed, and being assured that it was ascribed to the proper cause, mentioned it in a letter to Lady Liverpool. This lady communicated her authority to the London gossips, and the exposure of his proceedings through Colonel Cotton's inadvertence came to the prince's knowledge. He never forgave the indiscretion; so Colonel Cotton was no longer invited to the Pavilion, and on several occasions became convinced that the prince was unfavourable to his interests.

The Prince of Wales had taken a fancy to spend much of the winter season at Brighton, and there a camp was established to prevent any disembarkation of the French upon the Sussex coast Colonel Cotton's regiment, with the 18th Hussars, two infantry regiments of the line, and the Gloucester Militia, encamped on a high ground behind the level, where the Bedford Hotel now stands. The prince occupied the red house while the Pavilion was preparing. He gave daily dinner parties, and Colonel Cotton, before his unlucky indiscretion, was invited twice a week to join them, and regaled with music, chiefly duets, performed on two violoncellos, by the prince and Captain Bloomfield.

The latter was at that time a handsome and most agreeable young man, whose Irish vivacity was already tempered by the self-command of a courtly manner. He was then commanding a troop of horse artillery at Brighton, and the musical intimacy which had sprung up between the prince and him ripened into a friendship which endured for many years, securing for the princess friend all the advantages that royal favour confers, in the appreciation and kindness of society. Manly and upright, his honours decorated without deteriorating a superior nature. A patriotic objection to exact from the national generosity the cost of some splendid jewels, bestowed by the prince at his coronation upon another favourite, lost Lord Bloomfield the royal intimacy and patronage, which were withdrawn then for ever.

In 1802 Colonel Cotton was ordered to proceed with his regiment to Ireland. The night before his embarkation at Liverpool he was called out of his bed by the authorities, who required his men to extinguish a fire which raged at Goree, a suburb of the city. After several hours' exertion, the soldiers succeeded in stopping the conflagration and saving a great part of the town. Next day, as Colonel Cotton was going on board, he received a letter of thanks from the mayor and corporation, enclosing *ten pounds* for the men! This very munificent donation was indignantly returned with compliments and thanks.

On arriving in Ireland, the 16th was quartered for some months at the village of Gort, a miserable place in those days, where the only habitable house belonged to the clergyman. This was hired by Colonel Cotton for eighteen months, and there his first child was born, a son, who survived till 1821, and then died of sore throat, after having justified, by great application and abilities, the proudest hopes of a fond father for his future success in life. At the end of eighteen months the 16th was removed to Dublin, and while there witnessed some remarkable scenes in the melancholy drama enacted in July of the year 1803. It was then that took place the insane attempt at rebellion projected by a young man called Emmett, well known for his talents and many social attractions.

Robert Emmett was the son of a Dr. Emmett, from whom he had recently inherited a few thousand pounds, which he devoted to providing material for the rebellion that in his eyes assumed the aspect of a noble struggle against the oppressors of his country. He engaged a dilapidated house in an obscure street, where stores and ammunition were deposited, and nightly met the conspirators, who eagerly engaged to support him. Enthusiastic and eloquent, young Emmett persuaded himself and his accomplices that they were to establish a Utopian government by means of the populace of Dublin and the majority of the people throughout Ireland, who, inspirited by their enterprise and astonished at their courage, would, he fondly fancied, rally round leaders likely to ensure their liberty. For weeks, he had spent his time at a miserable house in Marshalsea-lane, surrounded by implements of destruction, and still accumulating more. In his room there was afterwards found a journal, from which the following passage is extracted:—

> I have little time to consider the thousand difficulties which still lie between me and the completion of my wishes. That these obstacles will be overcome, I have ardent and, I trust, rational hopes; but if such a result is not to be, I thank God for giving me a sanguine disposition, which will comfort in the worst emergencies.

Towards dusk, on the 23rd July, a concerted signal, the firing of a small piece of ordnance, called the chief insurgents out into streets thronged with country people, some of whom had come into town to keep an annual festival, and others, no doubt summoned by a general secret appeal, had repaired there to engage in the projected rebellion. The mystery and silence which shrouded the preparations for this assemblage proved how ready were the lower orders to engage in any proceedings directed against the government, and how implicitly they relied on Emmett's ability to lead them.

This misguided young man now sallied forth from the rendezvous of his chief adherents, and drawing his sword, placed himself at the head of a motley and unruly mob. Not long afterwards one of his followers, on perceiving an officer in uniform at a little distance, fired and shot him dead on the spot. The murdered man was Colonel Brown, just then passing quietly along the street on his way to attend a summons of the commander of the forces. Emmett's followers, totally regardless of his directions, next proceeded where they pleased. They attacked the gaol, and then making an onslaught on an isolated post, overpowered and killed the few soldiers who occupied it.

After an hour spent in reckless atrocities, which Emmett endeavoured vainly to check, the insurgents, entering Thomas-street, perceived the carriage of Lord Kilwarden, Lord Chief Justice of Ireland, approaching. Here was an object on whom to wreak their fury, for Lord Kilwarden had, after the late rebellion, taken an active part in convicting the prominent insurgents. He was now hailed by the mob with shouts and invectives, the horses were stopped, and the poor old man was dragged from his carriage and from the arms of his niece. Miss Wolf, who, echoing piteously his own entreaties for mercy, vainly tried to screen him from the attacks of the excited multitude. All was in vain. He, as well as a nephew who accompanied him, was felled to the ground, and pierced with innumerable wounds, which his assailants seemed to dispute the pleasure of inflicting.

While these atrocities were taking place, Miss Wolf, desired by the mob to escape, made her way to the castle with an account of the murderous act she had just witnessed. Lord Kilwarden was found still alive two hours afterwards, and was conveyed to an adjacent watch-house, where, in half an hour, he expired. On one of the persons who had rescued him exclaiming that the assassins ought to be executed the next day, the dying man, with almost his last breath, whispered, "Murder must be punished; but let no one suffer for my death, except on a fair trial and by the laws of his country"—a sentence that furnished the noblest of epitaphs for the murdered judge, and one which struck to the heart of Emmett when it was repeated to him at the trial.

Finding that the mob he had assembled were committing frightful enormities, the wretched Emmett, who had been weak enough to believe that he could direct them to some noble aim, left the city unobserved. He first proceeded with a few followers, all dressed as French officers, to a mountainous district near Dublin; but meeting with no encouragement, and dreading pursuit and detection, he returned to town with the view of temporary concealment till enabled to leave Ireland for ever. His disguises and retreat being however soon discovered, he was captured and committed to prison.

But to return to the adventures of our hero on that stirring occasion. The day on which Lord Kilwarden fell a victim to the ferocity of the mob a council was held by the Lord-Lieutenant, where he read an anonymous letter, received a few hours previously, stating that at eight o'clock that night the conspirators would assemble, headed by Emmett, in Thomas-street, where they would be supplied with arms concealed under logs of wood, in two houses appropriated for the purpose by their leaders.

Although many communications to the same effect had previously reached the authorities without being followed by the threatened disturbance, still Lord Hardwicke, the lord-lieutenant, considered it expedient to take some immediate precautions at the present juncture. Warned by his experience, and further alarmed by coincidences which confirmed the information given during the day, the commander-in-chief, General Fox, brother to Charles Fox, summoned all officers commanding regiments in Dublin to attend him on the evening of the 23rd, at the Royal Hospital.

Colonel Cotton was preparing to dine with the Cricket Club when the commander-in-chief's message reached him, and as it contained a recommendation that he should come privately to the conference. Colonel Cotton returned home immediately after dinner, and proceeded in a hackney coach to his destination. Colonels Vassal and Brown, commanding regiments stationed in the town, had started on foot to join the meeting, when the former was pursued to the gates of the Royal Hospital by the mob, escaping their fury with difficulty; while Colonel Brown, passing through a crowded street, was, as already related, shot dead by one of the rebels.

Colonel Cotton, prudent enough to avoid the public thoroughfares, proceeded along a street skirting that in which the mob had congregated, and reached the Royal Hospital in safety.

The commander-in-chief had just given his orders to the infantry colonels present, when Colonel Cotton arrived. He was desired to reinforce the guards at the bank, the castle, and the Royal Hospital, and to keep his men in barracks ready for any emergency. Then, mounting an orderly's horse, he tried to pass out of the court by a side gate; but finding it fastened, probably by some disorderly persons, he emerged through another opening into the street. On approaching Thomas-street the shouts of the mob warned him to change his course; so, turning aside into a more private road, he rode on unmolested, and reached the barracks in safety.

That night Colonel Cotton lost one of the best men in his regiment. The poor fellow was employed in conveying dispatches from the commander-in-chief to the lord-lieutenant, and while attempting to pass down Thomas-street, he found it so thronged with the mob, that, to save his dispatches as well as his life, he returned to the castle instead of proceeding to his destination. Some foolish *aides-de-camp* taunted him with being a coward, and declared that he could pass the crowd if he liked, without risk to himself or his charger. The poor man assured the young gentlemen that there was difficulty and danger in the attempt, but that, as they ordered him to proceed, he would do so. A few hours afterwards he was found dead, with seventeen pike wounds in his body.

After the disturbance had lasted for some hours, General Fox, chiefly influenced by Colonel Cotton's urgent representations, called out the military, fired on the mob, and at once restored tranquillity.

Poor Emmett's conviction and execution soon followed the suppression of this popular tumult. His personal merits had recommended him to society and endeared him to his many friends, who, while disclaiming the opinions which he advocated, still deplored the fate of a youth so talented, and hitherto so estimable. What added to the halo of romance by which he was surrounded was the circumstance that he was engaged to the lovely and gifted daughter of the celebrated Curran, and the sad separation of the young lovers excited universal sympathy.

Colonel Cotton's regiment kept the ground at Emmett's execution, and formed a cordon round the gallows erected in Thomas-street. The colonel himself was within this circle, and saw every particular of the melancholy transaction. It was supposed that an attempt would be made to rescue Emmett, who evidently expected it, for he constantly looked anxiously round during the preparations. His firmness here appeared as remarkable as his bearing during the trial. This gifted young man was as much pitied and admired as condemned, even by his political enemies.

Everyone knows the sad tale of the great orator's daughter, whose story Washington Irving has poetically related, and whose sorrows are equally immortalised by Moore. This unfortunate young lady inherited much of her father's talents, and also possessed other attractions, admiringly recognised in society and fondly appreciated by the young, enthusiastic Emmett. The intensity of his affection had long captivated hers before Curran consented to their union. He at first banished her from her home, and Emmett had only latterly been permitted to return preparatory to the marriage, which was to have taken place about the time of his conviction.

The alternation of hope and despair, the pride with which she heard of his eloquent defence, with its appeal to posterity and outburst of patriotism, coupled with the dread that it might exasperate his judges, cruelly racked her mind during the trial. His conviction paralysed her with the stunning shock of grief; but from this temporary apathy she started, with the painful certainty of her impending desolation. For days vibrating between the reality of grief and the uncertainty of hope, the poor girl's vital powers appeared to fail, and it was then believed that she would not long survive her lover's condemnation.

After mourning as if she had already been poor Emmett's wife, she yielded to the persuasion of friends, and again appeared in society, while her thoughts were far away in that time now past, which seemed only the darker from its contrast with the present scenes of pleasure that dazzled and bewildered her tear-bedimmed eyes. Her sad story was to be read in her expressive face—to be heard in the tender pathos of a voice which seemed to exhale sorrow, as she sung the plaintive airs of the country he loved so well, adding more touching charms to those that had captivated her dead lover. Many suitors vainly sought the hand which he had clasped, but she resolved to mourn through life the loss of her first and only love. Poor, weakly, unprotected, she was, however, at last, by the persuasion of friends and the assurance that he would try to conquer the love which she had hitherto denied him, induced to accept a worthy man, whose military duties called him to a southern climate, desirable for the recovery of her fading health.

They were married, and her husband took her to Sicily, where, by the most devoted attachment, he endeavoured to divert her mind from sorrowful memories. She seemed to rally, and tried to be cheerful and make his home happy, but it was not long to be brightened by her presence. Her constitution, already enfeebled, yielded to the encroachments of her insidious malady, of which the sufferer seemed to die, when it was the poor heart which, strained by the tension of grief, had only broken when sickness burdened it still further.

The melancholy romance of this poor girl's life cast a dark shadow over her grave, where the sentiments of admiration which she inspired did not bring a single mourner to deplore her untimely end. In a magazine of the time some traveller describes a funeral which he met on a narrow road leading to the obscure church of Newmarket, in Ireland, where she is interred.

A poor hearse, followed by a humble jaunting-car, bore the remains of her, once the idol of social adoration. Hurrying on to the little edifice, the irreverent haste of this mean procession induced the stranger to inquire who was thus deserted and left in charge of careless followers, apparently only anxious to release themselves from an irksome task. With surprise, he heard that this miserable funeral, with its faded hearse and broken-down car, was to consign to her native earth the fair object of poor Emmett's love, the impassioned vocalist whose strains had vibrated through many hearts, which had equally thrilled with sympathy for the patriot and the poet, the noble youth whose misdirected patriotism had hurried him along the fatal career which led to the scaffold.

Appointed Major-General October 30th, 1805, Stapleton Cotton was ordered to assume the command of a brigade of cavalry, stationed at Dorchester and Weymouth, under the Duke of Cumberland, who commanded the south-western district. This brigade, which consisted of the 14th and 16th Light Dragoons, was afterwards transferred to Norwich and Ipswich. In 1806, Major-General Cotton was elected member for Newark, in conjunction with Henry Willoughby, Esq. Again, in 1812, he was subsequently returned for the same place, which he represented till his elevation to the House of Lords, in 1814.

In May, 1807, Lady Anna Maria Cotton's health began to be a great source of distress to her husband. Young, high-spirited, and totally uncontrolled by the most indulgent of husbands, she would not relinquish the pleasures of her age for the relief of ailments which she deemed insignificant, but which her medical adviser knew to be of dangerous importance. She rode, drove, and danced as usual, until the insidious progress of pulmonary disease enforced the restrictions which her friends had hitherto in vain counselled.

The removal to a mild climate was recommended, and General Cotton accompanied her to Clifton, where he established her for the winter. Her weakness increased daily, but with the hopefulness of consumption she anticipated recovery and bright days to come, to be enlivened by the progress of her little child, who was now the solace of her quiet life. She fancied that its peaceful seclusion would be but temporary, till at the last, when awakened to the certainty of approaching death, she gave her thoughts unceasingly to religious aspirations. The Duke of Newcastle and her mother encouraged her in them, and, with her husband, sadly watched the waning life, the few remaining hours of which were chiefly spent in prayer.

It may be imagined how deeply General Cotton felt his bereavement, as with his sanguine temperament he to the last entertained hopes of her recovery. Overwhelmed with grief, he was comforted by the sympathy of another mourner nearly as much afflicted as himself; for the young Duke of Newcastle deplored his sister's death with all the tenderness of his nature. He accompanied General Cotton on his melancholy journey to Combermere Abbey, where Lady Anna Maria's remains were deposited in the family vault at the parish church of Wrenbury. The tenantry, dependents, and neighbours assembled there to mourn over the grave of the fair young creature for whose presence near the same spot the joy bells, which now tolled the funeral knell, had rung a merry peal but six years previously.

General Cotton was not long permitted to indulge in his natural grief, which was soon interrupted by the contagious excitement of military associates, all eagerly contemplating the coming contest in Spain. Vainly did his female relations endeavour to dissuade him from engaging in it, now that he was next heir to the family estates, and the proper guardian of his infant son. He, however, could not be tempted to forego his chosen career by the prospect of remaining in his loved old abbey, with its romantic associations, evoked by woods and water, the shelter and pleasure of his ancestors for centuries. At that time the domestic life of the Cottons in their old abbey, cheered by warm affection, and enlivened by the joyous spirits of a numerous family of brothers and sisters, was very different from that which we now call country retirement.

There was little county visiting then; there were no excursions for a week to the sea, no sudden rushes to London and to Paris; none of those extemporised journeys undertaken by restless people, with no ostensible object but to come back again. Country families were satisfied with country pleasures, which, if not enjoyed with natural zest, must have been accepted with that contentment which necessity prompts; for there were no others accessible. The very immovability of their position made our grandsires happy with the amusements within their reach; while we but feebly enjoy those which we command from a longing for something else that the habit of change accustoms us to look for.

In a collection of letters to her sister, Mrs. Stapleton, Lady Cotton describes the routine at Combermere Abbey with a minute precision, such as required for its details the sheet of large foolscap on which ladies of her day wrote to friends, when both letters and Mends were dearer than they are now. A single sheet, of whatever size, cost a certain sum; and that this outlay, where postage was paid for according to distance, might be remunerative, the paper, well filled with close writing, looked as intricate as a page of Bradshaw's hieroglyphics. Lady Cotton's accounts of the quiet, happy life at Combermere were written with the kindest simplicity, and they describe, in an unconsciously touching manner, the quiet pleasures and innocent pursuits of her children—all then grown up. In summer, they crossed the lake almost daily, to spend the morning at a beautiful cottage, buried in a wood beyond; or stopped at an island where some old spreading oaks shaded them, while they worked or drew, and afterwards prepared themselves the midday meal, to which their brothers often returned from walks or fishing excursions.

Rides and drives varied these mornings, day following day of such gentle pursuits; and when the winter arrived its natural amusements commenced. In these the tenants joined, if the young ladies (amongst whom Stapleton, when at home, was always foremost) gave a ball, or the young men exhibited in private theatricals for their entertainment. The line which now separates one class from the other was not then, in a certain sense, so strongly marked as now; for Lady Cotton describes, in one of her letters, a ball given by her daughters to the maids, when, dancing together in the absence of gentlemen, the party sat up till two o'clock in the morning.

The following letter belongs to this period, and gives such a pleasant picture of country life at the beginning of the century, that we have yielded to the temptation of inserting it:—

75

Cottage in the Wood, July 26th.

Dear Sister S., (Miss Stapleton)—I really thought I should have had plenty of time this week for writing, but I never yet knew it otherwise but that unexpected interruptions come when least expected, and your chance for a long letter this post again is but small. I meant to have come to this retired spot the moment I had breakfasted this morning, and employed myself in writing you a long letter, while overlooking the workmen at the dairy, as I am superintendent of them while the fine lady dairy-maids, (the Miss Cottons, her daughters, who had a little dairy at the Cottage), are dancing away at Knutsford; but before I was quite dressed comes Fanny (her eldest daughter, Viscountess Kilmorey), on horseback. At eleven she set out again, her father with her, and I then came over here, thinking to have an hour without interruption, when behold, at the water side (this side) I saw two young men standing, booted and spurred. They were two of the Dean of St. Asaph's sons, who, not finding anybody at home on the other side, had walked round to amuse themselves here. I could not be so rude as to write while they stayed, so my time is all dawdled away.

Lady Corbet, (Sir R. Cotton's sister), is coming to spend a day or two with me, to be consoled by me in her widowed state (she went with Sir Corbet Corbet to Nantwich early this morning on his way to the North), and to console me in the absence of my children, four of whom are gone for the whole week to Knutsford. I do not stand in need of consolation, though, for I am as happy as you can imagine in knowing that they are all well taken care of at Arley, and that they will be very much amused; they are the greatest of favourites with Sir Peter and Lady Warburton, besides other friends there. It is the most agreeable family that can be.

I set the girls off on Monday morning in their coach and four beautiful greys; their brothers did not go till yesterday; they and their father had an engagement on Monday to a beans and bacon feast at Wrenbury, I spent the whole day from breakfast till night here. This is really and truly the most enchanting place that ever was seen.

There cannot be greater luxury than sitting as I do now in the easiest of couches instead of chairs. We have a low couch that fits round the room, the arm-cushions stuffed with straw, covered with coarse calico and patch-work made out of old gowns. The sun never comes into the room, and it's always cool in summer and warm in winter. The sun shines upon the bank from the rising to the setting; yet, hot as it is today, and I think it cannot be much hotter, I am as cool as possible.

Viper, (her dog, whose remarkable sagacity is noticed in some work on the canine species), lies on one side, and your Viper on the other; *they say they* are very happy in the absence of their mistresses, one, will so rejoice to see them return. Sir J. and Lady H. Chetwode, who came, as I told you, they were on Thursday, begged to come here after dinner, and you cannot imagine how much they were delighted with it; the dairy is finished, and the last coat of paint Tommy is putting on now, Sally has churned three times, more excellent butter, better than a pound each time, and a little new milk cheese to surprise her mistresses when they return. The calf gets fat; in another week, poor little thing, it will be fit for the butcher. I don't like to look at it, it's a pretty little thing. I hope for your letter tonight, and will add what I can to this tomorrow morning.

Thursday,—Here I am again at my little paradise, where I shall write you a few more lines, and then send my letters over for the postman, who is in haste to go. I am most sadly disappointed, and should be alarmed if I let myself anticipate, at not hearing from you last night as usual, judging by myself. I should hope that Lady Chatham is better than when you wrote last; this lovely weather surely is in her favour, and in Mr. Glid's too, I hope. I will flatter myself every spare moment you have been enjoying the lovely hay-making—sure never was such a season, I regaled my nose last night. Lady Corbet and I, after drinking tea here, and enjoying the luxury of this cool pleasant room as the sun went down, and there was a cool breeze upon the water (though not enough to ruffle it, for it was like a mirror), crossed over, and I found her whisky at the door. I and my dogs got in with her; she set me down at the lodge, and drove herself home. I sat at the cottage door talking to Molly till just nine, the hay in the meadow just before my nose and eyes; it was quite delightful, and a sweet walk through it I had home again.

Lady C. comes again today, and stays till Saturday; a pleasanter companion there cannot be, affectionate, friendly, and kind to me and mine she ever is and ever has been, and I think I may venture to say, ever will be; for she is steady in her friendships. That she has her foibles—one I wish she had not—is true; but a good heart and good-nature overbalance them with her friends. To those who have not experienced the same friendship, affection, and kindness from her that I ever have, they do, I believe, sometimes make her enemies. Her nephews and nieces she loves almost as much as if they were her own children, particularly Bob, her first friend. She is, as you may suppose, happy enough with her neighbour, (Lady Kilmorey), and is very, very good and attentive to her. They are within two miles of each other, and seldom a day passes without their meeting.

The simple pleasures of home had great charms for Stapleton, whose love for the quiet country never varied, enhanced rather than lessened by the excitement of his busy life. During his stay at Combermere invitations poured in from all quarters. A handsome, agreeable widower, heir to a fine property, he was asked to join many pleasant parties, and his female relatives, anxious that he should leave the army and settle at home, vainly urged him to select a wife from amongst the county belles. But neither entreaties nor allurements could divert the gallant soldier from his purpose, and he started for Portugal, sailing from Falmouth in August, 1808, in command of a brigade consisting of the 16th and 14th regiments of Dragoons.

16TH LIGHT DRAGOONS

CHAPTER 5

The Peninsular War, 1808, 1809, and 1810

In the chapters relating to the Peninsular War we do not intend to attempt a sketch of that arduous struggle, but merely to confine ourselves to a narrative of the personal part borne in it by the subject of this memoir. Important and conspicuous as were his services, we yet experience great difficulties in bringing them before the public in the detailed shape they merit. In those days, there were no "own correspondents" to chronicle every incident and exploit of the campaign, and, so to speak, fill in the meagre outline furnished by the official dispatches. Neither did the British cavalry, from the paucity of their numbers and the nature of most of the battle fields, play so conspicuous a part as did that arm in Napoleon's army. As will be seen in the course of these pages, our dragoons had work and danger enough to satisfy the most indefatigable fire-eater; but, with few exceptions, it was chiefly the infantry who won the great and decisive actions in the field where Wellington gathered his luxuriant crop of laurels.

The result of these various circumstances is, that both Napier and other historians have passed over the deeds of the cavalry somewhat skimmingly. Lord Combermere himself, too, was a singularly modest man, and so content to leave his fame to the care of public justice, that he rarely preserved the slightest scrap or memorandum relating to the part he played as one of the most distinguished lieutenants of the great duke. Unlike some, he was singularly averse to talking about himself, or fighting his battles over again. Even his old age was not garrulous, and a recent acquaintance might live in his house for months without hearing anything from his own lips which would arouse the slightest suspicion that Lord Combermere had done anything more than draw his sovereign's pay for nearly three quarters of a century. The following chapters, therefore, are chiefly the fruit of incidental letters and occasional conversations held with him by his widow. Such as the materials are, however, they are authentic, and the great unwillingness of Lord Combermere to speak of self adds increased weight to what he did say, the purport of which was at once taken down by his biographer. But to proceed.

Early in December, 1808, Major-General Cotton sailed from Falmouth with the 14th Light Dragoons. Their destination was Vigo, from whence they were to march to join Sir John Moore's army. On approaching Vigo, after a five days' passage, they received orders directing them to prolong their voyage as far as Lisbon. On the 22nd December, they were disembarked at that port, and joined by two squadrons of the 20th Light Dragoons. It was at first intended to send the 14th to reinforce Sir John Moore in Spain by way of Almeida, but the insuperable difficulties in the matter of commissariat supplies for the march caused the idea to be abandoned. On the 12th January, Sir John Craddock, still striving most loyally to support Moore, even at the expense of his own command, embarked 600 of the 14th, under Cotton, and 1300 infantry, with a view to dispatching them to Vigo. Before, however, the transports had left the harbour, intelligence arrived of Sir John Moore's retreat.

The troops were accordingly disembarked, and General Cotton was now dispatched with the cavalry, the 9th Regiment, and subsequently two battalions of stragglers from Sir John's Moore's army, to occupy different posts between Lisbon and Coimbra, pushing forward advance posts even to the Vouga, in order to watch Marshal Soult. Cotton passed the winter sometimes with one portion of his command, sometimes with another. On the 80th April his brigade of cavalry, now consisting of the 14th, 16th, and 20th Light Dragoons, and the 3rd Light Dragoons (King's German Legion), were directed to concentrate on Coimbra, and on the 4th of May were all assembled at that place.

On the 7th, Cotton, with the cavalry, marched by the Oporto road towards the bridge over the Vouga. (Cotton commanded all the cavalry in the campaign in Portugal, Lieut.-General Payne not having as yet joined Sir Arthur Wellesley). On the 8th he halted, to enable the remaining portions of the army to place themselves in their proper positions; and on the 9th arrived on the banks of that river. Encamped in front, on the opposite side, was Franceschi, with some cavalry, as well as a small body of infantry, and Cotton was anxious to cross early in the night, in order the more certainly to surprise him. With this view, he had proceeded to Sir Arthur Wellesley's headquarters, to obtain permission to do so. Sir Arthur, probably fearing the risk of a night engagement—for his effective force of cavalry was small, and he dreaded the chance of diminishing the numbers of an arm so difficult to replace—anxious also to give time for his other columns to reach their destination, refused his consent to Cotton's enterprising plan, and it was arranged that the cavalry should not cross until about midnight. The result of thus deferring the passage of the cavalry was that Franceschi got wind of the intended movements of the British, and retreated during the night to a strong position near Albergaria Nova, where he rested the flank of his horsemen on a wood lined with infantry.

It may here be remarked, that throughout the war the Duke of Wellington was invariably very chary of engaging in cavalry combats, from the fact that the strength of that arm was always inadequate to the duties required of it, from his experience of the difficulty of obtaining reinforcements from home, and from the well-grounded conviction that any serious losses would at once entail an abandonment of the struggle on the part of the British Ministry.

But to resume the thread of our narrative. A little after midnight on the night of the 9th-10th, Cotton crossed the Vouga, which, though a narrow stream, of little depth, was rendered difficult by the pointed rocks over which its waters flowed. The French camp was deserted, and, misled by his guides. Cotton did not come up with the enemy till broad daylight, when he found them so strongly posted that he dared not attack. He was thus obliged to wait for the arrival of the infantry, who, under Sir Arthur Wellesley's personal superintendence, soon dislodged the French. They were then pursued, and the British cavalry, the superiority of which over that of the French was conspicuously manifested, took some prisoners. That evening Cotton halted at Oliveira. The next day the army continued its advance; and near Grijon again fell in with the enemy's advance guard, consisting of 4000 infantry and some squadrons of cavalry.

A short affair here took place, to the success of which two squadrons of Cotton's brigade, under Brigadier the Hon. Charles Stewart—the late Marquis of Londonderry—materially contributed. At the passage of the Douro on the morrow, the cavalry were not engaged, with the exception of two squadrons of the 14th Light Dragoons, under

Brigadier the Hon. Charles Stewart, who charged the retreating foe with considerable effect, and showed what great results might have been achieved had Sir Arthur thrown the whole of the cavalry across the river at Avintas. During the remainder of the Douro campaign, Cotton was not actually engaged, though after passing Montalegre a portion of his command followed the French up to the borders of Gallicia, capturing a few prisoners in the pursuit.

Cotton now returned to Braga, where he remained a few weeks. From thence he proceeded first to Thomar, subsequently following the army, which he joined in the neighbourhood of Talavera.

In that battle, the British cavalry was divided into three brigades, one of which was commanded by Major-General Cotton, Lieutenant-General Payne being at the head of the division.

On the evening of the 26th of July, Cotton came into the line of battle, being placed in rear of the redoubt, which was occupied by the British, and formed the point of junction between them and the Spaniards. It was dusk when Cotton arrived, and while passing through the Spanish army he was nearly fired at by some of the latter, who, in their bewilderment, mistook the party for foes. About three in the afternoon of the 27th, the advance guard, consisting of Mackenzie's division of infantry, and Anson's brigade of cavalry, was attacked at Salinas so vigorously and unexpectedly by the French that it was thrown into some confusion, and Sir Arthur himself, who happened to be in a house close by, was nearly captured. Soon, however, the British troops rallied, and supported by Anson's brigade of cavalry, reinforced by Cotton, who had been hurried to the front, retired in good order across the plain. Having effected this duty.

Cotton took post in rear of Campbell's division, the remainder of the cavalry being placed in the rear of the left of the position. During the rest of the action, Cotton had little opportunity of distinguishing himself; but, notwithstanding, he, in the only opportunity he had, displayed that promptitude which was so great a characteristic of the man. On the 28th the Guards, having followed an advantage too far, were thrown into momentary disorder; the German Legion were at the same time also in some confusion. In short, the British centre seemed broken. This was the critical moment, the turning point of the day, and victory seemed to be within the grasp of the French. Cotton, sitting immovable on his saddle in front of his gallant line of horsemen, saw the peril, observed the hostile waves rushing through the breach in the living wall before him, and determined to check the

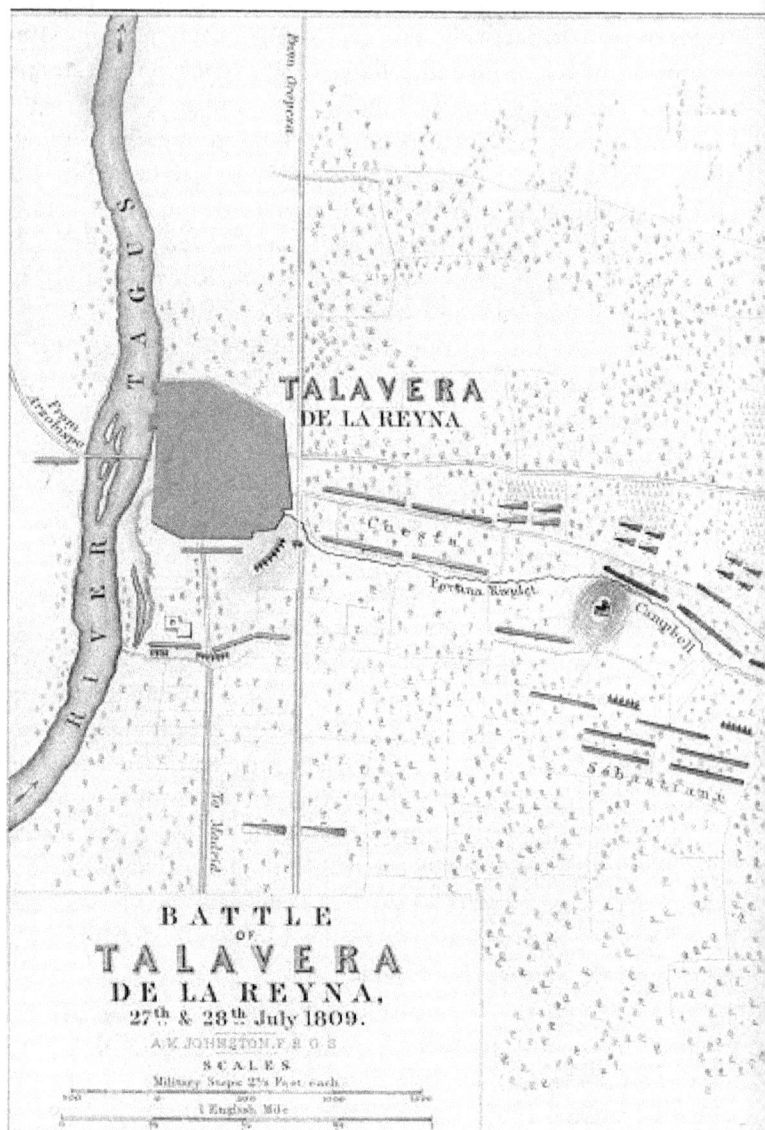

BATTLE
OF
TALAVERA
DE LA REYNA,
27th & 28th July 1809.
A.K. JOHNSTON, F.R.G.S

SCALES
Military Steps 2½ Feet each.
1 English Mile

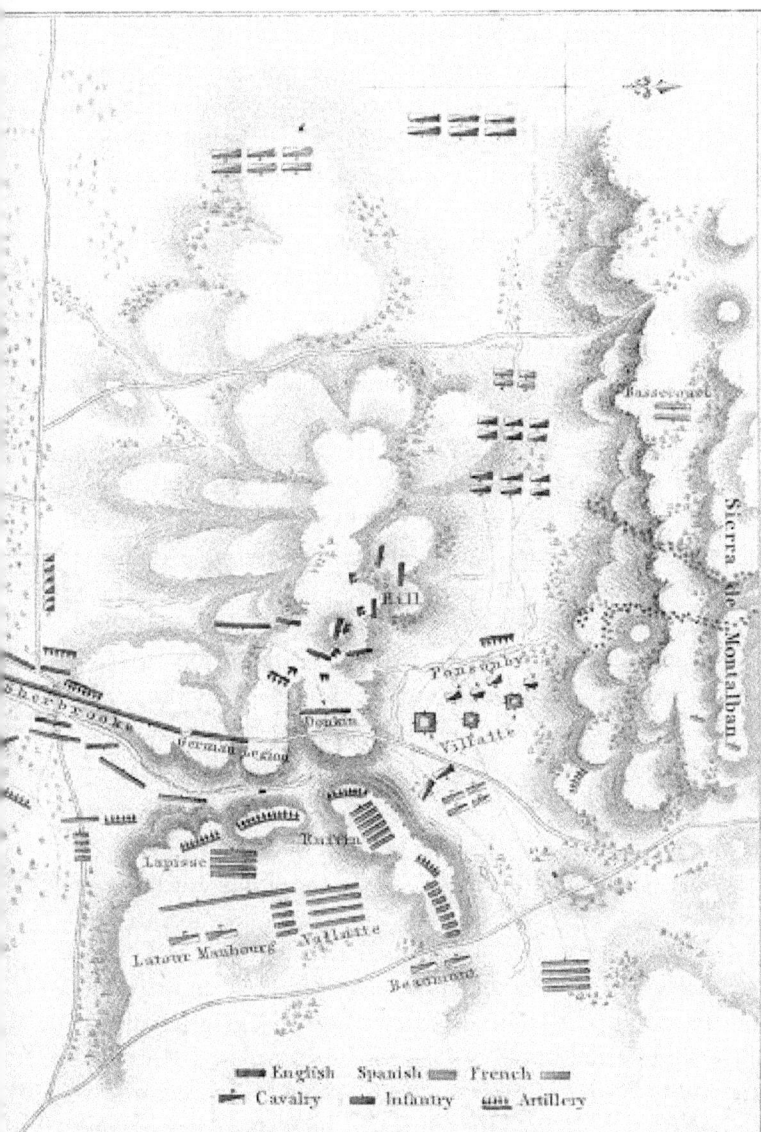

Sierra de Montalban

Bassecourt

Hill

Ponsonby

Villatte

Sherbrooke

German Legion

Donkin

Lapisse

Ruffin

Latour Maubourg   Vallatte

Beaumont

English   Spanish   French
Cavalry   Infantry   Artillery

advancing current. He had no orders from Sir Arthur to quit his post, but he was one of those who on such occasions are satisfied with the commands of honour alone, and he prepared to advance.

At that moment, a message came from Sir Arthur, whose powers of rapid military induction had, even before the event, discerned both it and the remedy, desiring Cotton to support the retreating infantry. Aided by the 48th, he did so, and the furious tide ebbed sullenly back, leaving behind it men and horses to mark where its track had been. The battle was saved. Though Cotton received the personal thanks of the commander-in-chief for this exploit, he was unmentioned in the official dispatch. The Duke of Wellington was never prodigal of praise.

Laurels, though gratifying, are an unsubstantial refreshment for the toil-worn soldier, and Cotton had at the close of this bloody day well-earned those creature comforts which are not disdained by the greatest heroes. He was destined to be disappointed. The Spaniards, who possessed the speed if not the courage of their Andalusian coursers, had plundered in their flight a great part of the English baggage, amongst others that of General Cotton. He was thus left so entirely destitute, that after the battle he was glad to purchase the canteen of Major-General Mackenzie, who had been killed the preceding evening.

Although the subjoined letter from Sir John, then Colonel Elley, to his sister, contains no reference to General Cotton, yet as in it is to be found an interesting allusion to the exploits of the cavalry at Talavera, and as, moreover, the writer afterwards became not only the adjutant-general of General Cotton, but also his intimate friend, we shall not apologize for inserting it:—

Badajos, Sept. 11th, 1809.
My Dear Sister,—Your letter, dated the 24th July, I received on the 8th inst.; it had been some time travelling, but was not less welcome. It afforded me very sincere gratification to find you were all in perfect health, particularly my father, who I am persuaded would feel gratified to hear a good account of me. I find the good people are disposed to give us great credit for our exertions at the Battle of Talavera. It was truly a serious day. The number of British troops did not exceed seventeen thousand. The French allowed themselves to be forty-five thousand. They took no notice whatever of the Spaniards, who stood quiet spectators of the most formidable battle, for the numbers engaged, that has been fought in modern times.

The loss of the enemy was immense: on our side, considerable; really every third man fell. I have before experienced an equally hot fire, but never one of such duration. From ten o'clock in the forenoon of the 27th to the close of day on the 28th (with the exception of a few hours at midnight), I was exposed to the enemy's shot. How I escaped everyone considered a miracle, and I even wondered myself, seeing so many continually falling around me.

The charge of cavalry, so much talked of in your newspapers, was led by your humble servant, at the head of two squadrons of the 23rd Light Dragoons, and so desperate was the undertaking, out of the two squadrons, consisting of about 160 men, all were either killed or wounded, with the exception of myself and six or seven dragoons.

This affair was witnessed by the whole British Army with a mixture of exultation, anxiety, and astonishment. I have said more about myself than I ought to do, but the reflection that I am writing to a beloved sister, who will communicate it to a revered father, I shall be excused so doing, well knowing the satisfaction he will have in saying he has a son who has done his duty in defence of the national honour of Great Britain, and that he bore a considerable part in the glorious achievements acquired on that memorable day. I have inducement for having mentioned myself, as it leads me to give you the following extract of a letter from my most worthy Colonel, the Duke of Northumberland. By a letter his Grace dates from Clifton, Bristol, 19th August:—

(extract.)

I congratulate you on your escape from being hurt, and from the great reputation and credit you have gained in this late action at Talavera de la Reyna; General Hill has written a letter to his brother, the major, wherein, after mentioning the slightness of his wound and other particulars relating to himself, he adds, "That he had the happiness to be able to observe from his position Colonel Elley lead on the British cavalry in a manner that did honour to his abilities and intrepidity."

(Signed)

Northumberland.

Pray tell my good father I rejoice from my heart to hear he is in good health, and I am persuaded it will be a satisfaction to you all to know that, in the midst of sickness, I am as well as at any period of my life. God bless you all! Remember me most affectionately to all the dear little folks, and to all visitors. To my father and Mr. Ellis say everything kind for me, and believe me to remain with true affection,

Your loving brother,

J. Elley.

Pray tell Mr. Ellis that the Spanish mule is the most dangerous animal in nature. He is so *vicious* and *uncertain*.

When Sir Arthur Wellesley marched to Oropesa in order to fight Soult, who was advancing from Placencia to cut off his retreat. Cotton was sent with his brigade to watch and check the advance of that marshal. He fell in with the French advanced guard, and kept it at bay. Afterwards learning that the English Army, on receipt of information that Soult's army was larger than had been thought, was passing the Tagus at Arozbispo, Cotton covered the movement, and was the last man to cross the bridge.

In this operation Cuesta might probably not have been so successful if when, on the first intelligence of Soult's advance, he was asked by Sir Arthur whether he would stay at Talavera and leave to the British the task of marching against that marshal, or the reverse, he had not accepted the first proposition. The firm attitude of Sir Arthur at Oropesa imposed on the French and allowed of a deliberate retreat. Had the Spaniards been in his place, circumstances might have been different. Sir Arthur was so sensible of the danger he had escaped, that soon after the passage of the Tagus he declared to some of his generals that he was the luckiest man alive; for if Cuesta, instead of remaining at Talavera, had proceeded to Oropesa, the British army must have been lost.

From Arozbispo the army retired to Jaraicejo, which place it reached on the 11th of August. On the 20th Sir Arthur, disgusted with the continued failure of the Spanish authorities to supply him with provisions, notwithstanding their magnificent promises, determined to abandon all thought of active operations for a time, and to withdraw to the frontier of Portugal. In pursuance of this determination, he marched to Badajos, and placed his troops in cantonments, in and near that city, on the line of the Guadiana. About this time Cotton, having been made a local lieutenant-general in Spain and Portugal, became ineligible for the command of a brigade; but Sir Arthur Wellesley, unwilling to lose his services, created a lieutenant-general's command for him at the advanced post of Merida, placing under his command a brigade of cavalry and some artillery.

The banks of the Guadiana are often visited by a bad contagious fever, which, in the autumn of that year, raged with great fury, causing terrible ravages in the British Army. The regiments which had recently joined from the Walcheren, being weakened by the fever which has given a mournful celebrity to that expedition, were specially susceptible to the epidemic, and were the first attacked. The loss of the army in these cantonments reached the large figure of 5000! The medical officers advised Sir Arthur to change his position, but he deemed himself unable to comply with their counsel. At Merida half the men and horses of General Cotton's force were at one time in hospital, and two hundred of the cavalry alone died. Although visiting the hospitals daily. Cotton himself escaped unscathed: an immunity which he always attributed to early rising, great temperance in eating and drinking, and taking a ride every day before breakfast.

With regard to the Walcheren expedition, Lord Wellington, one day, while riding with General Cotton near Badajos, observed that had the troops thus employed been sent to Spain, his success would have been certain. He added that Napoleon was quite aware of this circumstance. Lord Wellington had written to the same effect to Lord Castlereagh.

At the close of the year, news reached General Cotton that his father was dead, and that his presence at home had become necessary. He accordingly obtained leave of absence, and arrived in England in January, 1810. He was received in the most flattering manner by the House of Commons, of which he was still a member. The following is an extract from the journals:—

8th March, 1810.—Lieutenant-General Sir Stapleton Cotton, Baronet, being come to the House, Mr. Speaker acquainted them that the House had, upon the 1st day of February last, resolved, that the thanks of this House be given to him for his distinguished exertions on the 27th and 28th of July last, in the memorable Battle of Talavera, which terminated in the signal defeat of the forces of the enemy; and Mr. Speaker gave him the thanks of the House accordingly as follows:—

Lieutenant-General Sir Stapleton Cotton,

Upon your return from the eventful wars of Spain, whatever variance of opinion, whatever alternation of hopes and apprehensions you may have found to prevail in this country respecting the progress and final issue of that awful contest, nevertheless, your distinguished conduct and services have not failed to call forth one universal expression of applause and admiration.

The British cavalry has been long renowned in war. Victorious in other times over the troops of France, it feared not again to meet its former rivals, flushed even as they were with the pride of conquest and the spoil of many nations.

Led by your sword, it again displayed a strength and valour irresistible in the shock of arms, and renewed its ancient triumphs in the hard-fought field of Talavera. When the history of these memorable days shall be read by our latest descendants, be assured that your name will be repeated with exultation, and your deeds recounted in the list of those heroic achievements.

You serve not an ungrateful country. It well knows that military fame is national power. And this House, ever prompt to proclaim its gratitude for eminent services in war, has therefore conferred upon you the honour of its unanimous thanks. And I do now accordingly, in the name and by the command of the Commons of the United Kingdom, thank you for your distinguished exertions on the 27th and 28th days of July last, in the memorable Battle of Talavera, which terminated in the signal defeat of the forces of the enemy.

Upon which Lieutenant-General Sir Stapleton Cotton said:—

Mr. Speaker,

In endeavouring to express my sense of the very high honour which has been conferred upon me, and which has been communicated to me by you, Sir, in so flattering a manner, I fear I shall fall short of what my feelings are upon this occasion.

To receive the thanks of Parliament is one of the highest rewards to which a soldier can aspire; and believe me. Sir,

I shall ever consider it my greatest pride to have been so honoured. This, I may venture to say, is the feeling of all my brother officers and soldiers who had the good fortune to be commanded by one of the most able and distinguished generals that has adorned the annals of this country, and who will, I trust (should an opportunity offer), again prove to the world that a British Army is not to be beat by a French force of double its numbers.

One of his first cares on arriving in England was to comfortably establish his mother and his only unmarried sister at Combermere Abbey, displaying as ever the greatest consideration for their comfort. His female relations, especially his mother, to whom he had always been a most affectionate son, were earnest in their entreaties that he would remain at home and look after his estate. But Stapleton Cotton firmly resisted both their persuasions and the inducements afforded by his own tastes and social advantages. A man of fashion and well received in London, very fond of farming and shooting in the country, a baronet and the owner of a fine estate and a beautiful country house, his temptations to a home life were truly great. The education of his only son required his superintendence, and his property, which had somewhat suffered under Sir Robert's careless and wasteful management, demanded the eye of a master.

Still the patriotic spirit to which Mr. Abbott, the Speaker, alluded on the occasion, in a highly commendatory speech in the House of Commons, added strength to the same duty which recalled him to the seat of war, after but a few weeks' stay in England. When he rejoined the army, he was appointed first to the command of the First Division, and shortly afterwards, on the recall of Lieutenant-General Payne, to that of the cavalry. Ere we follow Sir Stapleton on the bright path now opened to him, let us pause for a moment to consider what manner of man this was who was entrusted with so important a command as that of the British cavalry in the most glorious of our wars.

At that time, he was thirty-five years of age, and a decidedly handsome man. Of middle height and strongly though somewhat slightly built, he possessed great activity of body, and was an excellent horseman. In his habits, he was temperate to an extent not frequently met with in those days, yet withal he was of a sociable disposition. Though naturally hot-tempered, he was universally liked; for, courteous and pleasing in manner, he had ever a kind word for those of his subordi-

AN OFFICER (LIEUT.-COL.) OF THE 14TH LIGHT DRAGOONS
IN PARADE DRESS

nates with whom he came in contact. Cheerful and fond of society, he frequently, during the intervals of active operations or in winter quarters, amused himself by assembling the ladies of the neighbourhood at those little parties called *tertullias* in the Peninsula, at which dancing, music, and flirtation all combine for the entertainment of the guests. Like his illustrious chief, he was a great dandy, though with more success. Resembling Murat in personal enterprise and fearlessness, he also resembled that prince of *beaux sabreurs* in carrying his love of dress into the very field of battle.

On the most perilous occasions, he was to be seen attired in the rich uniform of a general of hussars, and mounted on a horse covered with the most gorgeous trappings, exposing himself recklessly to a storm of shot. So notorious was this habit, that it obtained him in the army in Spain the name of the *Lion d'Or*. As calm and cool under the heaviest fire and at the most critical moments as at a ball, his gallantry was so conspicuous, that the writer of these pages heard one of Cotton's bravest officers liken, after the lapse of upwards of half a century, his lamented chief to Ney. Surely no soldier was ever honoured by a more noble panegyric. Yet his courage, which was as cool as it was ardent, never led him to subject his men to undue hazard; and on many occasions, he disregarded the chance of personal distinction rather than expose his troops to the risk of a heavy loss.

Among his many excellent qualifications for a leader one was preeminently conspicuous: however depressing and critical the circumstances in which he might be, he always maintained the same cheerful and spirited demeanour. His men were not slow to catch the contagion, and it tended in no slight degree to support them on many anxious occasions. Although he had risen so rapidly to the command of a regiment, there was not an adjutant in the service better acquainted with all the details of cavalry service than was Stapleton Cotton. He possessed a peculiar aptitude for the inspection of troops of all arms, but especially of those belonging to his own branch, the cavalry. With him an inspection was no matter of form and ceremony. Never troubling himself with trivial detail, he went straight to the leading and important points.

He considered it his duty to ascertain that the officers were practically acquainted with the routine of drill. He examined them closely as to their knowledge of this part of their duty, and may be quoted as the first inspecting general who called out officers from their places to manoeuvre the whole or any part of the regiment before him.

On these occasions, he was as ready to bestow praise as to administer censure, when either was deserved. His reports were short, clear, and faithful. Nor could any regiment undergo his inspection without the authorities at headquarters being made perfectly acquainted with the true condition of its discipline and its state of efficiency for the field. If wanting in either of these particulars, no smartness of appearance could deceive General Cotton, or induce him to pass over the absence of the more essential qualities. In his treatment of those under his command, he was equally just and discriminating, and a good officer might always feel safe in his hands and confident of a good report, if he deserved it.

Without being what is termed a genius, he possessed great common sense and a quick and acute perception of character. So judicious was his selection of those in whom to place confidence in military matters, that no general was ever better served in the field by his staff than he was. They, as well as all those under his command, knew that the only way to obtain his favour was to perform their duty with strictness and diligence. Never did he spare either time or exertion to promote the interests of those officers and men whom he believed to deserve advancement.

The Duke of Wellington thought most highly of his qualities as a cavalry general, and often was heard to remark that, when he gave an order to Sir Stapleton Cotton, he felt sure it would be obeyed, not only with zeal but with discretion.

After such a description, and considering the great reputation which Sir Stapleton Cotton acquired as the best cavalry officer mentioned in the military history of Great Britain, it will appear somewhat strange that so few incidents have been preserved of personal adventure in the greatest of our wars. It may be urged against the editors of these memoirs that they have failed to bring the individual with sufficient prominence before the reader, and that many anecdotes must exist concerning the deeds of one who may, without exaggeration, be termed the English Murat. To this we would reply, that no journals, and scarcely any letters, of the subject of our biography have been preserved; that he outlived all his contemporaries, and most of his juniors who took part in the Peninsular War, and that, consequently, his own disinclination to speak of himself cannot be supplemented by the memories of others.

Besides, as we have elsewhere remarked, the nature of the theatre of war in Spain and Portugal was such that cavalry movements on a large scale could seldom be attempted, even had the Duke of Wellington been less thrifty of that arm than he notoriously was. Moreover, it is alike unnecessary, and contrary to the genius of the English Army, for the general commanding the cavalry to take habitually a personal and prominent part in the charges which he directs. So much is this the case, that in the most complete history of the Peninsular war extant—Napier's—we do not find Sir Stapleton Cotton's name mentioned above half-a-dozen times, and then only casually, while, with all our industry, we have been unable to discover that, intrepid as he notoriously was, the subject of our biography ever once crossed swords with an enemy.

As we have before mentioned, we by no means pretend to write a history of the Peninsular war, but only to narrate the part borne in it by the subject of this memoir. We shall therefore not enter into any details concerning the cantonments of the British Army when Cotton joined headquarters at Celorico. Lord Wellington had taken up a position to cover Lisbon and check the invasion of Portugal. The main body of his infantry was at Viseu, Celorico, Guarda, and Pinhel. General Hill was at Abrantes and Portalegre with his division, to which was attached the 13th Light Dragoons. Craufurd, with another division, and three regiments of cavalry, held the advanced posts between the Coa and the Agueda, in front of Almeida; and Cotton, with the rest of the cavalry, was in cantonments in the valley of the Mondego. Opposed to Wellington was Massena, at the head of 80,000 veteran troops, threatening the fortresses of Ciudad Rodrigo and Almeida. To oppose him, the British General could not muster above 56,000 disposable troops, including the Portuguese garrisons, and, moreover, half his force consisted of Portuguese militia.

With the exception of a skirmish at the bridge of San Felices, on the Agueda, on the 19th March, between Craufurd and General Ferey, in which the latter was worsted, nothing of any importance took place for several months, the French confining themselves to mere demonstrations, and the British still maintaining their attitude of defensive watchfulness. At last, on the 8th June, 4000 French cavalry crossed the Agueda, and Craufurd, in consequence, withdrew his troops a short distance from that river, and concentrated them at Gallegos and Espeja. Nothing particular, however, occurred till the 4th July, when a skirmish took place, which is described in the following letter to General Cotton:—

Lines, near Fort Conception, 6th July, 1810,

My dear General,—Pen and ink were such scarce articles, in consequence of our separation from our baggage, that I was not able to write you yesterday, as I had intended, the account of our skirmish on the 4th. It is the only event which has occurred since you left us, (cavalry headquarters were at some distance to the rear), except, indeed, a very trifling affair a day or two after your departure, when the enemy drove us from some of our most advanced points, particularly the village of Carpio and the hill, where we reconnoitred, and obliged us to retire behind the brook. From that time till the 4th, Ciudad Rodrigo, spite of the French batteries and assaults repeated every night, continued to defend itself with unexpected obstinacy. At daybreak on that day the enemy attacked three of our picquets with columns of cavalry, supported by infantry and artillery. We always turned out before daybreak, so we were ready for them. We had Krokenburgh's squadron of hussars and our two squadrons. Our infantry, with the Spaniards, were in our rear, near Alameda.

Of course, we retreated as the enemy appeared. Fortunately, not a man of the picquets was cut off. Hay, Van Hagan, and Tomkinson, with a German officer, were on the different picquets, and Bellis captain of the day. In the rear of Gallegos, at the distance of about half a mile, you may recollect a bog with a narrow causeway across it. When we had retired beyond this, Krokenburgh, who commanded the skirmishers, collected them together, and made several dashes very gallantly at the French officers. A sergeant and some men were killed. We could have stopped them here longer in front had not their numbers enabled them to encircle our right. It is understood they had about 2000 cavalry. Our artillery was served very well, and with considerable effect.

I saw several shrapnels burst in the middle of the enemy's squadron. About a mile from the bridge the enemy were pressing us hard, when we met our infantry. We drew the enemy close to them, and Elder's *caçadores* poured a volley into them. This checked them completely, and we were no more annoyed. The enemy's artillery hardly ever got into action. Our whole loss consists of one 16th and four or five hussars wounded, two 16th horses killed, three or four 16th and as many hussar horses wounded. I do not think our infantry lost a man.

We are at present behind the little river which separates Spain from Portugal. One squadron 14th, one *do.* hussars, two *do.* 16th, are encamped here together; one squadron 14th, one *do.* hussars, form a chain to our left towards Barquillo, and the Spanish cavalry, under Colonel Mara, are to our right at Fuentes; our infantry are near Fort Conception. The enemy have retired and contented themselves with leaving a picquet in Gallegos, and patrolling by night from thence to Alameda. Their object in drawing us back was probably the forage near Gallegos. Ciudad Rodrigo still holds out.

This is the 13th day since the batteries opened, and three weeks at least since they began to break ground. We have been very well foraged since we have been here. We have generally had more than our allowance; sometimes wheat, sometimes Indian corn, sometimes rye, with plenty of green forage. The men have been well off, except for wine. A pipe, which we had just procured at Gallegos, we could not bring away, and were obliged to stave it. Some supplies of biscuit were also left behind. The horses have not fallen off, though they have been almost constantly saddled at Gallegos. Duty fell very hard, particularly on the subalterns: four were on picquet always out of ten.

Ever most faithfully yours,

E. Charles Cocks.

(Captain the Hon. E. C. Cocks, 16th Dragoons. He was afterwards killed at Burgos).

On the 11th July Craufurd endeavoured to capture a French foraging party of one hundred infantry and thirty cavalry. He had six squadrons of the 14th and 16th Light Dragoons, and the 1st German Hussars. Craufurd had besides infantry and artillery in reserve, for he expected to have to do with cavalry alone, and knew not that any French infantry had crossed the river. The British cavalry quickly killed, wounded, and captured those of the enemy, but were less fortunate against the infantry, who, forming square, steadily repulsed every attempt to break them, and eventually effected their escape before Craufurd's infantry supports could be brought up. The failure of the charge of a squadron of the 14th under Talbot is another instance, if it were wanted, that a square of steady infantry is impregnable against the best cavalry alone; for Talbot led so gallantly, and his men followed so devotedly, that Talbot himself and fourteen troopers fell close to the

CHARGE OF BRITISH LIGHT DRAGOONS

levelled bayonets which arrested them.

There was no lack of charging home here, for after the action the bipod was seen welling from wounds inflicted by bayonets, and it is asserted that he actually fell *on* them. After Talbot's death, another squadron of the 14th Dragoons prepared for a renewed assault, when cavalry was seen to advance both front and flank. These being supposed to be reinforcements for the enemy, the attack was arrested, and the two hundred gallant Frenchmen made good their retreat without the loss of a man.

It was afterwards ascertained that the cavalry in question were two of our own squadrons, which had been detached at an early hour to cut off the retreat of the French. The conduct of the French infantry on this occasion was beyond all praise. They allowed the British cavalry to approach within a dozen yards before they poured in a destructive volley. Colonel Talbot received eight bullet wounds, and Captain Brotherton, who commanded the squadron, had his charger shot under him.

The horse fell within a yard of the square, and such was the steadiness of the men composing it that not an individual left the ranks to kill or capture Captain Brotherton, who, entangled by his slain steed, lay completely at their mercy. It is only justice to that gallant band to record the regiment to which they belonged. It was the 66th of the line, and Marmont recognised their merit by instantly bestowing on every one of them the cross of the Legion of Honour.

When a few days later Captain Brotherton arrived at the French headquarters with a flag of truce for the purpose of obtaining the body of Colonel Talbot, he saw his late opponents already bearing the much-prized decorations on their breasts. (Part of the above account is derived from information kindly afforded by General Sir Thomas Brotherton, K.C.B., the Captain Brotherton mentioned as commanding the squadron which made the gallant but unsuccessful charge). The disastrous result of this affair gave rise to much gossip, and some most unfounded assertions were thrown out against the 16th Light Dragoons, to whose misconduct it was said the escape of the French was due. A rumour of this calumny having reached Sir Stapleton Cotton, who, from having formerly commanded the 16th Dragoons, felt a more than ordinary interest in the good name of that corps, he exerted himself to clear up the matter. The following letters, among the correspondence which took place on the occasion, have been preserved:—

Encampment, near Fuerte de la Concepcion,
12th July, 1810.

My Dear General,—Ciudad Rodrigo has at length fallen. It surrendered about six on the evening of the 10th, after a bombardment of sixteen days.

We endeavoured yesterday to cut off a party of the enemy. A troop of cavalry, covered by three or four companies of infantry, had for some days been in the habit of advancing by daybreak to a height near Villa de Puerco in order to reconnoitre our position. We moved a little before midnight (the night before last), and by daybreak got beyond Villa de Puerco. We had one squadron hussars, two squadrons 16th, and three squadrons 14th. Captain Gruben's squadron hussars was likewise to appear in another direction and co-operate.

As the sun rose we discovered the infantry beyond Villa de Puerco, and the cavalry to their right. The whole of the country was open in front, and to our left covered with com. To the right were some woods. We had a defile to pass, by the village, in order to get into the plain. We advanced in column of divisions from the right; the hussars first, followed by the 16th, and then the 14th. The infantry were just opposite the defile, behind the brow of a hill, and nearly concealed by the corn.

The hussars endeavoured to form to the front and charge, as did the 1st squadron (Ashworth's) of the 16th. They got a heavy volley, which knocked down thirteen or fourteen men and nearly as many horses. They then wheeled to the left, and made at the cavalry. The 3rd squadron (Bellis') followed their example. The sun was directly in our eyes, and from that circumstance and the dust we could see nothing, and, except the two squadrons who had charged, no one knew whence the volley had proceeded. Then three squadrons rode at the cavalry, and took nearly forty with their horses. Very few got away.

The 4th squadron (Brotherton of the 14th) was stopped by General Craufurd, and ordered to charge the infantry. It is impossible to do justice to the intrepidity of this body of men. They stood the second charge as well as the first, knocked down some by a running fire, and bayoneted others. Colonel Talbot led the squadron. When he saw the enemy had formed an oblong, he endeavoured to bring his right flank forward and charge the upper face of the square. He moved on like a lion, had his horse killed close to the enemy, and fell himself fighting sabre in hand in the middle of the square. This was not broken, and the 14th was repulsed. In the dust and confusion which ensued the enemy got off through the corn into the woods.

The 14th have lost, besides Colonel Talbot, one quartermaster and fifteen or sixteen men, and upwards of twenty horses killed or desperately wounded. We have escaped, being principally employed with the cavalry. We had one man badly wounded, and two horses killed and some wounded. The total of rank and file is thirty-two, of whom only two are likely to recover.

We had a report an hour ago that the enemy was advancing on Fuentes to our right, where Colonel Mara is encamped with the Spanish cavalry. Fort Conception is to be blown up; but the enemy is ignorant of this, and think our position very strong in consequence of the support we may derive from that fortress.

> Believe me, my dear general,
> Most truly yours,
> E. Charles Cocks.

Sir S. Cotton's Letter to General Cole.

15th July, 1810, near Povoa del Rey.

My Dear General,—I consider it very kind of you to inform me, through my friend Tweeddale, of the groundless, malicious reports circulated of misconduct of the 16th Dragoons in the affair of the 11th at Villa de Puerco. In consequence of Tweeddale communicating to me these and other similar reports which he heard at Alverca, I thought it my duty, from commanding the division to which that regiment belongs, to have the matter investigated, in order to bring those to whom blame or suspicion is attached to trial, or that, if there were no grounds for these evil reports, their unfavourable effect should be done away with.

I therefore made known to Lord Wellington that such were in circulation, and I received the following very satisfactory letter in return. But it is not sufficient that the corps and I should be satisfied, it is necessary that the actual conduct of the regiment should be generally known, and that the persons circulating these reports should be called to account for them.

If General Craufurd had blamed any particular corps it could not have been known that he did so, for the dispatch was not received till sometime after these reports were in circulation, and the good-natured authors of them declared that General Craufurd in his dispatch had thrown the blame on the cavalry, particularly on the 16th.

Now it appears that no blame could really be thrown on that regiment, nor, indeed, on any other, for the first squadron of the 16th were attached to the hussars, and under the orders of Captain Crawkenberg, who commanded them to attack the enemy's cavalry, which was moving off. He also sent orders to the next squadron, which was also of the 16th, to wheel to the left and cut off the enemy's cavalry, who would certainly have got away if the officer commanding that squadron had not promptly obeyed. General Craufurd then came up and made the next squadron (the 14th) charge the infantry, which poor Talbot did not see till the squadron got over the brow of the hill, and was close upon them.

The 6th squadron (14th) under Colonel Arenchildt, was then advancing to support Talbot, but upon seeing a squadron of the 1st Hussars in the distance approaching, and taking them for the enemy, he halted the 14th. The squadron of the 14th, headed by poor Talbot, failing in the attack, the infantry escaped through the corn to a wood on their left. These are the outlines of what I have learnt by letters as well as from officers who have been to the outposts.

Tweeddale, I expect back this evening or tomorrow. He has promised to send you any further particulars which he may collect, and you will oblige me particularly by showing Lord Wellington's letter as well as Tweeddale's, if you should hear any hints drop as to the misconduct of the 16th.

I have always endeavoured to be, and I believe I am, impartial, and although I commanded the 16th Dragoons some years ago, and of course must feel attached to the regiment, yet, if I knew that the corps, or any individual belonging to it, had been in fault, I should be as active in bringing the circumstance forward as if it happened in any of the other regiments belonging to my division.

I send you a rough sketch of the affair of the 11th. Believe me, ever your sincerely and obliged,

Stapleton Cotton.

P. S.—Will you have the goodness to send my letter and Lord

Wellington's to General Campbell, and request him to show both to Slade, who is near him.

Alvena, July 14, 1810.

My Dear Cotton, (Gurwood's *Dispatches*)—I have received your letter of this day, and I am much obliged to you for the perusal of Cocks' letter, which contains a very clear account of the events of the 11th.

I can show you Craufurd's letter to me, which does not throw any blame whatever on the 16th, and indeed I never had a doubt upon the subject. The cause of the failure to take the infantry as well as the cavalry, Craufurd states was that a body of our own cavalry, which I conclude was Grüben's Hussars, were seen coming out of Barcilla, and were taken by mistake for the enemy, which stopped the attack of the rear squadron. The 16th had nothing to do with this mistake, nor probably is anyone to blame for it. The French infantry appear to have behaved remarkably well, and probably were so posted that no efforts of cavalry could have forced them. It would really not be fair to the 16th to have any inquiry into their conduct in this affair. I have no doubt how it would turn out, but the very fact of inquiring upholds some grounds which, to suppose even, would be injurious, to them.

You may show this letter, if you please.

Ever yours most sincerely.

Wellington.

The following is from Captain Cocks to General Cotton on the subject:—

Encampment, near Fort Conception,
July 17th, 1810.

My Dear General,—I felt as much surprised as hurt when I received your letter mentioning the reports, which idle or ignorant men have presumed to spread in the rear. I had not heard one word of them here, nor do I believe that anything of that nature has been said at the outposts in any way whatever.

There are two circumstances which, if not fairly spoken of, might be supposed to give some colour to these injurious misrepresentations, namely, our having suffered so little, our being the only regiment which was not actually engaged with the infantry, and the idea that the squadrons here were about to be relieved so soon,

Our not being engaged personally with the enemy, and our consequent slight loss, I trust I explained in my letter of the 12th. Had Ashworth been allowed to remain in the rear of the hussars, where he had formed, he would have had an opportunity of making an effectual charge when the hussars opened out, in consequence of the fire; but he was ordered by some staff officer to form *in line* with the hussars, and as the latter outflanked the infantry on both flanks. Ashworth's squadron, which was to the left, of course, completely cleared the infantry, and was protected from their fire by the hussars filing round the flank of the enemy.

After the charge, therefore, they again formed. An order was given to form to the left and attack the cavalry. This order was given by Captain Krokenberg, whose character is well known, and who had the immediate command of the *two* leading squadrons. It appears perfectly natural, for the cavalry were dispersing and preparing to escape, *à la débandade,* and it was necessary to secure them instantly, particularly as we did not know whether Grüben's and Butler's squadrons were friend or foe. The infantry, on the contrary, derived their security only from their immobility and their position, and had they been inclined to move there were squadrons in the rear to look after them who were well situated for their attack, though not so handy for the cavalry.

When the two leading squadrons began to go off to the left, the next squadron (Bellis's) had not cleared the crest of the hill. It was more broken in the defile than the others, in consequence of having more ground to make up. It could not have seen the infantry, even had the dust cleared up, and as it followed Ashworth's squadron it was not opposite to them. The fire was independent, and no one of this squadron could tell whether it proceeded from infantry or cavalry. When, therefore, the order was passed down to move on the cavalry, it was obeyed with alacrity and without surprise, as they were the only enemy to be discerned.

The next squadron was prevented from following the example of the preceding only by the general who directed them to charge the infantry. Neither Colonel Talbot or Captain Brotherton saw them, and they were obliged to ask the general where they were. I am certain that any well-informed man could find nothing to blame in the conduct of any of the cavalry, except a too great persistency in the pursuit of the enemy's dragoons, which, however, was the more excusable, as the enemy did not resist, and as speed, not fighting, seemed likely to be the criterion of the number of our prisoners.

Should reports such as you mention be circulated here, I shall not be wanting to put a stop to them, and in such case, shall make use of Lord Wellington's letter; but should nothing of the sort be said, which will probably be the case when the facts are well known, I shall not enter on the subject. I am conscious of right; do not want precaution, but may be thought wrong.

Believe me, my dear general, we feel truly grateful for the kindness you have shown the regiment on this occasion. At a distance, it was necessary the facts should be made known. I received your letter yesterday, at the moment I was going on duty, which prevented my answering it till today.

Ever most faithfully yours,

E. Charles Cocks.

CHAPTER 6

Combat of the Coa

On the 21st July, Craufurd retired from the neighbourhood of Fort Conception to a position between Almeida and the Coa. Captain Brotherton's squadron of the 14th Dragoons formed the rear guard, and remained close to Fort Conception till that work was blown up. By the explosion he suffered some loss, both of men and horses, and had the pain of knowing that the body of Colonel Talbot, who had fallen on the 11th, and who had been buried on the glacis, had been blown up.

On the 24th July took place the disastrous but bravely disputed combat of the Coa, in which the cavalry of Craufurd's force took little or no part.

From the end of July till the arrival of the army at Torres Vedras, Sir Stapleton Cotton had charge of the outposts, and conducted that duty in the most satisfactory manner. In order to prepare for the re-treat that was in contemplation, the infantry divisions were moved to the rear, and the cavalry in advance to Alverca, on the Almeida road. Almeida was invested by the French, and the trenches were opened on the 18th August, but the want of energy displayed by the besiegers, and the small force employed by them in the operation, induced Lord Wellington to make an attempt to raise the siege, or at all events to bring off the garrison. This design was rendered abortive by the fall of Almeida on the 27th August. The infantry of the army was now again withdrawn to the rear into the valley of the Mondego, one division, however, being left at Guarda, and the cavalry under Cotton occupy-ing a line of outposts about Alverca. The following letters give an idea of the duties performed by them, and the manner in which they were carried out:—

Alverca, 28th August, 1810.

Sir,—I have the honour to report to you that about noon this day the enemy advanced from Carvalhal, and drove in the cavalry brigade stationed near Vendados. I charged the advanced party (consisting of cavalry and infantry, to the number of from one hundred to one hundred and fifty) with part of the inlying picquet of the Royal Dragoons. The enemy lost from eight to ten men in killed and wounded, and I have made five prisoners. Two men and one horse of the Royals were killed, and the same number wounded.

 I have the honour to be, Sir,

   Your very obedient humble Servant,

         John Slade, M.G.

Lieut.-General Sir Stapleton Cotton, Bart, &c. &c.

On the 3rd September, Wellington retired the infantry one march further to the rear, on account of some threatening movements of the enemy. On the 17th of the same month the retreat began in earnest, the cavalry covering the movement, and gradually withdrawing as the French pushed on.

       Daybreak, 10th September, 1810.

My Lord,—I had the honour to report yesterday at four p.m. that the enemy was advancing by Alfayates and Sabugal on Guarda, and had reached Pega at one p.m. I afterwards sent off an orderly at half-past five to report that the enemy was obliged to leave Guarda.

I think altogether I saw about 800 infantry and 50 or 60 dragoons. The infantry came out of the woods from two points, marching in files and straggling a good deal; the cavalry preceded them. When my picquet began to skirmish they fell back, and the infantry advanced. I observed two mounted men about three miles from Guarda, upon the Pena Maior road. I cannot tell whether they were flankers or the advance of another column, nor am I quite sure they were not peasants.

I am about a league from Guarda towards Mantugua. The peasants say the enemy talk of marching on to Celorico. I hope to find some point whence I can command that road perfectly.

I apprised Sir S. Cotton of the movements of the enemy. I brought with me every one of my party.

 I have the honour, &c.,

Almeida

PROBABLE FIRST POSITION OF CRAUFORD

To Val de Mula

To Junça or S. Pedro

To Junça or S. Pedro

R. Coa

R. Coa

E. Char. Cocks.
My patrol fell in with a patrol of the enemy just before day-break, between this and Guarda.

Convent of Busaco, 24th September, 1810.

My Dear Sir Stapleton,—Lord Wellington wishes that you should send a small patrol along the road that communicates between Mantagoa and Sardao.

This road, on leaving Mantagoa, passes through Gandera, Maceiro, Ferrestal, Boialvo, &c., to Sardao. The object is to obtain a report upon this road, and whether it is practicable and easy for artillery, and therefore an officer should be sent along with the patrol who is qualified to judge of it in that respect. The patrol had better enter the road somewhere near Boialvo, and proceed from thence towards Mantagoa. It is desirable, however, at the same time to avoid as much as possible showing the patrol to the enemy, or attracting his attention to the road in question.

I beg you will send me the observations made by the officer employed as soon as he returns. He may be directed not to fall back upon Boialvo, but to come to Villa Nova after finishing his reconnoissance, and to send up his report from thence. I suggest this as the means of saving time. When the cavalry are quartered I beg you will be so good as send me a list of their cantonments, or, at least, of the headquarters of the general officers, and of regiments, and of the troop of artillery.

Believe me, my dear Sir Stapleton,
Yours ever faithfully,
(Signed)
Geo. Murray.
Qr,-Mr. Genl.

Lieut.-General Sir Stapleton Cotton, Bart., &c. &c.

On the 27th September took place the Battle of Busaco, in which the cavalry, though present, took no part.

On the night of the 28th the army withdrew from the position of Busaco, still covered by the cavalry.

To retire day after day before a superior enemy is trying to the best troops, but Stapleton Cotton's calm energy and unvarying animation cheered up his followers and drove depression or discontent far from them. He fully justified the confidence which both Lord Wellington and his own men placed in him, and steadily kept the pursuers in check. His method of proceeding was to show such very light lines of skirmishers that the French thought they could easily ride them down. When, however, they attempted to do so, they soon found themselves in contact with the judiciously posted supports and reserves, and suffered heavily for their presumption. Almost daily were these affairs, which thoroughly established the superiority of the British over the French dragoon. As an instance of the amount of confidence thus generated in the former, we may give an extract from an old number of the *United Service Journal*.

Shortly before the Battle of Busaco, my gallant and lamented friend Captain White, with his single troop of the 13th Dragoons, attacked a superior body of the enemy, and not only overthrew them, but killed and captured every man of them.

During the whole retreat, from the time they quitted Alverca to the day on which they entered the lines of Torres Vedras, the cavalry were engaged almost daily with the enemy. The chief affairs were those of the passage of the Mondego on the 1st, of Alcoentre on the 8th, and of Quinta del Torre on the 9th October.

We cannot do better than give a literal extract from the journal of an officer (Colonel Tompkinson, formerly of the 16th Dragoons), who was present at these affairs. We are the rather induced to adopt this plan, because the account here given of the passage of the Mondego differs somewhat from that found in Napier.

October 1st.—We formed at daybreak in front of Fornos, and Sir Stapleton Cotton ordered General Anson not to retire unless he was attacked by infantry. This was the case, and I was sent to report it to Sir Stapleton, when the brigade retired before a large force of cavalry and infantry to the Coimbra plain. Here we joined the heavy cavalry brigade and Captain Bull's guns, which, by opening on the enemy, retarded their advance a little. The enemy pushed their infantry along the banks of the enclosures, when we were obliged to retire, and on our crossing the Mondego by a ford they pushed a squadron of cavalry over the river, which was charged by a squadron of the 16th and driven back, and the retreat was safely effected over the river. We marched, and bivouacked in the neighbourhood of Soure.

October 8th.—It rained nearly the whole night. In the morning, the troops moved off for Alquentre in the heaviest rain

I ever experienced. The left squadron of the 16th was left in Rio Maior as a rear guard. We marched, and bivouacked in the rear of Alquentre two leagues. Generals Cotton, Slade, and Anson, with the troop of horse artillery, were in the village with the two brigades in its rear. About two we heard some shots fired near the village, and Captain Cocks' squadron, being the first for duty, moved down as quick as possible with the first mounted dragoons we could collect, in all not fifty men. In our way down, we met five of the guns coming up in the greatest confusion, some with four, some with six horses to them, having got away how they could.

On the other side the village ran a considerable brook, which was not passable excepting at the bridge on the entrance into the town. The enemy had two regiments of cavalry close up, and Captain Murray's people were all withdrawn over the bridge. Our party formed up ready to charge down the street. There was a howitzer and two ammunition waggons without a horse to their commissariat mules and oxen in the greatest confusion. Colonel Elley, (Assistant Adjutant-General to the Cavalry Division), was standing half shaved at a window as we went in. The enemy did not long remain idle, and detached two squadrons from the 14th Dragoons into the village.

They passed the bridge, driving in Captain Murray's people, and came halfway up the street to where we were formed. The two squadrons were close to each other in sixes, completely filling up the street. From the bridge to where we were, the street makes a right-angle. The head of the column passed the turning; the other squadron in the rear not seeing how we were formed. In this situation they halted, when we charged them. They instantly went about and wished to retire.

There was the greatest noise and confusion with the enemy, their front wishing to get away, and their rear not seeing what was going on, stood still. They got so close together that it was impossible to get well at them. We took twelve and killed six, driving them over the bridge again, and by this means allowing time for what remained in the town to get clear away. The enemy dismounted their dragoons, and we retired through the town, forming on the heights on the other side. The cavalry retired to Quinta de Toro. Our squadron remained skirmishing with the enemy till dark, and then retired half a league in front of Quinta de Toro, where it remained on picquet.

October 9th.—Captain Cocks' squadron was on picquet. It rained the whole night. The enemy came on with a considerable force of cavalry about twelve o'clock, and attempted to drive us back. We charged three times down the road, and each time they retreated to their former ground; but they pushed a body on our flank, and we were obliged to retire to the high ground near the Quinta de Toro. We had covered the retreat the whole way from Coimbra, and having been three nights out in incessant rain, we were ordered to the rear, and the heavy brigade took the outpost duty.

Southey, in his *Peninsular War*, Vol. 2, asserts that at Quinta del Torre, Sir Stapleton Cotton lost six guns, and that they were recovered with the assistance of the 10th Hussars. Lord Combermere, on seeing this misstatement, wrote to the author to assure him that these guns had never been captured by the enemy in the first instance; and that the 10th Hussars, so far from recovering guns that had never been lost, were at the time quietly stationed at Hounslow.

The following is Lord Combermere's own account of the affair, which not only contradicts Southey's statement, but also acquits him of the charge of negligence which might be inferred from the extract from the journal given above:—

On the 9th October, the extreme rear guard consisted of a squadron of the 16th Light Dragoons under Captain Murray. After reconnoitring the enemy's front with this officer at noon at Lerea, Sir Stapleton Cotton perceived them making preparation for a day's halt. Their cooking arrangements seemed in progress, and the torrents of rain, which poured down incessantly, seemed to warrant Sir Stapleton in the belief that the French army would remain where they were till the next morning. Leaving Captain Murray at Lerea with his orders for the day, Sir Stapleton joined the main body, and on his arrival at Quinta del Torre, prepared to enjoy a quiet dinner.

His intentions were, however, soon defeated by the arrival, in hot haste, of an officer from Captain Murray, with the information that soon after Sir Stapleton's departure from Lerea the enemy were on the move, and that Captain Murray was retreating before a large body of their cavalry. At this juncture. Sir Stapleton learnt from his quartermaster-general. Lord Tweeddale, that, contrary to Sir Stapleton's general order, he had placed the guns of Bull's troop of horse artillery in the town itself.

Very much annoyed at this disregard of his instructions, Sir Stapleton desired Lord Tweeddale to order Captain Bull to get the guns out immediately, and with the artillery to join the rest of the troops in rear of the place. Sir Stapleton then commanded the 16th Regiment to take post at the top of the hill at the end of the main street, determined to keep the enemy at bay till the guns were reported safe. He now galloped off to join the squadron under Captain Murray's command. He found it in full trot, followed by the enemy. He promptly halted it, formed it across the road, and sent out skirmishers right and left. Captain Murray had assured him that, owing to the pouring rain, the pistols would not fire; but contrary to his assertions, they went off, and the manoeuvre was perfectly successful in keeping the enemy engaged until Lord Tweeddale reported the guns to be in safety behind the town.

Sir Stapleton now ordered Captain Murray to retire over the bridge and to turn out of the main street. This done, Sir Stapleton joined a supporting squadron of the 16th, and immediately charged with them down the hill, driving the enemy across the bridge. Thirty or forty were taken prisoners, with four or five superior officers, and a stop was put to the further advance of the enemy by a display of our force, drawn out to the greatest advantage on the heights behind the town. That night the captured colonel and three French officers dined with Sir Stapleton, and were well joked about the boast of their soldiers during the skirmish, who declared that they would reach Lisbon before the British forces arrived there.

It was in one of these skirmishes during this retreat that an incident took place, which, though trifling in itself, exemplifies very strongly the habitual coolness of the leader of Wellington's cavalry. Sir Stapleton was with the rear guard, which was skirmishing with the enemy, who were pressing sharply on it. A defile was between the British rear guard and the main body of the cavalry, and the French threatened to intercept the exposed squadron. Captain Brotherton, of the 14th Light Dragoons— an officer remarkable throughout the whole army for his intrepidity— was that day riding with Sir Stapleton. (Later General Sir T. Brotherton, K.C.B., one of Sir Ralph Abercrombie's soldiers, and had seen some service before the Peninsula). He, observing the critical position of the little party, and the impassibility of his leader, who was surveying the advancing foe as coolly as if watching a steeplechase, thought it advisable to suggest the propriety of retiring while it was yet time.

"I think. Sir Stapleton, we had better be off, or it will be too late," said Captain Brotherton.

Turning quietly in his saddle, Sir Stapleton replied, with a quiet and, as it were, pacifying smile, "Why, Brotherton, what a fuss you're in," and persisted in waiting till his object had been effected, and the advance of the enemy checked long enough, when he turned round and galloped off.

"I must say," said Sir Thomas Brotherton, "I was rather annoyed at the remark; for I was one of Sir Ralph Abercrombie's soldiers, and had seen some service before the Peninsula."

We should not be doing justice to our subject were we not to give an extract from a dispatch from Lord Wellington to Lord Liverpool, dated 20th September, 1810, in which he thus speaks of Sir Stapleton Cotton's conduct during the retreat:—

> I must take this opportunity of mentioning to your Lordship the obligations I am under to the British cavalry commanded by Lieutenant-General Sir Stapleton Cotton. Since the end of July they have alone done the duty of the outposts, and the enemy has never been out of sight of them; and on every occasion their superiority has been so great that the enemy does not use his cavalry, excepting when supported and protected by his infantry.

Another equally favourable mention occurs in another dispatch from Lord Wellington to Lord Liverpool, dated 13th October, 1810:—

> The movements of that part of the army under my own immediate command were covered by the British cavalry under Sir Stapleton Cotton; and that of the troops under Lieutenant-General Hill by the 13th Dragoons, and Portuguese cavalry under Major-General Fane.
> The British cavalry had several occasions of distinguishing themselves, upon which I enclose Sir S. Cotton's report, and I must add my sense of the obligation which I owe this body.

With reference to the superiority of the British cavalry over that of the French, it may be mentioned that though the latter were more numerous they were not so well mounted as our own. A French officer taken prisoner during the retreat complained bitterly of this in terms somewhat as follows:—

When we break you, we can't catch you; but when you break us, *il n'y a pas un pauvre diable qui s'échappey.*

The subjoined letters from the quartermaster-general to Sir Stapleton show what were the detailed arrangements for the celebrated retreat, how carefully Wellington watched over the execution of every part of his plan, and enable the student to trace with great certainty, day by day, each movement of the army. The successful result of the operation, moreover, was in great measure due to Sir Stapleton's skill and firmness; we do not therefore consider that we are obtruding irrelevant matter by inserting the letters bearing on the subject.

(Confidential)

(Gurwood's *Dispatches*)

Headquarters, 26th September, 1810.

In the event of the army being ordered to retire from the positions which it now occupies on the Serra of Busacos, the following are the roads by which the several divisions are to move.

No. 1.—The troops under the orders of Lieutenant-General Sir Brent Spencer will move by the Great Road, through Mealhada to Fornos, and thence into the great plain below Coimbra, and across the River Mondego, at the ford near Cazas Novas.

Sir Brent Spencer is already aware how his column is to avoid interfering with any other troops in passing through Fornos, and he will be pleased to place an officer that knows the turn that his column is to take in the village of Fornos (with a guard), in due time to prevent any part of his baggage or troops taking a wrong direction. The whole of this route is practicable for artillery, and Lieutenant-General Sir Brent Spencer will receive further orders in regard as to how he is to proceed after crossing the Mondego.

No. 2.—The 4th division will retire by a road which leads direct from Busacos to Fornos, through the village of Marmoleira. This road has been reconnoitred by Lieutenant Westmacot, of the Royal Staff Corps, and reported fit for British artillery. Lieutenant Westmacot will be sent to conduct this column. After reaching Fornos, the 4th division is to continue its march by the great Coimbra road. It will cross the Mondego by the bridge at Coimbra, and will ascend the hill upon the other side. Major-General Cole will not discontinue his march along the great road, after passing the Mondego, until he receives orders to that effect, it being necessary that he should move on to give room to the divisions in his rear.

No. 3.—The light division will retire by the road which passes through the village of Paul to Botao, and thence to Fornos. From Fornos the light division will take the Great Road to Coimbra, but it will halt before reaching the houses called Cazas do Canonigo Paes, at which point the troops under Major-General Picton are to enter the Great Road, and these troops are to be allowed to move into the Great Road before the light division resumes its march.

The road through Paul and Botao to Fornos has been reconnoitred by officers of the light division; and also by Captain Scovell, of the quartermaster-general's department, who will be attached to the light division during the march as far as Fornos. The whole of this road is reported practicable for British artillery. Brigadier-General Craufurd will receive further orders during the halt of his division between Fornos and Cazas do Canonigo Paes.

No. 4.—The troops under Major-General Picton will retire by the road which leads through Alegoa and Eiras, and join the Coimbra road at Cazas do Canonigo Paes. This road has been reconnoitred and reported fit for Portuguese artillery by Lieutenant Shanahan, of the Royal Staff Corps, who will be sent to conduct the column.

The troops under Major-General Picton will enter the Great Road at Cazas do Canonigo Paes after the 4th division has passed that place, taking their place in the column of march between the 4th division and the light division. After coming into the Great Road, Major-General Picton will continue to follow the 4th division until he receives further orders.

No. 5.—Major-General Leith's corps will retire by the road which leads through the village of Povoa to Dianteiro, and thence by the Quinta de Lugans do Seminario to the Convent of San Antonio dos Olivaes, above the town of Coimbra, where Major-General Leith will halt and wait for further orders.

The road has been reconnoitred and reported practicable for light artillery (aided by men at some steep ascents) by Lieutenant Shanahan, of the Royal Staff Corps. As that officer is to be attached, however, to the 3rd division during the march to Coimbra, Major-General Leith will lose no time in having the road reconnoitred by officers of his own corps.

The Nine-pounder Brigade, which was with Major-General Leith, having been attached this day to Lieutenant-General Hill, it will follow the movements of his corps.

6th.—The troops under Lieutenant-General Hill, which are on the position of Busacos, will (in the event of the army retiring) recross the Mondego at the Ford near Pena Cova, and will be placed between that point and the village of San Miguel de Poyares. A separate instruction will be given to Lieutenant-General Hill respecting the further operations of the above corps, and also of the other troops now in the neighbourhood of Ponte de Moulla.

7th.—Lieutenant-General Hill's corps, in retiring, will march by its right; all the other divisions above mentioned will move by their left.

8th.—The cavalry will retire by the Great Road through Mealhada to Fornos, and thence into the great plain below Coimbra, following Lieutenant-General Sir Brent Spencer's corps.

Lieutenant-General Sir Stapleton Cotton will send forward an officer and a small party of dragoons to Fornos to take post at that point where the road turns in that village to lead into the great plain, and to prevent any part of the division from taking a wrong direction, and interfering with the troops that are to move from Fornos by the Great Road to Coimbra. The officer stationed at this point by Sir Brent Spencer is not to quit it until relieved by the party of dragoons above mentioned.

Lieutenant-General Sir Stapleton Cotton will form the cavalry in the great plain, and will there wait for further orders.

9th.—It is clearly to be understood that no movement is to take place under these instructions, unless in the case of orders being received for the army to retire.

Geo. Murray,
Quartermaster-General.

Lieut.-General Sir Stapleton Cotton, Bart, &c. &c., Vanorossa.

Busaco, 28th September, 1810.

The army will retire from its present position this night.

The following arrangements will be attended to in addition to the general instructions of the 26th instant, circulated to the general officers commanding divisions.

Orders are to be immediately sent to the baggage in the rear to move off without delay from the places to which it has been already sent; and if any baggage remain with any of the corps, it is to be sent off immediately by the routes already pointed out for the several divisions. All the baggage is to cross the Mondego, and is not to halt till it arrives in the open olive groves on the top of the hill on the other side of the bridge of Coimbra, where it is to be packed, and to wait for further orders.

Such of the divisions as have not already supplied themselves with native guides, may be able probably to find, amongst the Portuguese corps in the divisions, officers or men who are acquainted with the country, or peasants who are in the lines.

The several divisions are to move off in the following order— The 1st division, including all the corps and artillery which marched up from Mealhada with Lieutenant-General Sir Brent Spencer, are to march first, and they will begin to move off without delay by the Great Road to Mealhada, as already pointed out in the general instructions.

Major-General Cole's division will march off at twelve (12) o'clock, through the village of Varsees, and close up near to the Mealhada Road, at Lameiro de San Pedro. As soon as the rear of Sir Brent Spencer's corps has gone by, Major-General Cole will cross the Mealhada Road at Lameiro de San Pedro, and proceed along the route which has been already pointed out for this column in the general instructions.

The picquets of Major-General Cole's division are to remain out till three o'clock in the morning, at which hour they are to be withdrawn by the field officer of the day, and to follow the route of the division. The field officer will report to Brigadier-General Craufurd at the chapel near the park wall of the Convent before he sends to draw in the picquets.

The Light Division, including Brigadier-General Pack's corps, will march off at two o'clock tomorrow morning. It will enter the Convent park at the gate near the chapel (excepting Brigadier-General Pack's corps, which will enter at the gate above that, and at the opening at the top of the hill) and it will pass out by the gate which leads out towards Paul.

The picquets of the division are to be called in at four in the morning, and after assembling at the chapel, they will follow and form the rear guard of the division.

Major-General Picton's division will move off at two o'clock in the morning, and the picquets will assemble and follow as a rear guard at four o'clock.

Major-General Picton will have one battalion and one light gun between the rear of the column and the picquets, as a support to the latter.

Major-General Leith will move off in the same manner and at the same hour with Major-General Picton.

Lieutenant-General Hill's corps will move off also at the same hours by the route already pointed out to him. He will be pleased to send an order to Major-General Fane to halt in the villages behind the Serra of Mocella, and to push his picquets and patrols to the other side of the Alva.

Care must be taken to keep up the communication with the advanced and the rear guard of each column.

The fires in the lines are to be kept up. All the arrangements and movements, particularly those of the artillery, are to be made with as much silence as possible, and no torches or other lights of that sort are to be shown until the troops are behind the Serra, when lights may be made use of to assist in finding the road, and in conducting the artillery.

No bullock carts of any description are to be suffered to move with the army; and if there are any now with any of the divisions the bullocks must be unyoked and the carts left behind. Every impediment met with on the line of march must be removed by the advanced guards of the several divisions.

Lieutenant-General Sir Stapleton Cotton will retire the cavalry tomorrow morning as circumstances may require. Falling back by Mealhada and Fornos into the great plain below Coimbra, as already directed. He will be so good as send reports from time to time through Fornos to headquarters at Coimbra.

Captain Bull's troop of horse artillery has been ordered to Mealhada this night, there to wait Sir Stapleton Cotton's further instructions. An order will be sent for the baggage of the cavalry to retire beyond the Mondego, which order, however, Sir Stapleton

Cotton had better repeat as soon as he receives this instruction. The detachment of cavalry near Busaco will be ordered to move with the light division. The detachment at Botao will be left to observe the road through that place, until otherwise instructed by Sir Stapleton Cotton.

Col. Geo. Murray,
Quartermaster-General.

Lieut.-General Sir Stapleton Cotton, Bart, &c. &c.

Coimbra, 30th September, 1810.

Lieutenant-General Sir Stapleton Cotton will be pleased to move the brigade of heavy cavalry today into the great plain below Coimbra, and bring one of the other two brigades of cavalry to this side of Fornos, keeping out the other brigade in front of that place. If pressed by the enemy, Sir Stapleton Cotton will move the whole of the cavalry division into the great plain, and, if necessary, he will retire across the Mondego by the fords near Casas Novas, near which place (on the left bank of the river) Lieutenant-General Sir Brent Spencer's corps is cantoned. In the event of the cavalry moving still further back, it is to march from Casas Novas through Pereira, Fermozelha, Granja, &c., to Soure, and Lieutenant-General Sir Stapleton Cotton will communicate with Sir Brent Spencer, whose corps is to move by the same route, and will regulate the length of his march as circumstances seem to render it necessary, apprising Sir Brent Spencer of anything extraordinary that occurs, and transmitting his reports to headquarters through Condeixa after he has passed the Mondego, until he is informed that the Sir Stapleton Cotton will endeavour to obtain intelligence whether the enemy is moving any troops in the direction of Tentugal, Monte More Velho, or any other place on the lower part of the River Mondego.

The troops under Brigadier-General Craufurd and Brigadier-General Pack, are ordered to move back this afternoon to within a short distance of Coimbra.

Col. Geo. Murray,
Qr.-Mr.-Genl.

To Lieut.-Gen. Sir Stapleton Cotton, Bart., &c.

Redinha, 1st October, 1810.

Lieutenant-General Sir Stapleton Cotton will be pleased to halt the cavalry tomorrow at the village of Almagaria, and other cantonments on the same side of the river between Almagaria and Pombal,

The Royal Dragoons will be directed to halt at Venda de Cruz, between Redinha and Pombal, and the detachment of dragoons under the orders at present of Brigadier-General Craufurd will be directed to rejoin the rest of the cavalry tomorrow afternoon.

Headquarters will be tomorrow night at Leyria, but Lord Wellington will be at Redinha or Pombal till late in the day.

(Signed)

Geo. Murray,
Qr.-Mr.-Genl.

Lieut.-Gen. Sir Stapleton Cotton, Bart., &c.

The Royals will have a picquet at Redinha.

(Signed)

G. M.

Leyria, 3rd October, 1810, 8 p.m.

My dear Sir Stapleton,—Whether or not the army shall move further back must depend in a great degree upon the intelligence received respecting the enemy. It is very desirable, therefore, that the posts you have at the points mentioned in your letter of today should be upon the alert, and that officers should be stationed with them who are capable of judging from appearances whether, when the enemy shows himself, he is actually in motion to advance in force, or is only pushing on patrols to reconnoitre or to collect supplies.

Perhaps it would be expedient to have some support between your outposts and the Rio Mandanilla, in order to give confidence to the most advanced parties, and enable them to stay longer out to make their observations upon the enemy as he comes forward.

If the enemy advances in force, you will be so good as draw back your advanced posts by degrees, and if necessary, you will also put the whole of the cavalry in motion to fall back according to the arrangement transmitted to you this day; and you will be pleased to apprise Brigadier-General Craufurd, that he may in like manner put the infantry under his order in motion also.

You will, of course, send the speediest intelligence to headquarters of the enemy's motions, as also of those which you find yourself obliged to make, in order that no time may be lost in putting the whole army in motion.

Believe me, my dear Sir Stapleton,

Ever faithfully yours,

(Signed)

Geo. Murray,

Qr.-Mr. Genl.

Lieut.-Gen. Sir Stapleton Cotton, Bart., &c.

I hope to be able to send you a survey of the country from Leyria to Lisbon tomorrow morning.

(Signed)

G. M.

Leyria, October 4.

My dear Cotton,—There is a report that there were stragglers, Portuguese as well as English, in the villages to the right and left of the road near where you are cantoned, and I shall be obliged if you will send out patrols, and take up all men of this description, and send them in here as prisoners. Murray will have sent you your instructions.

Keep yourself light in front, to observe the enemy, and don't engage in any affair with superior force. After this day's halt, the sooner the enemy advance the better. I have little doubt of the result.

Ever yours most sincerely,

Wellington.

(Gurwood's *Dispatches*).

5th October, 1810, ½-past 9

My dear Sir Stapleton,—I have received the pencil note you sent by the bearer for Lord Wellington, who is just gone for Alcobaça. You must have already received your instructions to fall back to one league beyond Leyria.

Yours ever,

G. Murray,

Qr.-Mr.-Genl.

Lieut.-Gen. Sir Stapleton Cotton, Bart.

Leyria, 5th October, 10 a.m.

My dear Sir Stapleton,—I conclude you will order the picquets you have towards Guia to fall back upon Monte Redondo and

Monte Real, and to communicate with the two squadrons you sent today to Marinhas.

Yours ever faithfully,

(Signed)

Geo, Murray,

Qr.-Mr.-Genl.

Lieut.-Gen. Sir Stapleton Cotton, Bart., &c.

Leyria, 5th October, 1810.

My Dear Sir Stapleton,—I beg you will be so good as send back a party of dragoons this forenoon to station itself at Aljubarotta, in order to establish your communication with certainty and celerity with headquarters at Alcobaça. The party sent to Aljubarotta should have a small post of three or four men at the place where the road turns off to go to Alcobaça, after passing Calvaria, in order to direct the dragoons or other persons you or Brigadier-General Craufurd may have occasion to send to Alcobaça either during the day or night.

Believe me, ever faithfully yours,

(Signed)

Geo. Murray,

Qr.-Mr.-Genl.

You will of course put yourself in communication with Brigadier-General Craufurd at Batalha.

Leyria, ½-past 12 a.m., 5th October, 1810.

My Dear Sir Stapleton,—In consequence of what you report in your letter to Lord Wellington, dated eight p.m., 4th October, and your letter to me received along with it, his Lordship has directed Brigadier-General Craufurd to fall back this morning upon Leyria. You will be so good as remain with the cavalry on the Rio Mandanilla, in order to ascertain as far as you can the force and intentions of the enemy, in case he continues to move forward.

If it should appear that he is actually upon the march forward in force, you will, of course, retire according to the instructions you already have from Lord Wellington.

If you are obliged to retire, I think you had better pass through here in two columns, one by the main street, through the town, and the other by the road Captain Scovell pointed out this afternoon to the officer you sent for that purpose.

Believe me, my dear Sir Stapleton,

 Ever faithfully yours,

Geo. Murray,
Qr.-Mr.-Genl.

I have given the bearer a letter for Brigadier-General Craufurd, and have directed him to produce to you the receipt for it.

G. M.

Leyria, 5th October, 1810.

My dear Sir Stapleton,—When the cavalry move further back (which will be tomorrow) you will be so good as separate one brigade from the rest, as the body of the cavalry is to travel by the Great Road through Rio Maior, and the brigade above mentioned by Alcobaça, Obidos, &c. Be so good as let me know as soon as possible which brigade you allot for the Alcobaça route, and you will be pleased to detach two squadrons from that brigade to be today at Marinhas and to have a look out towards Monte Beal, and the lower part of the Leyria River. Believe me, my dear Sir Stapleton,

 Ever faithfully yours,

Col. Geo. Murray,
Qr.-Mr.-Genl.

To Lieut.-Gen. Sir Stapleton Cotton, Bart., &c.

Rio Maior, 6th October, 1810.

My dear Sir Stapleton,—If the enemy does not continue to advance. Lord Wellington desires that you will move the two brigades of cavalry under your immediate orders, tomorrow, only to this place, and that you will order Colonel De Grey not to move his brigade further back than to Albergaria, which is a village about half way between Alcobaça and Caldas.

Colonel De Grey should have a look out at Alcobaça, and at Nazareth upon the coast, and you will probably think it expedient to observe the Great Road in the neighbourhood of Candeiros, as also the road which comes from Porto do Moz along the south side of the *sierra*, as well as to have a look from some advantageous point of the *sierra* itself. It may be as well to have a post also upon the road that leads from Rio Maior through Ronda to Pernes, as the whole of the troops under Lieutenant-General Hill will be coming in from that side tomorrow, and from Santarem towards Villa Franca.

Should the enemy again move forward, Colonel De Grey's brigade will fall back as already instructed to Obidos, and thence to Ramalhal, or to Torres Vedras if necessary. And the two brigades under your orders will fall back to Alcoentre and Tajano, and thence by the Great Road to Carregada and Castanheira. On the following day, whether the cavalry moves or not beyond this place tomorrow, the light division is to proceed as already ordered to Alcoentre and Tajano.

The headquarters will be tomorrow at ——

Believe me, my dear Sir Stapleton,

Ever faithfully yours,

Geo. Murray,
Qr.-Mr.-Genl.

I hear from a dragoon that the camp kettles of some of your regiments have gone beyond this place towards the rear, and I shall take the first opportunity that offers of sending an order along the road for their return to this place, to wait your further orders.

G. M.

Rio Maior, October 6th, 1810.

There is a road which comes from Porto do Moz along the south side of the *sierra* to this place, running parallel to the Great Road from Carvalhos, the *sierra* being between the two. Sir Stapleton Cotton will be so good as to send a picquet over the *sierra* by a road which crosses it from Candieros, and place it upon the road from Porto do Moz to Rio Maior above mentioned.

The officer sent with this picquet is to be instructed to report to Rio Maior by the direct road along the south of the *sierra*, as well as to Sir Stapleton Cotton, if he should see or have any intelligence of the enemy.

A picquet of infantry, upon which the cavalry picquet is to fall back, will be pushed out from Rio Maior, to a short distance along the road above mentioned.

Geo. Murray,
Qr.-Mr. Genl.

Lieut.-Gen. Sir Stapleton Cotton, Bart., &c.

The bearer of this has been directed to remain tonight; but Sir Stapleton Cotton is requested to let Colonel Murray know by the first opportunity that he sends in, whether he has received the distribution for tomorrow.

Rio Maior, 7th October, 1810.

My Dear Sir Stapleton,—If the enemy continue to advance, and you drive back the cavalry today to Alcoentre and Tajano, you will be pleased to fall back tomorrow to Carregada, to which place the Light Division is also ordered. If the enemy should not continue his advance so as to make it necessary for the cavalry to make the same marches with the Light Division, I am to request that you will keep Brigadier-General Craufurd constantly informed of your movements, as also of the intelligence you have of the enemy.

Believe me, ever faithfully yours,

Geo. Murray,
Qr.-Mr.-Genl.

Lieut.-Gen. Sir Stapleton Cotton, Bart, &c.

Alenquer, 8th October, 1810.

My dear Sir Stapleton,—It appears probable, from your latest reports of the advance of the enemy yesterday, that he will push his advanced guard today to Alcoentre, and bring the head of his column to Rio Maior. Lord Wellington desires, therefore, that you will halt the cavalry with you today at Quinta de Torre and Alba, having your outposts at N. S. Moxoema.

I wrote yesterday to direct that on quitting Alcoentre you would be pleased to send one regiment of cavalry to Abregada, with instructions to the commanding-officer to report to this place, and to fall back when necessary towards Sobral, reporting to Lieutenant-General Sir Brent Spencer at that place.

Major-General Fane will be today at Carregada and Custanheiros. He will be directed to leave his outposts at Villa Nova, and to communicate from thence with your right, near Quinta de Torre.

Brigadier-General Craufurd's headquarters will be today at Abregada.

The headquarters of the army move today to Aruda.

Believe me, my dear Sir Stapleton,

Ever faithfully yours,

Geo. Murray,
Qr.-Mr.-Genl.

Aruda, 9th October, 1810, 10 a.m.

If the enemy advances in force upon Carregada, Lieutenant-General Sir Stapleton Cotton will fall back, as it becomes necessary, upon Villa Franca, apprising Brigadier-General Craufurd, at Alenquer, and Brigadier-General Pack, at Carregada, of his movements. Major-General Fane, with three squadrons of cavalry, is at Castanhieros, and Lieutenant-General Hill (or the first division of his infantry) is at Villa Franca.

Sir Stapleton Cotton will be pleased to apprise these officers also of his movements, and of those of the enemy.

When Sir Stapleton Cotton falls back from Quinta de Torre, he will be pleased to detach two squadrons to Alenquer, with instructions to observe if the enemy moves anything in that direction, and to fall back along the *chaussée* from Alenquer to Sobral, as may be necessary, reporting to Sobral.

Sir Stapleton Cotton will, of course, transmit intelligence from time to time during the course of the day to headquarters, of his own situation and of that of the enemy.

Geo. Murray.

Qr.-Mr.-GenL

For Lieutenant-General Hill, and to be forwarded by General Hill, with as little delay as possible, to Major-General Fane, for his information, and thence to Sir Stapleton Cotton.

If the forage carts of the cavalry are at Villa Franca, they are to be ordered further back, as may appear necessary.

G. M.

On the 11th October, the whole army was within the lines of Torres Vedras. During the first few days the cavalry had frequent skirmishes with the French, in most of which they were the victors; but they were soon sent to the rear, both for convenience of forage, and because, in the rugged district occupied by the army, their services were of little use. When, in the middle of November, the army advanced from the lines against Massena, the cavalry accompanied it, but were not actively engaged during the remainder of 1810.

129

Chapter 7

Battle of Fuentes d'Onor

On the 1st January, 1811, Sir Stapleton Cotton proceeded to England on leave for the purpose of attending Parliament, rejoining the army in the field on the 19th April, 1811. He found it employed in blockading Almeida, with Sir Brent Spencer in command, Lord Wellington having a few days before left to superintend the siege of Badajos.

On the 28th April Lord Wellington returned to the army, and took the command from Sir Brent Spencer. It was about this time that a curious conversation took place between Wellington and Sir Brent Spencer, which is strongly illustrative of the extreme reserve practised by the former towards even the most trusted of his lieutenants. One day, the commander-in-chief and Spencer were riding out together, when Sir Brent took the opportunity of questioning Lord Wellington as to his plan of operations. The conversation ran nearly as follows:—

Sir Brent Spencer.—"We are about, my Lord, to engage in a very hazardous campaign, and no one can tell what may befall any one of us. I am sure I trust most sincerely that nothing will happen to your Lordship. It would be a great misfortune to the army if it were to lose you; but still you might be killed, and I think it necessary that I should ask you what are your plans, in order that I may be able to carry them out in case I should unfortunately succeed to the command of the army."

Lord Wellington.—"Plans?—ah, plans. I haven't got any plans, except that I mean to beat the French. If I can't do it in one way, I will in another."

Soon after his arrival Sir Stapleton Cotton was attacked by illness, but his indisposition did not last long, and in a few days he was again fit for work.

Indeed, Sir Stapleton had little leisure for a sickbed, for from the following letters he seems not only to have been in charge of the outposts, but also to have been entrusted with a general superintendence of that portion of the army nearest the enemy.

Villaformosa, 30th April, 1811.

My Dear Sir Stapleton,—I have just received your letter of this morning. Lord Wellington does not wish that the Light Division should be moved from its present cantonments at Gallegos and Espeja. When the advance of the enemy obliges the light division to fall back as mentioned in the accompanying memorandum, Lord Wellington wishes you to collect the body of the cavalry in the open country between Gallegos and Espeja, on this side of the rivulet, and to protect the retreat of the infantry. Lord Wellington is desirous that the squadrons of the cavalry on the left should protect the retreat of the 28th Regiment, which will retire across the Dois Casas River, and afterwards follow the ridge between Dois Casas and Torrein Rivers, until it joins the 5th division at Alobra do Bisfra.

I have just learnt that Don Julian will be today at El Bodon and neighbourhood. It will not be necessary, therefore, for the present to move the cantonments of the cavalry more towards the right.

Believe me, ever faithfully yours,

Geo. Murray,
Qr.-Mr.-Genl.

Lieut.-Gen. Sir Stapleton Cotton, Bart., &c.

Gallegos, 30th April, 1811.

My Dear Sir Stapleton,—I do not know exactly what the distribution of the cavalry is at present, but Lord Wellington seems to think we have rather too much of it on the left. I am inclined to think it is advisable, in case of the enemy advancing in force, that we should be prepared to collect our people towards the right. All we can do to the left of this place is, to observe the enemy and watch the passage of the Agueda, and communicate with and secure the retreat of what we have at Barba de Puerco. Lord Wellington thinks that two squadrons, or very little more, would be sufficient for these objects.

The lines of retreat which we must always keep open are upon Alfiates and Villa Maior. If the enemy moves their force from

131

Ciudad Rodrigo towards the right, we might be rather hurried in making a corresponding movement to meet him should he have much of a force to the left. But it will be much easier for us (should he move against our left and direct towards Almaida) to make a corresponding movement to oppose him in that quarter; and we shall be better placed to have our own lines of retreat perfectly open, and at the same time to threaten his line of retreat upon Ciudad Rodrigo, and to threaten also his left flank as he moves forward.

I wish you would turn this in your mind, and let me know what arrangement appears most expedient in your opinion for placing the cavalry more apart, to move in considerable force towards the right of our line.

Headquarters will be today at Villaformosa.

The line of retreat for the light division, in case the enemy should advance in force too great to be opposed in front—we should threaten its flanks—is to be upon Fuentes d'Onoro, in front of which place it will halt in the first instance, if not pressed.

I conclude that it rests with you to send orders to the troops at Barba de Puerco to fall back. They should retire by the road between Dois Casas River and the Turon River, unless expressly ordered at the time to follow some other line of retreat.

Believe me, ever faithfully yours,

Geo. Murray,
Qr.-Mr.-Genl.

Lieut.-Gen. Sir Stapleton Cotton, Bart., &c.

On the 3rd, 4th, and 5th of May took place the Battle of Fuentes d'Onoro. Sir Stapleton was not called upon to play an important part in the affair, owing to the numerical inferiority of our cavalry to that of the French. Still that arm was partially engaged. The insertion here, therefore, of an extract from the private journal of Colonel Elley, Adjutant-General of Cavalry, may not be considered out of place:—

Friday, 3rd May.—This morning was ushered in by an early movement of the enemy, commencing evidently by a ruse. Drumming was heard unceasingly on our left, to imply the movement of a considerable force towards Alameida and Barkilla; whereas the great force of the enemy remained in the vicinity of Especa. About eight or nine a.m. a prodigious force of cavalry appeared at the corner of the wood, leading from Especa by the road from thence, to Fuentes d'Onoro, which obliged us to fall back gradually to the left of the rivulet which divides the plain, running from S. to N. The enemy's cavalry remained on the opposite bank, and upon our rear guard opened a cannonade which lost us a horse, killed by reason of the reserve to our skirmishers being improperly placed. The cavalry and light division retired to the high ground between Fuentes d'Onoro and Villa Formosa, leaving picquets only on the plain on the right bank of the Dos Casas.

About noon the enemy advanced, our picquets retired, and were pressed at the head of the defile leading to Fuentes d'Onoro, the walls of which were occupied by some riflemen of the 60th, who brought some of the cavalry down and checked the remainder. In the afternoon of this day the enemy made his first attack on the village, under a heavy and well-directed fire of artillery. The success was never doubtful; the enemy suffered considerably, and were finally driven from the village. The attack did not evince much spirit. The weather was fine, and the night moonlight.

Saturday, 4th May, 1811.—Nothing took place on either side this day. Weather fine.

Sunday, 5th May,—At an early hour this morning , the enemy were in motion in columns of manoeuvre between Pozo Velha, and the country towards the road leading from Nave d'Aver to Freynada. To oppose this movement the entire cavalry and Captain Bull's troop of horse-artillery advanced, also General Houston's division supported by the light division. During this advance, the enemy's columns were concentrating behind a hill above the ground occupied by General Houston's division, and which completely looked into it, and on sending on a reconnoissance it was discovered the enemy was prepared to make his attack with artillery, cavalry, and infantry. On being discovered, some squadrons, supposed to be drunk, rushed forward without order or method, and mixing (called charging) with our squadrons, both went bodily to the rear. The cavalry so mixed was fired upon in passing General Houston's division, which division immediately commenced a retreat over the partly enclosed and partly open country towards the position General

Horse artillery at Fuentes d'Onor

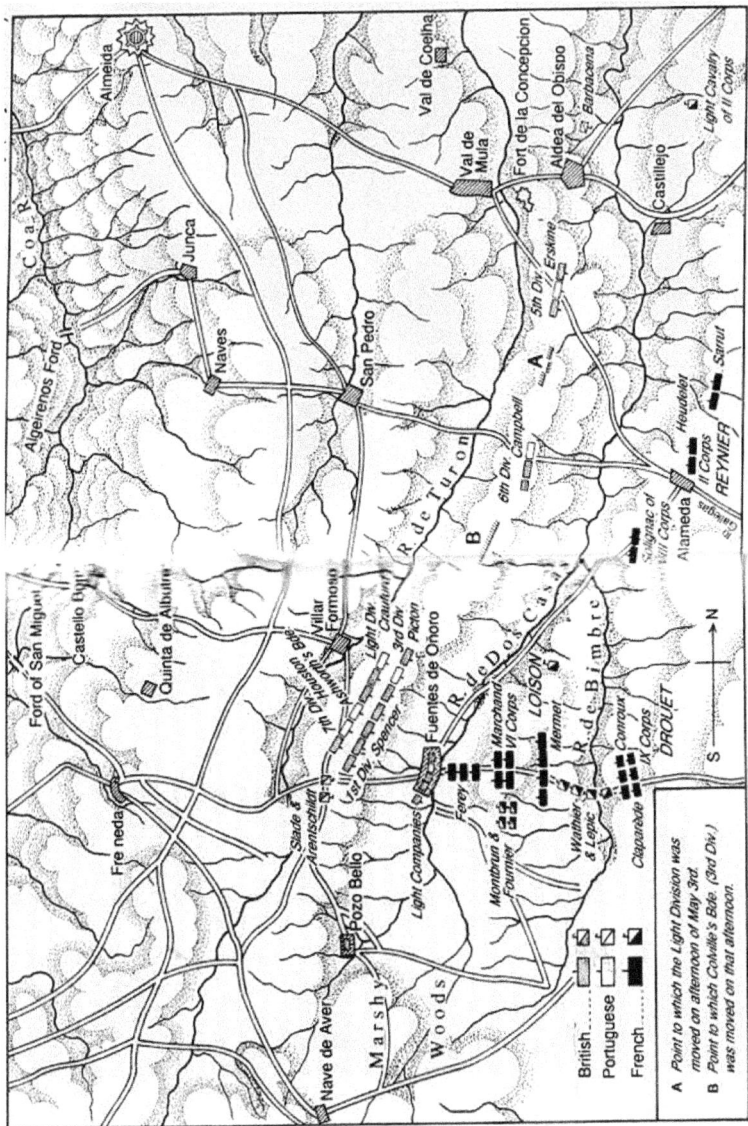

FUENTES D'ONOR POSITIONS ON THE FIRST DAY, MAY 3RD 1811

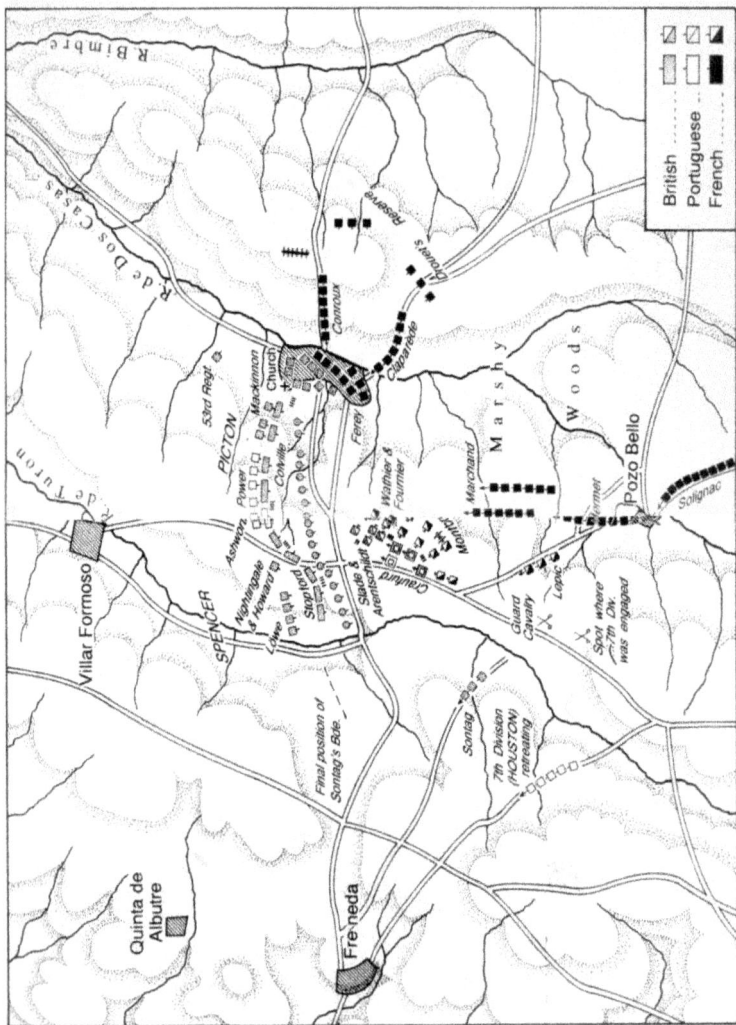

Fuentes d'Onor May 5th 1811

Houston afterwards occupied on the hill commanding the road to Almeida, on the left bank of the Turon River, and about two miles from Freynada.

The cavalry were ordered to retire covering; General Houston on the right, Colonel Nixon's Portuguese on the left, retiring from Pozo Velha, and the light division in square in our rear. The left of the cavalry was much exposed by the advanced infantry of the enemy's columns moving from Pozo Velha. The whole retired into position without suffering so much as might have been expected. Had the enemy made a very brisk attack on our centre and left at the time General Houston's and the light division were so far advanced, the French cavalry, numerous as it was, showing a becoming spirit at the same time by advancing, our situation would, I think, have been rendered doubtful. This opportunity lost by the enemy did not return. The attacks of the enemy that followed, by cannon, covered by their cavalry on the right and by infantry on Fuentes d'Onoro, failed altogether, and towards the afternoon the firing ceased.

Lord Wellington thus speaks of Sir Stapleton Cotton's conduct:—

The movement of the troops upon this occasion was well conducted, although under very critical circumstances, by Major General Houston, Brigadier-General Craufurd, and Lieutenant-General Sir S. Cotton.

Massena, in his official account of the battle, which is to this day claimed by the French as a victory, thus speaks of the charge of cavalry alluded to by Sir John Elley:—

In spite of the protection of the artillery and infantry concealed in the rocks, he, General Montbrun, overthrew successively the twenty English squadrons, and drove them before him for more than a league.

On the 6th and 7th the enemy contented himself with demonstrations, and on the 8th, finding that any attempt to force his way to Almeida would be useless, retreated. Almeida was now more closely invested than ever. General Campbell, at his own especial request, being entrusted with the charge of the operations. He showed himself unequal to the duty, and by his negligence enabled General Brennier to escape by night from the beleaguered fortress.

Lord Wellington expressed pretty plainly his displeasure with General Campbell, yet cast the chief part of the blame on another officer, who felt the censure of the commander-in-chief so acutely that he soon after committed suicide. The above statement is, it may be observed, given on the authority of the late Lord Combermere.

On the 14th May, Lord Wellington quitted the neighbourhood of Almeida for Elvas, in order to superintend the siege of Badajos, and on the 24th Sir Stapleton Cotton left for the same destination, arriving at Elvas on the 1st June. He found that the siege of Badajos, which had been temporarily raised by Beresford for the purpose of fighting the uselessly glorious or the gloriously useless Battle of Albuera, had been re-established by Lord Wellington. Sir Stapleton employed himself in visiting the various advanced posts occupied by the cavalry, and exercising a general superintendence over that arm, which was very actively employed in reconnoissances, patrol, and picquet duty.

On the 12th, the assault of the 9th having failed, the siege was raised.

The following letters and memoranda have, we believe, never before been published. They may be interesting to the military student, and the civilian can, if he likes, pass them over:—

Near Elvas, 9th June, 1811.

My Dear Sir Stapleton,—I received your letter of the 6th instant yesterday, on my return home. I had met Captain Cocks in the morning in the trenches on the other side of the Guadiana, and learnt from him that you had given him leave to be absent for two or three days. I think it very likely that he may wish to stay to see the end of matters at Badajos, but I shall apprise him that you are anxious for his return.

Lord Wellington approves of your sending an officer of the heavy brigade to meet Colonel Gumming. As yet, however, I have no intimation of the 11th having begun to move from Lisbon.

You seem not to be perfectly aware of the footing on which the Spanish cavalry are. It consists of two separate and distinct bodies. The one is under the command of Count Penne Villemur, and belongs to the army of General Castaños, who allows this body to act for the present in connexion with our cavalry.

The other body of Spanish cavalry, commanded by Brigadier-General Lago, belongs to the army of General Blake, who has not placed it in connexion with us.

You will observe, therefore, that even the first-mentioned body is not placed in a formal manner under the orders of the senior general officer of the British cavalry, although there is no doubt that Count Penne Villemur will act on all occasions of importance in the same manner as if that were the case, and that in regard to the cavalry of General Blake's army, as mutual communication and co-operation is (strictly speaking) all that can be required, Brigadier-General Lago will no doubt see the propriety of carrying this understanding as far as possible, but he will not expect to receive any direct order from the general commanding the British cavalry,

I think you will understand this from Lord Wellington's memorandum of the 29th of May, and my letter of the 2nd instant, addressed to Sir William Erskine, but I have thought it as well to state the matter, as I have done above, to guard against any misunderstanding arising.

In regard to the latter portion, it will be better (as I have mentioned in a former letter) that you should station one at Talavera la Beal.

You mention a letter party being at Solano, which has to go all the way to the camp before Badajos, but you will perceive that I understood Corté de Pelias to be the intermediate station between Almendralejo and the camp before Badajos in that line. As my letters frequently remain some time at the post-office, I beg you will write "immediate" upon such as are of importance and relate to the enemy's movements.

I conclude you have already moved forward the 2nd Hussars from Lobau, in consequence of my letter of the 5th instant to that effect.

Believe me, my dear Sir Stapleton,
        Very faithfully yours,
                        Geo. Murray,
                        Q.-M.-Genl.
Lieut.-Gen. Sir Stapleton Cotton, Bart., &c.

        Albuera, 14th June, 1811.
My Dear Sir Stapleton,—Lord Wellington wishes that you should not have the body of the cavalry further out than Solano, and that you should have only posts of observation at Almendralejo, Azanihal, &c., and a post at Santa Martha. If the

movement you proposed making, mentioned last night in your letter of yesterday evening, dated half-past six, was not carried as far back as I have mentioned. Lord Wellington desires that you will draw back your people accordingly this day.

If the cavalry were kept further out it might happen that they would be cut off from this position. Should the enemy advance rapidly by Santa Martha, and even from Solano, the retreat to this place is fully as long as the march of the enemy from Santa Martha here would be.

Be so good as to give directions that the officer at Santa Martha sends reports direct to this place, as well as to your headquarters. I beg you will also establish a direct communication between yourself and Albuera, and send in reports of what has occurred and what you have learnt of the enemy's movements since yesterday.

Believe me, ever faithfully yours,

Geo. Murray,
Qr.-Mr.-Genl.

Lieut.-Gen. Sir Stapleton Cotton, Bart., &c.

Arrangements for Retiring the Army.
1st March.

Headquarters, La Albuera, 15th June, 1811.

It is proposed that the Spanish troops under His Excellency General Blake should move to Valverde, their advance guard occupying Almendral and La Parre, and having posts of observation at Nogales, and upon the roads that lead to La Parre and to Sta. Martha, and communicating with the cavalry under Lieutenant-General Sir Stapleton Cotton at Albuera.

The infantry under Lieutenant-General Hill, 2nd and 4th divisions, and Major-General Alten's brigade of light infantry, will fall back to the rivulet on the edge of the pine forest, between Valverde and Badajos.

The cavalry under Sir Stapleton Cotton will fall back to Albuera, communicating on the right with the Spanish troops at Almendral, and on the left with Brigadier-General Madden's brigade at Talavera Beal. Sir Stapleton Cotton throws forward such posts of observation as he deems necessary towards St. Martha, Solano, &c.

Major-General Hamilton's division of Portuguese infantry will march to the camp in front of Badajos, and resume its former position there: General Hamilton reporting to Major-General Picton.

The Spanish troops now before Badajos will march to Villa Beal, near Juremanha, where Major-General Hamilton's division has arrived to take their place; but General Giron will be so good as have out his picquets and other posts towards the town of Badajos until they are regularly relieved by the Portuguese division, and they will then follow to Villa Real.

The 3rd and 7th divisions will continue in their present positions before Badajos; but Major-General Houston will send out a picquet of cavalry toward Montijo, which will put itself in communication with Brigadier-General Madden at Talavera. Brigadier-General Madden will report direct to Major-General Picton, as well as to Sir Stapleton Cotton.

Major-General Houston and Brigadier-General Madden will send out officers; the former to Montijo and La Roca, the latter towards Merida, to endeavour to gain information of the arrival, force, and other particulars respecting the troops of the enemy, which are expected from Truxillo.

Geo. Murray,
Qr.-Mr.-Genl.

It is probable that Lieutenant-General Hill will move from Albuera this evening or during the night.

G. M.

Headquarters, 15th June, 1811.

It is intended that the cavalry should continue during tomorrow to hold Albuera with its right, and Talavera la Real with its left (Brigadier-General Madden's brigade), if circumstances permit.

Sir Stapleton Cotton will keep up a continued communication between these two points, and will observe the country in front of that line.

Should the enemy press forward, so as to oblige the cavalry on the left to fall back, it will retire toward Badajos, passing to the right bank of the Guadiana as soon as it conveniently can. Major-General Picton is to be immediately apprised of the retreat of the cavalry from Talavera, that it may lose no time in crossing the Guadiana at the ford above Badajos, and proceeding to the neighbourhood of the 7th division. The cavalry from Talavera will join the 3rd division during the march, and afterwards continue with it.

Should it be necessary to retire further than the position of the 7th division, all the troops on that side will fall back towards Campo Maior.

In the above case of the left of the cavalry being forced in, Major-General Hamilton's division will pass the Guadiana at the ford below Badajos, and proceed in the direction of Elvas to the right bank of the Caia.

The right and centre of the cavalry will, in this case, fall back through the forest between Valverde and Badajos, and will pass the Guadiana at the fords leading towards Elvas, and afterwards join Major-General Hamilton's division on the right bank of the Caia.

Should the enemy force back the right or centre of the line occupied by the cavalry, it will retire by the Great Road from Albuera to within about three miles of Badajos, and will then keep to the left, so as to pass along the open heathy heights that lie to the south of Badajos, crossing the Guadiana afterwards at the fords below Badajos.

Major-General Picton and Major-General Hamilton must equally, in this case, be apprised of the retreat of the cavalry, that they may lose no time in passing the Guadiana, as already mentioned; and the cavalry on the left will also retire as above pointed out.

Besides the communication to be made as above to Major-General Picton and Major-General Hamilton, Sir Stapleton Cotton will also communicate with Lieutenant-General Hill, whose corps will be on the edge of the pine forest between Badajos and Valverde, and apprise him of everything important that occurs, and in particular of the movements of the cavalry, in the event of its being obliged to retire.

Should the enemy attempt to press at all upon the troops on passing the fords of the Guadiana, such dispositions are to be made by the several corps at hand as may enable the cavalry and infantry to give the most effectual aid to each other on covering the passage of the river.

In case the enemy does not press forward so as to render it necessary for the cavalry to fall back from the line of the Albuera rivulet, the infantry before Badajos will retain during tomorrow their present ground.

Geo. Murray,
Qr.-Mr.-Genl.

Lieut.-Gen. Sir Stapleton Cotton, Bart., &c.
Commanding the Cavalry.

On the 16th the cavalry began to fall back towards the new position taken up by Lord Wellington, for the purpose of covering the Alemtejo, on the banks of the Caia.

Albuera, 16th June, 1811.

The arrangement, dated at ten o'clock last night, provides for the case of the enemy's movements obliging the cavalry and the division before Badajos to pass in the course of this day to the right bank of the Guadiana, either by the cavalry on the left being forced back from Talavera Real, or by that on the right or centre having to give up the line of the Albuera rivulet.

Should the advance of the enemy, however, not be such as to render it necessary to make the movements above referred to in the course of the day, the troops on the left of the Guadiana will retire across the river, at all events, tomorrow morning, and will begin their movements for that purpose as soon as the moon has risen.

The cavalry on the left at Talavera and the 3rd division will pass the Guadiana, above Badajos, as directed in the former arrangements, and proceed to unite themselves with the 7th division. The whole of the troops will afterwards fall back to the neighbourhood of Campo Maior, except the 17th Portuguese Regiment, which Major-General Houston has been already instructed to send to Elvas.

The division of Major-General Hamilton will at the same time pass the Guadiana at the ford below Badajos, and proceed as directed by the former arrangement to the right bank of the River Caia, falling back afterwards in the course of the day to the olive grounds in the front of Elvas.

The troops under Lieutenant-General Hill will move at the same time from their present bivouac through the forest, and will pass the Guadiana at the ford called Puerto de Chico, falling back afterwards in the course of the day to the olive grounds in front of Fort St. Lucia.

The cavalry on the right at Albuera, &c., will fall back to the bivouac at present occupied by Lieutenant-General Hill's troops, continuing their march from thence through the forest to the open country near the Guadiana. It will afterwards pass the river at Puerto de Chico, and other fords between that and the conflux of the Caia with the Guadiana, and proceed to the olive grounds, in the neighbourhood of Elvas.

Sir Stapleton Cotton will establish a line of cavalry outposts, in front of the corps, at, and near, Elvas, which will communicate on the left at the River Caia with the cavalry outposts placed in front of the corps at Campo Maior. These cavalry outposts will have such a support of infantry from the two corps as may appear to be necessary.

Headquarters will be, on the 17th, at Elvas.

It is proposed that the Spanish troops, under His Excellency General Blake, shall be on the 17th instant at Jurumenha, having an advance guard at Olivearca.

Geo. Murray,
Q.M.Gl.

Lieut.-General Sir Stapleton Cotton, Bart., &c.

Elvas, 17th June, 1811.

My Dear Sir Stapleton,—It is not intended to make any general movements of the troops tomorrow, unless some circumstances should come to render it necessary.

The following arrangements are intended respecting the cavalry:—

The 13th Light Dragoons to go into cantonments at St. Olaia and Barbucena, and to move there either tomorrow or on the 19th, as you judge most expedient.

Brigadier-General Otway's brigade of Portuguese cavalry (the 1st and 7th regiments) to join Brigadier-General Madden at Campo Maior, and form a part of his brigade, consisting at present of the 6th and 8th regiments.

This movement to take place either tomorrow or next day, as you think proper.

The 11th Light Dragoons to continue for the present at Elvas and neighbourhood.

The Spanish cavalry, under Count Penne Villemur, to move to Onguella, and extend from thence, so as to watch the country on the left of the enemy, in the direction of Albuquerque, La Roca, &c., and to communicate on the right with the troops at and near Campo Maior.

The remainder of the cavalry to bivouac in the road upon the bank of the Caia, near Torre de Mouro, which is about a league from Campo Maior, on the road towards St. Olaia.

The line of outposts of the cavalry to be maintained in front of Campo Maior, towards Badajos, and from thence to the right, in front of Elvas.

The greater part of the infantry will also be in the bivouac near Torre de Mouro.

The troops that are to occupy that bivouac will probably be ordered to move there on the 19th instant, and an officer of the quartermaster-general's department will be directed to point out the ground.

Believe me ever, faithfully yours,

Geo. Murray,
Q.M.Gl.

Lieut.-General Sir Stapleton Cotton, Bart., &c.

Niza, 31st July, 1811.

My Dear Sir Stapleton,—I did not receive your letter of yesterday's date till this afternoon at this place.

My note of yesterday would apprise you that Lord Wellington expected you to cross the Tagus, as the body of the cavalry is moving in that direction. I should have been more explicit on that point, but understood that Lord Wellington's letter of a prior date would have made you aware of his intentions.

It is understood also that Major-General Anson is to accompany the 16th, although the other regiment of his brigade does not move.

It would be hardly worthwhile to make the 13th shift their quarters for one night, to let the 16th into Assumar, as the former regiment will certainly have to bivouac sometimes on its present march.

The 14th are not to move from Major-General Long's brigade at present, but you must have observed by the reports sent yon, that the heavy brigade (Major-General de Grey's) comes to Portalegre, where it will arrive from Coria upon the 4th August.

I beg you will give orders for letter parties being kept up by

Assumar to Villa Viciosa, to communicate with General Hill. There are guides at Palahgra.

Believe me, ever faithfully yours,

Geo. Murray,
Q.M.Gl.

Lieut.-General Sir Stapleton Cotton, Bart, &c.

Till the 2nd of August, Sir Stapleton remained in this camp, and then marched with the cavalry, following the rest of the army towards Ciudad Rodrigo, which place Lord Wellington entertained hopes of capturing.

Headquarters, Sabugal, August 8th, 1811.

My Dear Sir Stapleton,—The reason of sending so large a detachment towards Ledesma, &c., was that General Slade's report mentioned that forage was abundant in that direction. There is no reason why it should not be diminished to whatever you find sufficient to keep a look-out upon the part of the frontier about Segura, Salvaterra, &c.

The cavalry under General Slade is today at Albergaria, Fuente, Guinaldo, Espeja, &c., and will continue tomorrow in the same situation, merely leaving posts at El Bodon, Campio, and something at Peñapanda.

Major-General Alten's brigade to remain about Val di Lebo, &c. I beg you will let me know whether there is any forage to be had there.

I am very sorry to hear of your complaining, but I hope it will go off, as the weather must soon begin to cool a little. In the meantime, I doubt our having anything to do that would prevent your taking care of yourself.

Headquarters are to be tomorrow at Casalhas de Flores. I beg there may be a letter party *here* from Major-General Alten's brigade, and another at Pedrigao, to communicate with the 16th. General Slade will have one at Alfaiates. There will be a daily communication from headquarters to Portalegre by Scovell's guides, but it is necessary, as we now stand, to have two strings to our bow,

Believe me, ever faithfully yours,

Geo. Murray,
Q.M.Gl.

Lieut.-Gen. Sir Stapleton Cotton, Bart, &c.

On the 11th August Sir Stapleton arrived at the neighbourhood of Ciudad Rodrigo, and the same day accompanied Lord Wellington on a reconnoissance, riding altogether from thirty to thirty-six miles.

It is needless to enter into a detail of the operations which ensued, as Sir Stapleton, though a portion of the cavalry played a gallant part in them, was not himself conspicuously engaged. It suffices for the continuity of our narrative to say that, after maintaining a distant blockade of Ciudad Rodrigo, Lord Wellington saw himself obliged to fall back before Massena. During this operation, he, with two brigades, gave battle at El Bodon to the French—who had one division of infantry, thirty squadrons and twelve guns—in order to afford time for the rest of his forces to concentrate at Fuente Guinaldo.

From there the British withdrew to the heights beyond Coita; Marmont shortly after, having revictualled Ciudad Rodrigo, but failed to defeat the English Army, fell back upon the Tagus. In consequence of this movement. Lord Wellington, on the 29th of September, placed the bulk of his forces in cantonments on the banks of the Coa, sending at the same time a portion of his troops to observe, and threaten, Ciudad Rodrigo. A period of inaction now ensued, from the sickness prevailing in the army, which rendered it incapable of active operations.

During this interval of forced inaction, the officers sought to amuse themselves by shooting and hunting. The Marquis of Tweeddale received a pack of hounds from England, and we find Lord Wellington mentioning the circumstance in a letter to Sir Stapleton, and asking him to come over and have a day's hunting. Soon, however, the rainy weather set in, sickness increased, and outdoor sports were put a stop to. On the 6th December Sir Stapleton Cotton left for Lisbon.

The following letters and memoranda relate to the period the events of which we have briefly summarised:—

Fte. Guinaldo, 19th September, 1811.

My Dear Sir Stapleton,—It is expedient that the several brigades of cavalry should hold themselves in readiness to move on a short notice, and that there should be no encumbrance with the troops that would at all embarrass and impede their movements.

Major-General Campbell will probably draw in the infantry from Salisco this afternoon or tomorrow, and it will be necessary for the cavalry to withdraw at the same time or probably soon after.

The forage carts of the advanced brigades had better be sent a little to the rear as soon as the enemy advances towards the Agueda, and those of the other brigades should not be brought forward unless the regiments move up towards the front.

Yours faithfully,

Geo. Murray,
Q.M.Gl.

Lieut.-Gen. Sir Stapleton Cotton, Bart, &c.

Frenada, October 9th, 1811.

My Dear Sir Stapleton,—Lord Wellington has no objection to your relieving Major-General Alten's brigade by Major-General Anson's when you think it expedient to do so.

The 2nd Hussars have received a route for the Alemtejo from Lieutenant-General Hill, who had been authorised to call for them when he thought it necessary.

Lord Wellington is of opinion that the cavalry in front must be able to find some of that long grass still remaining which he saw about the banks of the Azava, and in other places in that part of the country.

Believe me faithfully yours,

Geo. Murray,
Q.M.Gl.

Lieut.-Gen. Sir Stapleton Cotton, Bart., &c.

Frenada, October 13th, 1811.

My Dear Sir Stapleton,—Lord Wellington wishes you to send Major-General Anson's brigade to relieve Major-General Alten's; allowing General Slade's to remain where it is, doing, as at present, the outpost parties in the direction of Penales, San Martin, &c. You will be good enough to make an arrangement also for furnishing the cavalry duty on the right of the Agueda; for the vicinity of the cantonments the light division is ordered to occupy in that quarter.

I enclose for your perusal a letter I have had from Major-General Craufurd on this subject, which I beg you will return. I am to observe, however, that Lord Wellington does not wish Portuguese cavalry to be sent, as suggested by Major-General Craufurd.

There is no objection to the 1st Hussars going back to the valley of the Zezere whenever you relieve General Alten's brigade.

The 11th may also be moved in that direction if you think it expedient to keep the brigade together.

Believe me, ever faithfully yours,

Geo. Murray,
Q.M.Gl.

Lieut.-Gen. Sir Stapleton Cotton, Bart, &c.

Frenada, October 25th, 1811.

My dear Sir Stapleton,—Lord Wellington thinks of sending General Le Marchant's brigade into the valley of the Zezere. I am, therefore, to request that you will suspend the intended march of General Alten's brigade in that direction.

Lord Wellington's idea is, that it is of importance to put the newly arrived regiments into the most quiet and comfortable cantonments we can give them. Perhaps you would, upon this ground, recommend the villages towards Lamego; but the objection, to these is their distance to the left in case anything should occur to make it necessary to reinforce suddenly the corps in the Alemtejo.

I hope to have reports from you soon about the supply of forage in the valley of the Zezere.

Very faithfully yours,

Geo. Murray,
Q.M.Gl..

Lieut.-Gen. Sir Stapleton Cotton, Bart., &c.

Frenada, October 31st, 1811.

My Dear Sir Stapleton,—I have sent direct to Alten respecting the movement of the brigade tomorrow.

The French are collecting in force upon the Tormes, to move forward upon Ciudad Rodrigo, for the purpose of putting in another garrison and some more cattle.

Let me hear if you move your own quarters. Perhaps you will find it convenient to be at or near Minsilha, as we may have to move further forward. I beg you will send the enclosed to General Graham.

Ever faithfully yours,

Geo. Murray.

Frenada, 31st October, 1811.

Movements to take place on the 1st November.

Major-General Alten's brigade to move to Navé, Soito, Bismuhla, Alfaiates, &c.

Major-General Anson's brigade, and Captain Bull's troop of horse artillery to move to Minselha, Marmaliero, and adjacent villages.

Both the brigades of cavalry to have a letter party at Villa Maior to communicate with headquarters.

Geo. Murray,
Q.M.Gl.

Lieut.-Gen. Sir Stapleton Cotton, Bart., &c. Alveria.

Frenada, 15th November, 1811.

My Dear Sir Stapleton,—Lord Wellington appears to concur entirely in your proposal of sending the heavy brigade to Cea, &c., and does not apprehend any want of long forage in that quarter. The only doubt seems to be whether the commissariat have not made their arrangements with a view to drawing their forage more from the Douro than the Mondego. I shall write to Mr. Bisset about this, and let you know his answer. As to the forage carts, the way will be for you to send me an official statement upon the subject, representing the disadvantages of the old system, and suggesting the remedy by the adoption of the portable forges, either entirely or in part, as you think best. As the business leads to an entire alteration of the existing establishment, we must proceed in form in it.

Believe me, faithfully yours,

Geo. Murray,
Q.M.Gl.

CHAPTER 8

Fall of Ciudad Rodrigo

On the 8th January Lord Wellington, seizing the opportunity of Marmont's having moved from Placencia and Talavera towards Toledo, and Dorsenne, with the army of the centre, in the direction of Burgos, crossed the Agueda, and invested Ciudad Rodrigo, which fell on the 19th of the same month. During this siege, as on many other occasions, the services of the cavalry, though not of a nature to be mentioned in dispatches or recorded in history, were not the less useful in picquet and patrol duty. In war, as in many other circumstances, the solid is often overlaid by the brilliant, and because trumpets did not always sound, or swords flash in the charge, many will think that, save on isolated occasions, the British cavalry and their gallant leader did not contribute much to the triumphs of the Peninsula. Such, however, was not the case, and it must be remembered that the most arduous duties of cavalry are those which prepare the road for the action of the other arms. But to return to the subject of our biography.

On the 17th January, 1812, Sir Stapleton rejoined the army from Lisbon, whither he had proceeded on a few weeks' leave. He found Lord Wellington occupied with the siege of Ciudad Rodrigo, and two days after his arrival that place fell. Sir Stapleton did not fail to send his mother an account of the interesting yet bloody drama which had been acted before him. Unfortunately, that letter no longer exists; but we are able to give another addressed to his sister in which some few allusions are made to the topic of the hour.

> Villa de Curvas, near Ciudad Rodrigo,
> January 29th, 1812.

My Dear Sister,—I wrote my mother last week an account of the siege and fall of Ciudad Rodrigo. The enemy advanced a few leagues on this side of Salamanca; but finding that the place had fallen he retraced his steps, and I believe will fall back as far as Valladolid, and we shall go into winter-quarters, although, probably, but for a few weeks, as Badajos must be attacked before the enemy receives reinforcements.

Poor General R. Craufurd died of his wounds last Friday, and we all attended his funeral the next day. His remains were deposited near the breach where he received the wound during the assault on the night of the 19th. The other general officer whom we lost, McKinnon, was blown up. I saw the explosion, but little thought that what arose in the air were the bodies of poor McKinnon and forty men.

This has been, and still is a most severe winter; but the troops, although much exposed to the weather during the siege, have not suffered much. I have moved about so constantly, that no time could be found to build a chimney anywhere. The houses are cool and pleasant in summer, but not comfortable in winter, as you may imagine, without glass windows or fireplaces. The Estrella mountains and the Sierra de Gata are now covered with snow and beautiful; but the sight does not warm one. You will have a letter from me in the course of two or three months, complaining of heat. What a famous windfall Lord Harrington has got! The Duchess of Newcastle has not been forgotten by General Craig. I was in hopes that the old gentleman would have left me some of his fine paintings. He had a good, though small collection.

I will write to dear Robert in a day or two.

Duty and love to all, from, dear Hester,

Your most affectionate brother,

S. Cotton.

Feasts were sometimes in the Peninsula strangely mixed up with fights, and in Sir John Elley's journal we learn that on the 17th February Sir Stapleton Cotton gave a ball at Cavilhan. But sterner work was at hand; and on the 26th he left for the vicinity of Badajos, which town Lord Wellington intended to besiege. On the 16th March, the day that the place was invested, a force, commanded by Sir Thomas Graham, (afterwards Lord Lynedoch), consisting of three divisions of infantry, with two brigades of cavalry under Sir Stapleton Cotton, was dispatched towards Llerena to act as a covering army. A portion

Sieges of the Forts
and Operations round
SALAMANCA,
1812.

of the cavalry occupied posts at some distance in advance of the main body. While employed on this duty Sir Stapleton was brought much into contact with Sir Thomas Graham, whose shrewd, yet simple and hearty disposition, is thoroughly shown in the following letters:—

Villa Franca, 22nd March, 1812.

My Dear Sir Stapleton,—The contents of the intercepted letter to General Raymond, at Fregenal, proving that a previous provisional order had been given him to move all his troops for the purpose of occupying Fregenal on hearing of the evacuation of Zaffra, and information received yesterday morning that at least part of the infantry and cavalry had marched from Hornachos on Valentia de las Torres, from whence they might easily have gone on Llerena, made me rather anxious about Colonel Mitchell's small detachment.

I therefore rode over to Ribeira, and got General Slade to send on a squadron under Sir George Calcraft, by Usagré towards Villa Franca, to give support to the squadron already advanced, and to Colonel Mitchell's infantry. I likewise sent on an *aide-de-camp* to desire Colonel Michell to leave Llerena if he had entered it yesterday evening, and by a report just received I find he did so. Some of the enemy's infantry and a small body of cavalry are stated to have been yesterday at Canta Gallo, which must be those coming from Tregenal.

I regret not having sent a larger force to Llerena, which might have enabled the officers to try to cut off them; but with so small a detachment it would have been imprudent to have attempted anything.

I shall not recall the infantry from Usagré till I hear more particularly about the state of the enemy's force, and about their indication on this side of the *sierra*; and I shall leave it entirely to you to send directions relative to those two squadrons which will probably be likewise today at Usagré.

The reports concerning forage should be a material consideration, I think, in the distribution of the cavalry.

I enclose you Scovell's arrangement of communication with the camp; any letters of yours should be here an hour or two before six, that the bag may be dispatched exactly every evening from this at that hour.

By Lord Wellington's account they go on well notwithstanding

the rain; on the 19th the enemy made a sortie, and were driven back with very considerable loss, and Philippon greatly alarmed lest our people should have followed into the garrison. Picton's *aide-de-camp*, Cuthbert, was killed, and Colonel Fletcher slightly wounded. By the last accounts I have received, a part of the enemy's infantry went over the mountains from Hornachos towards Zalemca; there still remains a small portion there, which we will dislodge when our light, (cavalry is doubtless meant), may go there to obtain information.—*Adieu.*
Ever most truly yours,

Thos. Graham.

Lieut.-Gen. Sir Stapleton Cotton, &c.
P. S,—Would you be kind enough to desire your servant to get a small bag of rice for me, and to send it by the first orderly that happens to come? There is not an ounce to be got here.

On the 25th March Graham made an attempt to surprise a French detachment in Llerena. We insert Sir John Elley's narrative of the expedition:—

About 8 o'clock a.m., the three divisions of infantry and two brigades of cavalry moved in separate columns to surprise about 1500 infantry and 200 cavalry at Llerena, under General of Brigade, Guiotte. In order to keep the movement as secret as possible, the heads of the columns were not allowed to exceed each other. The 7th division moved upon the high road, with four cavalry only allowed to be in front. The consequence was a patrol of the enemy's cavalry came suddenly within a hundred yards of the column on the road, by which the head of the 7th division became panic struck, and commenced firing. We arrived at Llerena in time to see the enemy's column file out of the gate of La Reyna, taking the mountain road by Tracoira to Guadalcanal.
Sir S. Cotton and staff occupied two houses during the day, going to V. Garcia in the evening.

Sir Thomas Graham received reports about this time of the probable advance of Soult to relieve Badajos. He consequently withdrew his infantry a short distance to the rear, in accordance with Lord Wellington's instructions, who intended that battle should be given to Soult, if he ventured to approach, in the position of Albuera.

Beolanga, 1st April, 1812, 9 a.m.

My Dear Sir Stapleton,—I met the dragoon sergeant with your letter of this morning as I was patrolling on to meet you in front of this place.

You have done perfectly well to remain today under the circumstances, as certainly, as long as the enemy can be kept in uncertainty with regard to our having returned to the former cantonment the better. These deserters from the camp last night will give them the information, probably, though they might perhaps not know in what direction the troops were to move this morning.

I do not feel myself at liberty to delay the march of the infantry, and indeed, unless a part at least was to be countermarched as far as Assuaga and Maguilla, I do not think any advantage would result from any change of what has been fixed according to the memo. I sent you yesterday.

No positive scheme of cantonment for Anson's brigade has yet been made out; I merely told Ponsonby, in the note I sent by Lord William Russell, what you proposed in your memorandum yesterday, and which I think will do perfectly well.

It is so important to gain authentic information concerning Soult and the troops from Seville, that the longer Captain Erskine can remain at Guadalcanal the better.

I desired General Slade to occupy Maguilla today with one squadron, that the Zalamca road on the left may be watched. He has another squadron at Llerena, but as he means to see the bearer of this himself you can settle with him any arrangement you think best.

I shall be today at Valentia de los Torres, and shall go tomorrow to Villa Franca to be more in communication with General Hill, from whom I heard this morning. It appears part of Foy's division of Marmont's army has come up to Croute by Castel Blanco and Puebla de Alcocer.

I remain very truly yours,

Thos. Graham.

To Sir Stapleton Cotton, Bart., &c.

P. S.—I have not yet had any account of Anson's brigade and the 11th Light Dragoons having actually passed the river, but from his former letter I think they must have followed the infantry that De Lancey sent me notice of yesterday.

Llera, 2nd April, 1812.

My Dear Sir Stapleton,—On examining the country yesterday, I find there is an excellent carriage road, from Guadalcanal through Verlanga and Valentia de los Torres to this place, and so on to Ribeira.

It was by this road that Drouet sent some of his loaded carts; the tracks of the wheels are to be seen all the way. The country people all say it is much the shortest way, and being so practicable, even for artillery, it will require being watched as much as the Usagré road from Llerena should, though the Great Road, perhaps, from Guadalcanal is not better than this in dry weather. I think therefore, you should reinforce this post on your left, giving the officer commanding, (orders omitted, no doubt), to patrol to his front and flanks, and during the day to look out frequently himself with a glass from the height of Sta. Martin de Fee, a conical hill that lies to the left of Valentia de las Torres, and which overlooks all the plain.

There can be no occasion for the letter party at Valentia after this. You will let me know those you establish back to Villa Franca.

From the information, I received this morning, Soult has probably left Seville by this time with the troops assembled there from the south and east of Andalusia. They will probably come by Constantina and Guadalcanal, in order to effect a junction easier with Drouet. Two of the German Legion deserted from Maguilla yesterday, and were brought in to me this morning at Valentia by some Spaniards from Campillo.

It will be well to give all your posts orders to look out for such rascals.

I had not received any reports this morning from any quarter before I set out. *Adieu.*

Ever truly yours,

Thos. Graham.

Lieut.-Gen. Sir S. Cotton, Bart., &c.

I sent to Llerena this morning, to try if the hospital stores can be brought away.

Villa Franca, 2nd April, 1812, 4 p.m.

My Dear Sir Stapleton,—By a letter I found here from Lord Wellington, it is not his intention that any kind of affair with the enemy should be brought on till the army is collected at Albuhera. I think, therefore, it would be best to send back Bull's troop to Villalba, where the rest of the artillery will be assembled ready to move at once by the Great Road at St. Martha to the position of the army.

The road I mentioned to you in my note this morning from Llera is perfectly good, and certainly, the shortest that the troops can take, coming from Llera here, where part of the carriages, &c., belonging to it now are.

The squadron that was at Hornachos was withdrawn, but by some mistake a company of the 61st regiment that ought to have gone there from Ribeira has remained all this time at Ribeira. Hornachos, therefore, is quite unoccupied. It should be patrolled too, frequently, from Llera, and from Ribeira, when the cavalry gets there, and I shall see tomorrow myself whether a good bivouac for an infantry picquet can be found on this side of the river, on the road from Ribeira to Hornachos.

I am very anxious to hear what intelligence has been obtained of the enemy's movements and force in different quarters; while Lord Wellington desires to have the most frequent reports of it sent to him whenever the information appears to be authentic and of consequence.

Adieu, my dear Sir Stapleton.

Ever faithfully yours,

Thomas Graham.

The peasants near Llera said it was reported the enemy were in Campillo, but I do not believe it.

Villa Franca, 3rd April, 1812, ½ past 6 p.m.
My Dear Sir Stapleton,—Though it is not probable that the enemy is ready to advance in such force as Captain Heathcote seems to believe, yet, as I have every reason to believe that Soult left Seville with 8000 or 10,000 men on the 31st *ult.*, or at latest on the 1st instant (this came from Ct. Penne Villemur and a confidential correspondent of Lord Wellington's, at Xerez de las Cabalheros) for Constantina, Drouet must endeavour to cover the *débouche* of Guadalcanal as soon as he can.

I have therefore determined to close the infantry to within one march of the road in front of Albuhera, which Lord Wellington desires me to occupy in the first instance whenever the enemy collect in any force on the plain.

This will leave Los Santos, Fuentes de Maestre, Ribeira, and this place open for the cavalry. The 6th and 7th Dragoons remain at Almendralejo and Azauchal until further orders,

Cavalry will not march till tomorrow morning from the Torre d'Almendral, &c., to which place I sent off Lord Wm. Russell as soon as I got your letter. I have since forwarded your last. I have directed him to march tomorrow on Fuentes de Maestre, as the most centrical to move from in any direction that may be advisable. Will you meet him here to dinner at six o'clock tomorrow? His people will have had enough of it to Fuentes de Maestre.

  I remain, ever truly yours,

Thomas Graham.

Sir S. Cotton, &c.

Villa Franca, 3rd April, 1812, ½ past 7.

My dear Sir Stapleton,—Lord Wellington seems anxious that you should not expose the post of Guadalcanal, &c., to risk by keeping them out too long.

At the same time, it is of much consequence to endeavour to learn, with as much certainty as possible, what is Soult's line of march, and with what numbers he comes.

Lord Wellington thinks from his information that he will come by the Great Road of Ronquilla, &c. It is not, however, impossible that his march by this line may have been discomposed by our being so forward as we were the other day.

Captain Clarke, who was at Campillo, seems to be a very intelligent officer. Perhaps if he could be spared for a few days it might be worthwhile to have him at Fuentes de Cantos, so as to try to get intelligence from the Great Road in front.

I send some letters brought here from headquarters. I believe Lord Wm. says they go on well. I have ordered the letter party from Fuentes de Maestre to Almendralejo, to keep up the communication with General Hill. Indeed, I did not know till yesterday, when a dragoon of his came all the way through, that that party had been withdrawn.

The direct line from headquarters will now be by Albuhera, Sta. Martha, Villa Franca.

You will let me know what others you think necessary.

I remain, ever truly yours,

Thos. Graham.

Lieut.-Gen. Sir Stapleton Cotton, &c.

Villa Franca, 4th April, 1812.

My Dear Sir Stapleton,—By General Slade's report, received at two a.m. this morning, it appears that the enemy advanced, in considerable force of cavalry, to Berlanga yesterday. Your posts of observation on the right must therefore be drawn in, so as to be in hand, in case of the enemy pushing strong patrols across the roads within them.

It is not probable that the enemy will push on this way till Soult arrives. You do not say upon what authority you speak of his not having marched from Seville till the 2nd. He may not have left it himself till that day, but I am inclined to think that his troops marched sooner, and therefore may soon arrive at Guadalcanal.

Till the arrival of the light brigade, which cannot be till tomorrow, I should think it would be advisable to keep the cavalry, all but the posts of observation, so as to be able to unite it quickly. I am rather inclined to think that Lord Wellington has let Ponsonby and Harvey both remain in camp. Of course, they will join their troops today.

I send back the officer you sent to show Ponsonby the posts, as probably a different disposition of the light cavalry will be necessary tomorrow when they come up.

I shall ride out by-and-by to the heights beyond Ribeira.

A squadron of Slade's is all that can be spared today for Almendralejo. I have directed him to send one.

The attempt to blow up the dam of the inundation did not succeed.

Yours truly,

T. Graham.

Sir S. Cotton, &c.

Villa Franca, 4th April, 1812, 12 at Noon.

My Dear Sir Stapleton,—I have received your letter half an hour ago, and Ponsonby is not come in from Almendral. His people will be at Fuentes de Maestri about four p.m., this afternoon.

We shall ride out together by-and-by in the hopes of meeting you. The arrangements made for the infantry is according to the enclosed; but Feria La Parra, La Morera, and Nogales will hold General Le Marchant's brigade, and afford plenty of green forage till the infantry move into the wood, which may probably be the next day.

As the enemy is placed, he may either move from his right on Medellin, or advance this way. Lord Wellington does not think it improbable that Soult will attempt the relief by the right bank of the river.

All information concerning this movement, therefore, becomes very interesting, and I beg you will direct the attention of the people employed to observe, to this object. From the account of their artillery (if correct), and of the reinforcement following, would make one suppose Soult could not be ready to move forward for a day or two.

The enemy may mask his movements by driving back your posts, which will always be in his power by means of infantry; this would on a common occasion have induced me to leave batteries to support your cavalry, but, under Lord Wellington's instructions, I could not risk the infantry in partial affairs.

There must be more troops employed by the enemy before he can hope to relieve the place, however, should the attack that is expected to take place fail. *Adieu.*

My dear Sir Stapleton,

I remain very truly yours,

Thos. Graham.

I have ordered back two of Captain Macdonald's 6-pounders, to be at hand should you want them.

Villalba, 9 a.m., 6th April, 1812.

My Dear Sir Stapleton,—I was on the road to Villa Franca when I met the dragoon with yours, at half-past six morning. I shall not now go from this, that I may not be out of the way when any reports are sent. I should hear directly from General Le Marchant of what is coming by Los Santos. In the evening, I shall go to Sta. Martha.

You seem to think the enemy is not yet ready to advance rapidly.

Lord Wellington thinks Soult will be in the woods before Albuhera tomorrow; and certainly, if his troops, &c. are collected, there is nothing in the distance to hinder him. Lord Wellington calculates his numbers at thirty thousand. You must, therefore, be prepared, so as to fall back the cavalry at leisure, that the horses may be fresh for next day, should there be a battle on the old ground at Albuhera.

Let the enemy's movements be well watched with small posts of observation, and without harassing the bulk of the cavalry. When Soult gets within a certain distance, you may depend on a very rapid forward movement, if he means to fight on the 8th; and if it is ascertained that infantry is coming by Los Santos, he certainly does not intend to move on Merida.

Pray keep General Hill well informed. *Adieu.*

Ever truly yours,

Thos. Graham.

Sir S. Cotton, &c.

P. S.—Should the intelligence you now send be confirmed by your next reports, I should wish the bulk of the cavalry to be behind the Sta. Martha River by tomorrow morning or sooner. The eight guns here are going there now. The right of General Le Marchant's brigade might fall back to Torre d'Almendral. Nothing from camp this morning. The firing continues.

Villalba, ¼ past 1 a.m. 6th April, 1812.

My Dear Sir Stapleton,—It does not appear by Captain Clarke's report, that the enemy have begun to move on in force; it is probable all the advanced posts will be already driven back, and we may expect that Soult will push on as rapidly as possible, either towards Merida or Albuhera.

It becomes, therefore, of the utmost consequence to keep both General Hill and me informed of the enemy's movements. General Hill has his corps collected on this side of the Guadiana, at Arroyo de Servan, Calamonte, and the woods near, with his cavalry looking out on the roads to Almendralejo and Zarza. He has besides sent two officers to Almendralejo, to give him the earliest notice of the intelligence from the front.

If Soult means to fight, he will be in front of Albuhera tomorrow night; but he may manoeuvre by the right bank of the Guadiana, I hope, in every case, too late to save the place, which there is every reason to believe will be attacked tonight, though everything were not in the state as we wished.

Adieu. Pray let me hear often, and send a letter party of at least six men, for I have only my orderlies.

I sent back this morning the corpl. and 4 to Long's brigade, as General Hill wished; and I desired Ponsonby to send two of his as orderlies, but I don't believe they are come. *Adieu*.

    Ever yours,

                        Thos. Graham.

Sir S. Cotton, &c.

                   Sta. Martha, 6th April, 1812.

My Dear Sir Stapleton,—I have got yours of this day, one p.m., and Captain White has sent me Lieutenant Anderson's second report of eleven a.m., which leaves no doubt of the enemy coming on in force by both roads: I should suppose by Los Santos and Ribeira, this evening, so that then there should be no time lost in falling back the gross of the cavalry.

I enclose this open to the officer commanding at Fuentes de Maestré, that he may forward it, and that he may be prepared to move.

I remain,

    Ever truly yours,

                        Thos. Graham.

Lieut.-Gen. Sir Stapleton Cotton, &c.

                Villalba, 4 p.m., 6th April, 1812.

My dear Sir Stapleton,—From the reports yet received from Captain Clarke, &c., nothing more can be inferred than that the enemy is concentrating his forces on the Usagré road.

I presume he will still move on in force this evening, and therefore I can only recommend to your attention to have your cavalry in time behind the Sta. Martha River to prevent the risk of its being harassed by any rapid movement of the enemy. At the same time, it is of consequence to keep up the communication with General Hill as long as may be. I think he will retire on Lobon in the course of this evening.

    I remain, very truly yours,

                        Thos. Graham.

Sir Stapleton Cotton, &c.

Be so good as to send directly to Sta. Martha, as there will be no letter party here, and pray give notice to General Le Marchant of my going there, in case of having to send any direct report from the Los Santos road.

Sta. Martha, 7th April, ½ past 7 a.m.
My Dear Sir Stapleton,—I must begin by telling you that
Badajos is taken, by escalade both of the castle and the town, by
the 3rd and 5th divisions; the light and 4th being repulsed from
the breaches and having suffered much. Colonel M'Leod, 43rd,
killed, and several generals wounded.
The attack began at ten at night, and it was two hours before
the castle was carried.
I received your letter of yesterday, one p.m., at four this morning, and I have got yours of two this morning, an hour ago, with
Soult's note. When the men come I will send them all on to
Lord Wellington.
It is an odd reflection in such a communication—"*Du moins
il en est grandement tems*"—calculated for *effect*, if it fell into our
hands, if not so intended.
I don't at all know what Lord Wellington's plans will be. He has
ordered General Hill back by Lobon.
Soult at first will not believe the reports, and will probably
come on, which may give us an opportunity of striking a blow
against him. *Adieu.*

Ever yours,

Thos. Graham.

Torre d'Almendral, 9th April, 1812,
near 12 at night.
My Dear General,—It will be advisable to support the light
brigade, which will continue to follow the enemy tomorrow
till further orders from headquarters. Be so good, therefore, to
move your brigade on Los Santos *early, sending on this note immediately to Sir S. Cotton,* who will be the best judge, from the
information he receives, how far he can go with safety. He will
order General Slade and the horse artillery to follow him; and
at all events it may be of consequence to *spread the report that the
whole army is in motion*; for though I am afraid Lord Wellington
cannot follow Soult, yet it may be of use in the present moment that Soult should expect it; for Ballasteros has got hold of
Seville, and if circumstances would permit of our supporting
him the enemy would be forced to raise the blockade of Cadiz.
I was to have broken up the camp and to have put the infantry

into cantonments to the rear this morning. I shall delay it, and shall order a brigade forward to Villalba in the morning.

Yours truly,

Thomas Graham.

General Le Marchant, &c.

A Spanish officer is just come in from Bancarotta with the news of Seville being in their hands. No details. I have sent him on to Lord Wellington.

When Badajos fell, Lord Wellington, anxious for the safety of Ciudad Rodrigo, threatened by Marmont, and not placed by the Spaniards in the state of defence which had been ordered, hastened to the north. Before starting, however, he determined on an attempt to impress Soult (who, finding he was too late to prevent the fall of Badajos, retreated) that he was about to march on Seville. With this view he dispatched an order, which was received by Sir Stapleton, at Zaffra, on the afternoon of the 11th of April:—

Torre d'Almendral, 10th April, 1813,
½ past 3 a.m.

My Dear Sir Stapleton,—As Lord Wellington has no objection to the cavalry pressing a little on Soult's rear guard without overworking the horses, I have ordered the heavy brigade up— as you would probably learn from General Le Marchant—and Bull's troop, meanwhile, to Fuentes de Maestré. I enclose you the movements I have ordered, and am just going to camp to see Lord Wellington and to know if he will allow of any further advance of the infantry. At all events, it will be well to spread the report of our marching on Seville, and I shall send a commissary to bespeak biscuit in quantity, and rations for a large force, at Zaffra.

Adieu. Let me hear from you at Sta. Martha.

Yours truly,

Thomas Graham.

I have ordered Slade to Villa Franca.

Sta. Martha, 10th April, 1812.
In the evening.

Mr Dear Sir Stapleton,—On my return here from headquarters I found both yours of yesterday and this day, with the enclosures.

I was not without hopes that we might have been able to support Ballasteros a little in reality. Circumstances will not admit of it; and, therefore, as there is scarcely any chance of being able to do anything against the enemy's rear guard, all that seems advisable, and in conformity to Lord Wellington's wish, is by pushing on, with proper caution, intelligent officers with parties of observation, to try to get the most accurate information of the routes by which the enemy has moved, and the number and quality of the troops that have gone by them respectively, I shall stay here tomorrow, and shall forward any intelligence you may send immediately to Lord Wellington.

If you can safely push on something as far as Monasterio it may tend in some degree to create some alarm to the enemy.

But both Ballasteros and Penne Villemur are already aware, by communications from Lord Wellington, that the affairs of the north will not allow of his giving them the assistance which it would be so beneficial to afford at the present time.

There is, too, some doubt of the authenticity of the report about Seville having been occupied by the Spaniards, no official account having been transmitted by Penne Villemur, as might be expected.

If Llerena should be evacuated, patrols might be sent towards Maguilla, Berlanga, and Guadalcanal, for the object above mentioned. *Adieu.*

Ever most faithfully yours,

Thomas Graham.

Lieut.-Gen. Sir S. Cotton, &c.

The result of Sir Thomas Graham's interview with Lord Wellington was that Sir Stapleton was desired to make a demonstration in the direction of Seville, with discretionary power to attack if he should deem it advisable. He was, moreover, directed to issue orders for rations for 40,000 men, and to do everything calculated to impress the French with the idea that the whole British Army was about to move in that direction.

Immediately on receipt of this letter Sir Stapleton mounted his horse, and accompanied by the Assistant Adjutant-General, Colonel Elley, rode off to Bienvenida, about twenty miles off. On the steeple of the church of that place an officer and two dragoons had been posted, for the purpose of watching the enemy's movements. Arrived there.

Sir Stapleton himself mounted the steeple, and ascertained that the French occupied Llerena in force, and had a strong body of cavalry bivouacking in a wood at Villa Garcia, about five miles in advance of Llerena. After carefully examining their position he hastened back to Zaffra, where he found General Le Marchant in bed. Going to his room, he roused the General from sleep, and desired him to assemble his brigade, which was at Los Santos, and march so as to arrive at Bienvenida an hour before daybreak.

He also sent orders to Lieutenant-Colonel the Hon. F. Ponsonby, who commanded Anson's brigade, desiring him to march that afternoon from Villa Franca on Usagré, and the next day on Villa Garcia. Ponsonby moved that afternoon with the 12th and 14th Light Dragoons; the 16th Light Dragoons, belonging to the same brigade, not having received their rations, did not start till midnight. The inhabitants of the town gave a ball that night, and the officers of the 16th were flirting and dancing with the Spanish beauties till the very moment when the trumpet called them to mount and march, to honour certainly, and death perhaps.

Sir Stapleton's plan was to occupy the attention of the enemy in front with Anson's brigade, while with Le Marchant's he cut him from Llerena. Slade's brigade was to act as a reserve. The strength of the French cavalry was 2000, under Pierre Soult, and D'Erlon had 10,000 or 12,000 infantry, with a due proportion of artillery, in Llerena itself. At daybreak Sir Stapleton, with Le Marchant's brigade and the 16th, arrived at Villa Garcia, and found, to his annoyance, the French cavalry drawn up in order of battle, while opposed to them were only the six hundred sabres of the 12th and 14th Light Dragoons.

The cause of the enemy being thus prepared was that Ponsonby, not having received the cautionary order above alluded to, and neglecting to use his own discretion, drove in the enemy's picquet, and displaying his whole force, brought on the affair prematurely.

Sir Stapleton immediately dispatched Colonel Elley to guide Le Marchant's brigade—the 5th Dragoon Guards in advance, supported by the 3rd and 4th Dragoons—behind a mountain ridge which separates the two roads leading from Llerena to Usagré and Bienvenida. In the meantime, the French skirmished with Ponsonby's brigade, till, seeing the inferiority of the latter in numbers, they advanced against them.

Ponsonby retired slowly into a narrow defile between some stone walls, and the French, encouraged by his retreat, were on the point of charging, when the scene suddenly changed. The 16th, coming over the brow of the hill on the proper right of the rest of the brigade, beheld the French advancing and about a quarter of a mile distant. The latter paid little attention to this reinforcement; for between them and the enemy ran at the bottom of the hill a low stone wall, which appeared to render a direct advance of the 16th impossible. They little knew what obstacles British horses, ridden by British horsemen, can surmount, when a foe is on the other side. Trotting steadily down the hill, the 16th leapt the wall in line, without allowing it to check their onset for a moment, and dashed impetuously against the French.

At the same moment, the 5th Dragoon Guards came galloping along the valley on the right. On seeing this, both Ponsonby and the French, by a common impulse, faced about, Cotton charging with the former, and in a moment the British horsemen were on the flank and rear of the enemy, sabring and capturing in every direction. With proper caution.

Cotton, after a short time, halted his men for the purpose of reforming their ranks, much disordered by the charge. The French seized this opportunity of rallying behind a large ditch about half way between Villa Garcia and Llerena, and about two miles from each place. They were soon dislodged, however, for Cotton sent off two squadrons of the 16th to turn their left, charging in front at the same time with the 12th and 14th, supported by Le Marchant.

The French fled at once, and what an officer, (General the Right Honourable Sir Edward Oust), present in the affair terms in his journal "the finest chevy I ever had in my life," was continued. The flying horsemen were pursued up to, and even into, the very streets of Llerena, an officer of the 16th being killed in the town itself. D'Erlon, who had drawn up his infantry in one large square, supported by guns outside the town, fired a few round shot over the mingled mass of friends and foes bearing down upon him. The hint was taken, and after a little distant skirmishing Cotton fell back on Bienvenida and Usagré, having accomplished one of the most brilliant cavalry enterprises of the war. The French were so much impressed by the hardihood of the attack, that they thought that the whole British Army was at Cotton's back; and as soon as he left they retreated with all expedition towards Seville.

Our loss on this occasion was comparatively slight—57 of all ranks killed, wounded, and missing; while that of the enemy was about 50 killed: 1 lieutenant-colonel, 2 captains, 1 lieutenant, 132 rank and file, with a due proportion of horses, captured, and over 200 men wounded.

During the charge. Sir Stapleton's remarkably handsome charger, which he had ridden during all the preceding campaigns in the Peninsula, fell in charging a gully, bringing his rider heavily to the ground. Sir Stapleton was quit for some rather severe contusions, but his gallant charger dislocated his shoulder, and it was necessary to shoot him. On his return that day. Sir Stapleton must have completed about fifty miles—no bad exploit, considering that a sharp action was included in the performance.

This affair has been but little noticed by military historians; yet when we consider that Sir Stapleton was inferior in numbers and had no guns, and bear in mind the promptitude with which he recognised the failure of his original plan—caused through no fault of his own—and at once conceived another, it will, we think, be admitted that the affair of Llerena was one of the most distinguished episodes in a distinguished military career. No one but an eminently cool, and at the same time daring officer, could have handled his troops as he did on that day; yet the commander-in-chief speaks of the action in the following coldly formal manner:—

> And I have only to add my commendation of the conduct of Lieutenant-General Sir S. Cotton, Major-General Le Marchant, and the officers and troops under their command.
>
> Guinaldo, June 4th, 1812.
>
> Sir,(Gurwood's *Dispatches*)—I have the honour to transmit to you, by the directions of the Earl of Wellington, the enclosed extract of a dispatch from the Secretary of State, conveying to his Lordship the satisfaction which has been felt by His Royal Highness the Prince Regent at receiving the accounts of the success of the British cavalry under your orders at Villa Garcia, on the 11th of April last.
>
> I have the honour to be,
>
> Sir,
>
> Your most obedient servant,
>
> Fitzroy Somerset.
>
> Lieut.-Gen. Sir Stapleton Cotton, Bart.

Extract of a dispatch from the Earl of Liverpool to the Earl of Wellington, dated London, May 16th, 1812:—

> His Royal Highness the Prince Regent has read with satisfac-

tion the report of Sir Stapleton Cotton's very creditable action at Villa Garcia, where the French cavalry were completely defeated by an inferior number of British dragoons, commanded by the above officer.

The government showed themselves by no means prompt in recognising his services, and it was not till after Salamanca that he received the coveted red ribbon of the Bath. It had been most mortifying to him to have been invited on the preceding 12th March to attend a dinner given by Lord Wellington, after which Generals Hill and Graham were invested with the insignia of the Bath. On that very occasion Sir Stapleton had in his pocket a letter from Lord Wellington, thanking him for his services in covering the retreat to Torres Vedras; and it may be added that Sir Stapleton was subsequently thanked in his place in Parliament for his success at Llerena.

The following is the dispatch written by Sir Stapleton, giving an account of the affair of Llerena, which, though it has already appeared in Colonel Gurwood's *Dispatches* of the Duke of Wellington, could not, we think, be with propriety omitted here:—

Villa Garcia, April 11th, 1812.
Sir,—I have the honour to report to you that, having received information of the cavalry of General Drouet's corps (2600 strong) being encamped between Usagré and this place, I ordered Major-General Anson's (commanded by Lieutenant-Colonel the Hon. F. Ponsonby) and Major-General Le Marchant's brigades to move in the course of the night from Villa Franca and Los Santos, so as to arrive at daybreak, the former at Usagré the latter at Bienvenida, determining to attack the enemy at or soon after dawn, with General Anson's brigade in front, whilst Major-General Le Marchant's, by a flank movement from Bienvenida, should cut off his retreat upon Llerena. The advanced guards of Major-General Anson's brigade drove in the enemy's picquets from Usagré two hours sooner than I intended, and General Le Marchant's brigade had not time to get into the rear of the enemy, who fell back a sufficient distance to secure his retreat upon Llerena.
Lieutenant-Colonel Ponsonby followed the enemy through Villa Garcia, and his advanced guard was skirmishing with him, when General Le Marchant's brigade arrived on the other side of the heights between the Llerena road and Bienvenida. I

desired Colonel Ponsonby to show only three squadrons, and to endeavour to occupy the enemy in front until General Le Marchant's brigade (which I had sent Colonel Elley to conduct under cover of the heights) was prepared to attack the enemy in flank. This succeeded admirably, and the enemy being at the same moment vigorously attacked in front and flank, retired in the greatest confusion and disorder.

I pursued him with Lieutenant-General Anson's brigade, and one regiment of Lieutenant-General Le Marchant's (the 5th Dragoon Guards) supported by the 3rd and 4th Dragoons, to near Llerena, a distance of four miles, during which the enemy's loss in killed was very considerable; and about 150 prisoners, including a lieutenant-colonel, two captains, and one lieutenant, with about 130 horses, were brought off the field. The enemy's cavalry then formed on the right, and in rear of seven guns and between eight and ten thousand infantry, which had taken up a position on the left of and close to the town. The whole soon after retired upon Berlonga and Assuega, to the former of which places my patrols followed them.

I cannot say too much in praise of the gallantry and regularity of the four regiments which attacked and pursued the enemy, nor could anything have exceeded the steadiness and good discipline of the 3rd and 4th Dragoons (commanded by Major Clowes and Colonel Lord E. Somerset) who supported them. I have to recommend strongly to your notice Lieutenant-General Le Marchant and Lieutenant-Colonel Ponsonby, who commanded the two brigades with so much gallantry and judgment; and I have great pleasure in assuring you of the good conduct of Lieutenant-Colonel Hervey, commanding the 14th Light Dragoons, Major Prescott, commanding the 6th Dragoon Guards, Captain Dickens, commanding the 12th Light Dragoons, Captain Murray, commanding the 16th Light Dragoons, and the Hon. Major Cocks, commanding detachments of the 12th and 14th Light Dragoons.

To Lieutenant-Colonel Elley, my A.A.G., I am much indebted for the very great assistance which I derived from him, particularly in conducting my right column to the point of attack. I derived every assistance from Captain White, my D.A.Q.M.G., and Captain Baron Decken. Herewith I send a list of the killed and wounded, which I am happy to find is small, considering the very superior force of the enemy.

    I have the honour to be, Sir,

        Your most obed't humble Servant,

                Stapleton Cotton,

          Lt.-Gen. Commanding the Cavalry.

To Lieut.-Gen. Sir Thomas Graham, K.B., &c.

UNIFORM OF A MAJOR-GENERAL OF LIGHT DRAGOONS

CHAPTER 9

Wellington's Advance Against Marmont

On the 12th Sir Stapleton re-established his headquarters at Zaffra. The following day, notwithstanding the fatigue and exertions he had just gone through and the shock of his fall, the chivalrous hussar, as gay as gallant, gave a ball. On the morrow, he commenced his march to join the rest of the army, which was concentrating on the banks of the Agueda. Lord Wellington, after allowing his troops a few weeks' rest, broke up from his cantonments and advanced against Marmont in the direction of Salamanca. On the 13th of June, he crossed the Agueda, and on the 17th, passing the Tormes, entered Salamanca, and invested the forts. The 20th, Marmont marched to raise the siege with about twenty-five thousand men. The English Army was drawn up on the heights of St. Christoval, covered on the left by the light cavalry which, by a partial charge, defeated the enemy's attempt to turn that flank. The rest of the operations were confined to an affair of outposts, and a distant cannonade.

On seven following days, with the exception of the 23rd, similar skirmishes took place, the French marshal manoeuvring either to relieve the forts or to delay their capture till the arrival of reinforcements should enable him to give battle, which he expected to be in a position to do on the 28th. Wellington, on his side, was content to cover the siege, and steadfastly resisted the temptation, which was at least once offered him, of falling on the French with advantage. On the 27th the forts fell, and that evening Marmont retired towards the Douro. During the whole of these operations, and up to the date of his wound at the battle of Salamanca, Sir Stapleton was, by an order of the 1 9th of June, placed in charge of the outposts of the army. This duty he performed admirably, and it was one of equal importance and difficulty, for cavalry were employed freely on both sides for outposts and reconnoissances, and were frequently engaged.

Wellington, quitting Salamanca on the 29th of June, followed Marmont leisurely in his retreat, and on the 30th of June encamped on the banks of the Guarena.

From the Guarena he marched next day, 1st July, to Trabancos, and the next day to Villa Verde. Sir Stapleton now appears to have been entrusted with the command of the advanced guard, consisting of the light division. Pack's Portuguese brigade of infantry, four brigades of cavalry, a proportion of field batteries attached to the infantry, and a troop of horse artillery to the cavalry.

This column was directed to move, on the 2nd, on Torrecilla, and La Nava del Rey. The following day the two brigades of heavy cavalry were removed from his command, in order to be otherwise employed; and Sir Stapleton was desired with the remainder to move on the bridge of Tordesillas, but not to allow himself to be drawn into a serious engagement.

The instructions he received on the occasion are annexed:—

Headquarters, Villa Verde, July 2nd, 1812.
Sir,—The Commander of the Forces has directed that part of the army should make a movement tomorrow morning, the 3rd of July, for the purpose of alarming the enemy at the ford of Pollos and the bridge of Tordesillas.

To execute this operation, M. General Le Marchant's and M. General Bock's brigades of cavalry, and the 3rd division with B. General Bradford's infantry, and the cavalry and infantry under Don Carlos d'Espagné, are to move from their encamping ground of this day at half-past four o'clock tomorrow morning, to the ford of the river Duero, near Pollos, about two leagues below Tordesillas; and in aid of this movement the Commander of the Forces requests that the picquets of the light division and B. General Pack's infantry may be placed before day tomorrow, on the ground where his Lordship was last stationed that day to observe the enemy when Lt.-Colonel Elley was present; and the light division, with B. General Pack's infantry and the two brigades of light cavalry should be shown on the heights tomorrow morning, where the latter halted this day.

As soon as you hear a firing tomorrow morning near to Pollos,

175

you will be pleased to cause the cavalry and infantry to move towards the bridge of Tordesillas, endeavouring to conceal from the enemy the numbers of the troops, and not to expose them to any attack of the enemy, should he pass the bridge with that intention.

In the event of the bridge being destroyed by the enemy this night, the Commander of the Forces requests that you will give him the earliest information.

I have the honour to be. Sir,

Your obedient Servant,

Wm. De Lancey,

D.Q.M.G.

To Lieut.-Gen. Sir Stapleton Cotton, Bart., &c.

Sir Stapleton, in obedience to this order, proceeded to Tordesillas, and drove the French rear-guard over the bridge in great confusion and with some loss.

Wellington remained in his position for some days, hoping both that the fords would become more passable and allow him to cross the Douro, and that the operations of the Spaniards in the French rear would cripple Marmont's means of support, or at all events oblige the latter to make detachments for the sake of subsistence, and thus weaken his strong line of defence. The Spaniards were, however, inert, the country occupied by the enemy fertile, and on the 16th July Marmont crossed two divisions over the river at Toro and threatened the English left.

To oppose this movement. Lord Wellington, in the course of the night of the 16th concentrated the mass of his army at Canizal on the Guarena, believing that his left was the real point of attack.

Movements of the Troops on the 16th July, 1812.

The light division (with the exception of the British brigade at Rueda) and B. General Pack's brigade of Portuguese infantry, to move this evening at seven o'clock from their present encampment, by the valley of the Zapardiel River to Medina del Campo, and encamp near that town. The troops are to be placed during the day in the houses of the town, according to the former orders given on that subject.

The 4th division to move at half-past seven o'clock this evening from its present encampment to Villa Verde, and to encamp near to that village. It is desirable that the division should move on a road distinct from that on which the light division and B. General Pack proceed. The troops are to be placed in the village of Villa Verde during the day time, and to conform to the former orders given on the subject of occupying the villages during the day, and of encamping during the night time.

The 3rd division, with the exception of a proportion of British and Portuguese troops, equal in numbers to a common brigade of infantry, to move at eight o'clock this evening, from Pollos to Eban d'Arriba, and to encamp near that village. These troops are to enter the villages of Eban d'Arriba, Eban d'Abaxo, and Siete Egleisias, if necessary, during the daytime, and to assemble and encamp at night in the vicinity of Eban d'Arriba, until further orders. The troops remaining at Pollos are to have guns attached to them; the remainder of the brigade of artillery is to move to Eban d'Arriba.

Wm. De Lancey
D.Q.M.G.

To Lieut.-Gen. Sir Stapleton Cotton, Bart., &c.
The duties of observing and guarding the ford of Pollos and Herreros to be continued by the cavalry and infantry at Pollos.

W. D. L.

Headquarters, Nava del Rey, July 16th, 1812.
Dear Sir,—Notwithstanding any former order received, the light division, with the brigade of infantry at Rueda, and Brigadier-General Pack's brigade of infantry, are to move this evening at seven o'clock to Villa Verde. Lord Wellington desires me to acquaint you that he has received the most certain intelligence this evening that the enemy intends to move upon our left, and oblige us to quit the position we occupy near to river Duero. He therefore requests that you will move in General Anson's brigade of cavalry this evening to Medina del Campo (with the exception of the picquets you may have out), and keep the brigade in readiness at Medina del Campo, to move at the shortest notice.

I have the honour to be, dear Sir,
Your obedient faithful Servant,

Wm. De Lancey,
D.Q.M.G.

To Lieut.-Gen. Sir Stapleton Cotton, Bart, &c.

To be prepared, however, for every contingency, Lord Wellington ordered Cotton, with Anson's brigade of cavalry, and the 4th and light divisions of infantry—who, in accordance with his directions, were falling back—to halt at Rueda till one p.m. on the 17th, when, if no enemy appeared, he was to proceed to join the rest of the army. At the above-named hour, seeing no signs of the French in his front. Sir Stapleton retired to Castrejon, on the left bank of the Trabancos, where he bivouacked for the night.

The next morning, he rode out accompanied by his staff, to obtain intelligence, and towards evening learnt that Marmont was approaching. He at once sent off the information to Lord Wellington by three separate bearers, to insure safe delivery. That night Marmont, with about 50,000 men, and 64 guns, occupied Nava del Rey, a small town on the right bank of the Trabancos, and close in front of Cotton's position. At daybreak next morning, Cotton's outposts being driven in, he drew up his two infantry divisions in rear of the village of Castrejon, separated, however, unfortunately, by a wide ravine. Immediately in front he placed his cavalry and a troop of horse artillery. Napier says:—

The country was open and hilly, like the downs of England, with here and there water-gullies, dry hollows, and bold naked heads of land, and behind the most prominent of these last, on the other side of the Trabancos, lay the whole French Army.

The bluff above mentioned concealed the mass of Marmont's troops, and Cotton, seeing nothing but horsemen in his front, advanced his cavalry cautiously by his right along some high table-land towards the river. A heavy fire, both of cannon and musketry, was then opened on him, to which he replied with his horse artillery. Being now separated from his infantry by a marshy ravine, he brought up the 43rd Regiment to the support of the cavalry. A severe skirmish ensued, but, notwithstanding his exposed position, and the superiority of the enemy, Cotton maintained his post with but little loss, till at seven a.m., Wellington, accompanied by Beresford, arrived to judge for himself and support Cotton. On Wellington's arrival, he was at once exposed to one of the most imminent perils which he encountered during the whole war. A small body of French cavalry, at first supposed to be deserters, rushed across the valley of the Trabancos, mounted the tableland on which was Cotton's left wing, and drove in the cavalry skirmishers.

Wellington, ere leaving his headquarters, had ordered the 5th division to Torrecilla de la Orden and three brigades of cavalry to Alaejos, each place being about six miles in rear of Castrejon, to act as a support to Cotton. Some of the cavalry came up at this conjuncture, and soon arrested the fury of this partial and unsustained attack; but thirty or forty French horsemen detached themselves from their companions, and galloping over the brow just as Wellington was ascending the slope, perceived two guns escorted by a squadron of light cavalry. They hesitated a moment, and then charging, drove the English cavalry through the guns, and swept Lord Wellington, entangled in the *mêlée*, to the bottom of the hill. Lord Wellington and his staff, drawing their swords, with some difficulty extricated themselves from the mixed mass of friends and foes by which they were surrounded, and another squadron of British dragoons coming up, destroyed or captured almost to a man, the desperate band which had so nearly quenched the light of England's glory.

Marmont, now discovering his enemy's weakness, crossed the Trabancos in two columns and moved on Alaejos, hoping to cut the English off from the Guarena. Wellington returned by Torrecilla de la Orden, covered on his flanks and rear by the cavalry. It became a race between the English and French as to who should first reach the Guarena, and for ten miles the hostile columns moved on almost parallel lines, only half musket-shot, from each other. So close were they, indeed, that the officers on both sides touched their caps and waved their hands to each other in courteous recognition. The French vexed the march of the British with a desultory fire of artillery, but not a shot was fired in return by the latter. At length, the fords of the river were reached, and the retreating force just managed to avoid being intercepted. So close an affair indeed was it, that as the British reached the middle of the stream, forty French guns sent a shower of grape among them.

Marmont now directed Clausel to cross the river at Castrillo, on his right, in order to distract the attention of the defenders, while he collected his artillery in front, hoping to be able, by direct attack, to force the passage opposed to him, and seize the table-land of Vallesa. Wellington, however, was prepared, and had already sent his remaining divisions to the Vallesa plateau, and they arrived there before Marmont's infantry, exhausted by their forced marches, had sufficiently recovered to attempt the passage.

Nor did matters fare much better for the French on their right. Clausel pushed, it is true, Carier's brigade of cavalry, supported by a column of infantry, across the river at Castrillo. General Alten's brigade of cavalry were on the other side, supported by the 4th division, and ought not to have allowed the enemy to cross, for the banks were sedgy and difficult. Alten, however, was slow, and did not see his advantage. He, therefore, not only allowed the French cavalry to cross without opposition, but when he did attack only launched successive squadrons against them. Matters were at one time looking unfavourable for our cavalry, who were much vexed by the enemy's infantry; but, eventually, Carier was taken and the French cavalry retired.

At this moment, the 27th and 40th Regiments charged and broke the French infantry. Alten now pursued, and took two hundred and forty prisoners.

Thus, ended the affair which had commenced at Castrejon, and the success of which was principally owing to the firm and skilful manner in which Cotton held the whole French army at bay, with only two divisions of infantry and one brigade of cavalry, from daybreak till seven a.m., thus giving Wellington time to come to his assistance. Nor did the subsequent retreat to the Guarena, which was covered by the cavalry, do him less credit. Indeed, it may be with justice said that this was one of the most useful, though perhaps not the most brilliant day's work, he performed throughout the whole Peninsular war. Yet he never received any but verbal thanks from Wellington for his services on the occasion; and in the dispatch to Lord Bathurst, giving an account of the affair, merely this meagre remark occurs:—

Sir S. Cotton maintained the post without suffering any loss till the cavalry had joined him.

Yet Cotton possessed in great perfection a quality highly appreciated by Wellington—that of obedience; and in a letter of the 3rd June, 1812, to Lord Liverpool, he says:—

Sir S. Cotton commands the cavalry very well.

It would appear from what we can gather, that, though always on friendly terms with Lord Combermere, and fully appreciating his value, Wellington entertained no personal regard for him—perhaps, indeed, slightly the contrary. The French did more justice to Cotton's conduct at Castrejon. Soult, in a dispatch, states that had it not been for the opposition Marmont met with from General Cotton, the British army would have been surprised and attacked before Lord Wellington could have made a good position to oppose him.

AN OFFICER OF THE LIGHT DRAGOONS IN REVIEW ORDER

On the day following no movement took place on either side till evening, when Marmont massed his troops on the left, near Tarragona. Wellington, fearing for his right, withdrew his troops over a branch of the Guarena, and took up a position on the table-land above Vallesa and El Olmo. This movement was executed without interruption, and the day would have closed without an interchange of shots had not Sir Stapleton ordered Captain Ross, (later General Sir Hew Ross, G.C.B.), of the horse artillery, to fire at a group of French officers. The result of this order was a reply from twelve eight-pounders—Ross's guns were only six-pounders—which caused some loss, and compelled the light division to withdraw several hundred yards to the rear. Writing at this time to his uncle by marriage—Sir Corbet Corbet—Cotton shows clearly how much the campaign in the Peninsula was affected by Napoleon's designs against Russia:—

La Seca, near Valladolid, July 12, 1812.
My Dear Sir Corbet,—We have made some progress since I last wrote to you, and I was in hopes that we should have entered Valladolid by this time; but Marmont having been reinforced, and having taken up a strong position on the Douro, we are likely to stay looking at each other across that river for some time, neither party seeming to think itself strong enough for offensive operations.

If affairs in the North take a favourable turn, we may push the enemy behind the Ebro before winter; but if, on the contrary, Buonaparte settles matters amicably with Russia, we must re-trace our steps, and linger out another winter in Portugal. The Spaniards will do nothing. The enemy, by this movement of Lord Wellington, has been obliged to concentrate his forces, yet the Dons do not take advantage of his absence from Leon, Gallicia, and the Asturias, and we have no Spanish Army coop-erating with us.

At this moment, had they a disciplined force, it might enter Madrid while Lord Wellington kept Marmont in check. Soult and Suché, (thus in the original. "Suchet" is meant), cannot move from the south. In short, if our allies had anything like an army much might be done now.

I think the enclosed will amuse you. Owen is now the oldest lieutenant in the 16th. I hope that he will get a troop soon without purchase. I shall then recommend him to join, if Beresford will not give him a majority in the Portuguese cavalry. Pray give my best love to her Ladyship; and believe me, my dear Sir Corbet,

Your most sincere and affectionate,

Stapleton Cotton.

To Sir Corbet Corbet, Bart.

(Uncle to Sir Stapleton Cotton).

To detail the manoeuvres of the next two days which preceded the Battle of Salamanca does not fall within the purpose of our work; we shall hasten, therefore, to the morning of the 22nd July, which saw the English Army drawn up in order of battle, but prepared to retreat unless attacked, or unless the enemy committed some flagrant fault.

The following extract from the journal of an officer, (Lieut.-Colonel Tompkinson, then Captain), of the 16th Light Dragoons gives an interesting account of the night before the battle:—

General Anson's brigade bivouacked near Santa Martha. Dreadful thunder an hour after dark. The greatest number of the horses of the 6th Dragoon Guards ran away over the men sleeping at their heads, by which 18 men in the brigade were wounded, and 31 horses not found the following morning. (We saw the different columns very plainly from the lightning reflecting on their muskets, which at that time of night was beautiful.) The loss was said to have been accounted for on 22nd. By each flash we saw the columns of infantry marching to their ground for the night. Colonel and Mrs. Dalbiac, of the 4th Dragoons, were sitting down on the ground in front of the brigade. We had just time to carry her under a gun, which stopped the horses and saved them both.

After some skirmishing and numerous manoeuvres and counter-manoeuvres, Marmont, by detaching his left, in order to turn the English right, gave Wellington the opportunity he had so eagerly looked for. How fiercely and effectively the decisive blow was struck is brilliantly described by Napier. We purpose here only to follow Cotton and his gallant horsemen through this, with the exception of Waterloo, the most splendid day in the annals of the British cavalry. When, at about half-past three in the afternoon, Pakenham, with the 3rd division, sprang at the French left, Cotton, with Bull's troop of horse artillery, and Le Marchant's, Anson's, and Alten's brigades of cavalry, followed on his left rear. Pakenham had pushed the French over a slight eminence, the slope of which was steeper on the side of the latter than on that of the British, when Cotton, who had been desired by Wellington to take advantage of any opportunity to charge, rode up the hill to reconnoitre. He perceived on the other side a division of French infantry. Riding back to his men, he formed them in three lines: Le Marchant first, Anson second, and Victor Alten third; and then, accompanied by his staff and followed by his splendid horsemen, ascended the slope.

On reaching the summit, he saw that the French had weakened that part of their line opposed to him, in order to strengthen their right, at that time sharply engaged with Cole. Seeing that the decisive moment had arrived, he ordered Le Marchant to attack. That officer, in doubt as to the line of advance (for from the frequent changes of position made by both armies it was difficult to know where the enemy were) asked in what direction he should front. Cotton, losing his temper, replied, sharply, "To the enemy. Sir." High words ensued, and but for Le Marchant's death the matter would not have ended where it did. As it was, the necessity for action cut short this dispute; the charge was sounded, and, like an avalanche, Le Marchant's heavy dragoons crashed down on the enemy, who were drawn up in several lines.

The imposing nature and suddenness of the onset seemed to paralyse them; the division was pierced through in less time than has been required to write these lines; and the French soldiers cast away their arms, and running blindly between the British squadrons, piteously demanded quarter. Le Marchant and many officers had fallen, still Cotton hurled the remnants on with unrelenting fury, and in another minute, had broken with terrible slaughter a fresh column of infantry and captured five guns.

Lord Wellington, who, as usual, was always present at the decisive point, now rode up to Sir Stapleton, and fired with unusual enthusiasm by the brilliant feat which had just taken place, said, "By G—d, Cotton, I never saw anything more beautiful in my life!—the day is *yours*." Clausel, who, on the fall of Marmont, desperately wounded, had succeeded to the command, was making vigorous efforts, first to change the fortune of the day, and afterwards to effect an orderly retreat. D'Urban's brigade of cavalry relieved Le Marchant's dragoons, whose arms were wearied and swords blunted by striking; and onward still swept the death-laden cloud, which at once enveloped and announced the advance of Cotton and his horsemen. Anson's brigade led the way, D'Urban's followed in support, while Victor Alten's Germans formed the reserve, sweeping impetuously through the wood which lay between the English right and the ford of Alba over the Tormes, and nearly 2000 of the enemy here threw down their arms. On emerging into the open ground, Anson found about sunset a strong body of French artillery and infantry drawn up on a rise. The latter received our cavalry with so heavy a fire that they were obliged to retire a short distance. After a time, the French withdrew, and Anson's brigade then continued the pursuit to within a short distance of the Tormes, having been in one continued gallop from half-past four in the afternoon till sunset.

As soon as the defeat of the French was secured. Cotton received an order to join Lord Wellington with as much of the cavalry as he could collect. He did so, and overtook the commander-in-chief, who, at the head of the 1st division, was following the routed enemy. On arriving at a point where the road separates, one branch leading to the ford of Huerta, and another to the bridge of Alba, Lord Wellington remarked to Sir Stapleton that the French would cross the river at the former point. Sir Stapleton replied that he thought it more likely that they would make for Alba. The commander-in-chief persisted in his opinion, without for some time giving any reason for it. At length, however, he informed Sir Stapleton that he had stationed a body of Spaniards to intercept them at Alba, and destroy the bridge at that place, so as to oblige them to cross at Huerta.

Lord Wellington then desired Sir Stapleton to take a portion of the cavalry and patrol along the river in the direction of Alba. He did so, and after placing small posts of observation at different points on the banks, was returning, when he was fired at by a Portuguese picquet, who, in the darkness of the night, mistook his party for a body of the enemy. By this unlucky volley Cotton s orderly was wounded, several horses struck, and he himself received a bullet in the left arm, shattering one of the small bones. Though badly hurt. Sir Stapleton contrived to ride on to the village of Calvariza de Bajo. On arriving there he was carried from his horse into a miserable pillaged hovel, and placed in a pig trough, the most comfortable place that could be found.

Soon after Lord Wellington rode up to inquire into the nature of the accident, and on learning what had occurred sent for the surgeon of the 14th Dragoons. The latter advised immediate amputation, but Sir Stapleton steadily refused to consent to it until the opinion of the principal medical officer of the army—Dr. McGregor—had been obtained. Cotton suffered much during the night; his wound bled considerably through the bandages, and the pain he endured was greatly aggravated by the prospect of amputation on the morrow. Next morning Dr. McGregor visited him, and, to his patient's intense relief, declared that the arm might be saved, which it was, though to the end of his life it remained partially disabled. In his official dispatch to Lord Bathurst, Lord Wellington thus speaks of Sir Stapleton Cotton:—

> The cavalry under Lieutenant-General Sir S. Cotton made a most gallant and successful charge against a body of the enemy's infantry, which they overthrew and cut to pieces.
> I am much indebted to Marshal Sir W. Beresford, for his friendly countenance and assistance, both previous to and during the action; to Lieutenant-Generals Sir S. Cotton, Leith, and Cole, and Major-Generals Clinton and the Hon. E. Pakenham, for the manner in which they led the divisions of cavalry and infantry under their command respectively.

In a private letter to Lord Bathurst of the same date occurs the following passage:—

> I am very anxious that a mark of His Royal Highnesses favour should be conferred upon Sir S. Cotton. I believe he would be much gratified at receiving the red riband. No cavalry could act better than ours did in the action; and I must say for Sir Stapleton, that I don't know where we could find an officer that would command our cavalry in this country as well as he does.

The Order of the Bath here alluded to, Cotton received, as will be mentioned in the proper place. He also obtained—fourteen months later—an additional clasp to his gold medal; the Order of the Tower and Sword, from the King of Portugal; an additional crest, consisting of a mounted dragoon, with the word "Salamanca" beneath; and last, though not least, the thanks of both Houses of Parliament. Nor in the midst of these public testimonials of his services were the congratulations of his friends wanting.

The following warm-hearted letter is from the Duke of Newcastle, the brother of his deceased wife:—

Cowes, August 23, 1812.

Well done, my dear Cotton, you have indeed laid it on pretty thick—as the vulgar saying goes. You have covered yourself in such a manner with laurels, that you cannot be incommoded by the sunbeams of Castile. Such a friendly shelter will, I trust, contribute to your speedy recovery.

I cannot deny myself the pleasure of informing you that every tongue is loud in your praise; and after Lord Wellington you are voted the hero of the day. I have not ceased to admire your generalship and your gallantry. In my opinion Lord Wellington is indebted to you for this unexampled victory, ensured by your conduct on the 18th; nothing has distinguished you more than that. The Prince Regent has made you a Knight of the Bath. I am outrageous that he has not gone further. Your claims to this honour were sufficiently established previous to the 22nd. Taking all circumstances into consideration, you have a right to sit in our House.

Lord Bathurst mentions you in the highest possible terms, and styles your success as 'signal and eminent services,' &c. &c. This is no ordinary victory; it is a battle, in my opinion, superior to Blenheim. Direct in future to Collyers. I shall be at Clumber in November. All well—send kind remembrances and congratulations. Ever your most affectionate and most truly attached

Newcastle.

As a proof that it was not merely the partiality of connexions which prompted these eulogistic phrases, we add an extract from a letter of Lieutenant Owen, 16th Dragoons, to Sir Corbet Corbet, uncle to Sir Stapleton:—

Do not be alarmed—slightly is Sir Stapleton wounded in the arm. It could not be otherwise; he is so desperate in exposing his life. It is, perhaps, a fortunate circumstance for his family and friends that he is impeded in his glorious but too dangerous career. He never goes into action but in the richest of dresses, puts himself at the head of everything, and courts danger like a soldier of fortune whose future welfare depends upon a single dash. All this is very well for myself—to do my duty today and be forgotten tomorrow. But Sir Stapleton's conduct is admirable, and the lowest soldiers revere him. If we lose him, the British cavalry will be in a wretched plight.

His hours of pain and sickness must have been cheered with the thought that he had earned the approbation of his great commander. In a letter to Sir Stapleton, (Gurwood's *Dispatches*), the day after his arrival at Madrid, Lord Wellington thus expresses himself:—

> Madrid, 13th August, 1812.
>
> I have long intended to write to you, but I really have not had time to write to anybody. I was much concerned to learn that you were so unwell; but I hope that you will soon be better, as I am very anxious to have you again with the army.

The following letters from Sir William Beresford and Sir Stapleton Cotton, though they have already appeared in the *Supplementary Dispatches* of the Duke of Wellington, may, we think, be reproduced here with propriety:—

Sir W. C. Beresford to General the Earl of Wellington.

> Salamanca, 3rd August, 1812.
>
> My Dear Lord,—I have nothing to say but on a very uninteresting subject, *viz.*, self. I am continuing in a progressive state of amelioration towards my cure, and every appearance is favourable; still the doctors do not seem willing to admit any chance of my being out of doors before a month. The only pain I now experience is after being some time in bed, where being obliged to remain in the same posture, and indeed, unable to change it, is most wearisome and disagreeable. I hope a short time will enable me to take a turn, and that will be then a luxury.
>
> Cotton has had some pieces of the bone come off, and he has suffered a little pain, but, with the others, is going on well—Cole most surprisingly so.
>
> Believe me, my dear Lord, yours most sincerely,
>
> W. C. Beresford.

Sir S. Cotton to General the Earl of Wellington.

> Salamanca, 5th August, 1812.
>
> My Dear Lord,—I was in hopes I should have been able by this time to have given you a more favourable account of my wound. The small bone is shattered a good deal, and pieces of bone come from my wound every day: this causes great pain. The discharge has been so great that I am much reduced, and being kept away from the army frets me very much. When all the splinters of bone have come away I trust the wound will soon heal, and the moment I can get on horseback I shall start for the army by easy stages. Should you be able to spare a mo-

ment, my dear Lord, it will be the greatest comfort for me to hear from you.

Ever your very faithful and sincere

Stapleton Cotton.

Before quitting altogether, the subject of the Battle of Salamanca, we cannot resist giving the following anecdote related to us by one who bore a part in that day's glory. It is, in our opinion, a remarkable instance of what great results may be produced in war by the merest trifles:—

The 61st Regiment had received their new clothing a few days before the battle, and were consequently very conspicuous by the side of their dingy comrades. The French, struck by the sight of their gaudy-looking coats, conceived they were young troops, or, as some of the prisoners stated, militia from England. With this persuasion, they made a vigorous attack on them, but soon found they had burnt their fingers, for the 61st received them in a most gallant manner, and quickly swept away their assailants, though not without a heavy loss to themselves.

CHAPTER 10

Cotton Recovers, and Rejoins the Army

When Lord Wellington proceeded to Burgos, he left Dr. Littledale, the surgeon attached to his personal staff, to take charge of Sir Stapleton Cotton, who returned to Salamanca and took possession of the house belonging to the Marquis Seralbo, lately occupied by the commander-in-chief. His host was most kind and attentive, and occasionally entertained Sir Stapleton and his staff at dinner. As soon as he became convalescent, Sir Stapleton Cotton returned this courtesy, and the *marquis* and *marquesa* became his guests. In the meantime, Dr. Littledale most zealously assisted his overworked professional brethren in the performance of their arduous duties, in attendance on the crowds of sick and wounded who thronged the various hospitals and churches of the town. Fatigue, anxiety, and fever quickly disabled many of the surgeons, and Dr. Littledale exerted himself so much to supply the deficiencies thus caused, that at last he too fell ill.

This was, in one sense, a favourable circumstance for Sir Stapleton, who, had he not been detained by the sickness of his medical attendant, would have yielded to his impatience to join the army, and have started sooner than prudence or his doctor would have sanctioned. At length, Dr. Littledale having somewhat improved in health, and Sir Stapleton being now sufficiently recovered, the day for their departure was fixed. On learning this, a Spanish *grandee* from La Seca, where Cotton had been quartered the previous year, arrived at Salamanca with a carriage drawn by four mules, and placed them at his disposal. While at Salamanca, Sir Stapleton received frequent visits from Dr. Curtis, an Irishman, who was head of a priests' college there, and subsequently became Bishop of Armagh. Though he had been many years in Spain, he had not lost his native brogue or patriotic feelings. During the occupation of Salamanca by the French, he used to send continual reports of their proceedings to the British headquarters. A few days before the evacuation of the town he was dining with Marmont, when an officer present remarked how strange it was that the English commander-in-chief should be so accurately informed of all that was going on in the French camp, and of plans supposed to be known only to a few of the marshal's intimates. All eyes were at once fixed on Dr. Curtis, whose alarm became excessive. Nothing further, however, took place then, but the next day the doctor was thrown into prison. His fate was fixed and he would have been hanged to a certainty, had not the approach of the English army diverted the attention of the French from Dr. Curtis to more pressing matters.

In the Peninsula, spies were of all ranks and classes of society. At Madrid, a Spanish *marquesa* was in communication with Lord Wellington, to whom she sent valuable information. This patriotic lady, when asked which she preferred, the English or French, replied she would like to see the latter hung *"collos tripos"* of the former.

Taking advantage of the hospitable grandee's offer of a carriage, Cotton and Dr. Littledale started for Burgos, riding in the early morning and taking refuge in the carriage from the mid-day heat. They travelled in this manner for three days, when on the fourth, about noon, as they were seated in the carriage, Dr. Littledale, who had been complaining of illness the preceding evening, suddenly fell on Sir Stapleton's shoulder in a fit. The carriage was at once stopped, water procured, and every effort made to restore consciousness, but in vain. Finding all their efforts useless. Sir Stapleton hurried on with the still insensible doctor to the nearest town, which was Tordesillas. There the latter was put to bed, and Sir Stapleton sent off his *aide-decamp*. Baron Decken, to Valladolid for a staff surgeon. In the meantime, a Spanish doctor was called in, who prescribed strong remedies, which seemed at first successful, for towards evening the patient rallied. He subsequently, however, became worse, and in the course of the night died. The staff-surgeon not arriving till all was over.

After this sad event, Sir Stapleton continued his journey, and rejoined the army on the road to Burgos, towards which place Lord Wellington had advanced from Madrid at the end of August. Either on the road, or before leaving Salamanca, Sir Stapleton received a letter, dated 7th September, from Lord Wellington, to the effect that he had received the orders of the Prince Regent to invest Sir Stapleton with the Order of the Bath, and promising to try and pay him a visit for that purpose, should the latter not be well enough to come to headquarters. This was followed by another from Lord Wellington, in which he says, "I wish to God you were well." On rejoining the army. Sir Stapleton had the pleasure of learning that his name occurred in Lord Bathurst's official congratulations to Lord Wellington on the victory of Salamanca.

> Your Lordship will convey His Royal Highnesses especial thanks to Marshal Sir William Beresford, to Lieutenant-Generals Sir Stapleton Cotton, Leith, and Cole, to the Major-Generals and other commanding-officers named in your Lordship's dispatches.

About the same time the following document was placed in his hands:—

> Downing-street, 21st August, 1812.
> Sir,—His Royal Highness the Prince Regent having been pleased to nominate you to be a knight companion of the most honourable Order of the Bath, the insignia of which order are herewith forwarded to you, I am to acquaint you that the Marquis of Wellington has received His Royal Highnesses commands to avail himself of the first opportunity to invest you therewith in a manner suitable to the occasion.
>> I have the honour to be, Sir,
>>> Your obedient servant,
>>>> Bathurst.
> To Lieut.-Gen. Sir Stapleton Cotton, K.B., &c.,
> They will be sent with the duplicate by next mail.

Shortly after his arrival at Burgos, Sir Stapleton Cotton was invited by Lord Wellington to a dinner given to celebrate the investiture of the former with the Bath. As Sir Stapleton was still far from well. Lord Wellington, anxious to save him fatigue, sent a large old Spanish coach, drawn by four mules, to bring him to headquarters, which was so close to the citadel that on one occasion a round shot struck it. After dinner the investiture took place, to the appropriate accompaniment of the warlike sounds without which announced the progress of the siege. On returning in the evening, over a very bad road, in the coach above mentioned, which Lord Wellington had placed at his disposal during his convalescence, the lumbering old vehicle upset. Sir

Stapleton, being fortunately thrown on his right side, escaped with a few bruises; had he fallen on his left side the consequences might have been serious.

On the night of the 21st October Wellington raised the siege of the Castle of Burgos, to avoid having to give battle, both in his own person and that of Hill, who was covering Madrid, to the vastly superior hostile forces who were concentrating on these two important points. Late on the 22nd the enemy followed the British army, and on the 23rd some sharp rear-guard fighting took place. The retreat was covered by Sir Stapleton Cotton, who had under his command two battalions of infantry, two brigades of cavalry, two troops of horse artillery, and the *partidas* of Marquinez and Sanchez. The cavalry picquets were driven back on their reserves at the Hormaza stream, the passage of which they vainly disputed. Cotton then took up a position behind Cellada Camino, on a plain intersected by a marshy stream which cut the main road. This stream was only passable at one point, by a bridge. In front of this stream was a broad ditch, also crossed by a single bridge.

Cotton's right was covered by the Arlanzan, on the other side of which was Julian Sanchez, while on a range of hills to his left was Marquinez. Cotton placed Anson's brigade, one troop of horse artillery, and the two battalions of infantry as a rear-guard on the further side of the ditch, and drew up Bock's brigade and the other troop of horse artillery behind the rivulet.

When the French approached, two squadrons of the 11th Dragoons charged with success, but being outflanked Anson fell back, and the guns passed the bridge over the rivulet. Marquinez's *partidas* appeared fleeing in disorder, and the 11th again charged and drove the first line of the enemy's cavalry on to the second line. These being now united were too strong for the 11th, and pushed them over the ditch in confusion, the passage of which was, however, effected with little loss under cover of the fire of the two battalions of infantry, who, by this time, had been drawn up in rear of the bridge.

A brigade of French cavalry now turned the ditch in the hills, and following up the flying *partidas*, pursuers and pursued dashed into the flank of the 16th Dragoons, under cover of whom Anson was seeking to cross the rivulet. At the same moment, the enemy in front charged the 11th, and that regiment was driven back in confusion on the rest of the brigade. With great promptness, however, Anson took advantage of the time occupied by the French in reforming after the charge to cross the rivulet, on the other side of which he found the remainder of the rear-guard drawn up in an imposing attitude. Reinforcements now joined the enemy, who, in spite of a heavy fire of artillery crossed the bridge. Bock, unfortunately, let too many of them pass before he charged; so, when he did attack, despite courage and hard fighting, he was driven back in disorder.

Ten squadrons of French dragoons had by this time turned the stream by the hills, and poured down on the left of Anson, who, previously outflanked, out-numbered, and deprived of the assistance of Bock's Germans, was already retiring. Both brigades now became mixed up, and were driven to the rear, till the Germans, rallying, drew up on the left of the road, and Anson then formed on them. The Germans charged again, but by dint of numbers were again overcome, and only owed their safety to the superior swiftness of their horses. The whole of the cavalry, though unsuccessful, were most cool and steady, and soon formed up again, yet once more were they broken. The infantry and guns, however, the former being charged three times by the French cavalry, checked the further advance of the enemy, and in the evening the cavalry retreated without being disturbed to near the banks of the Pisuerga.

Though the events of this day were, to a certain extent, unsuccessful, yet it was not without honour to the cavalry, as well as the other troops under Cotton's command. In spite of the rout of Marquinez's *partidas*, the difficult nature of the ground, and the superior numbers of the enemy, the courage, steadiness, and coolness of the British were abundantly manifest, and though both sides suffered much, the loss of the French was greater than our own. Nor, in adjudging well-merited praise to the troops, must we forget their commander. On that trying occasion he seems to have displayed all the coolness for which he was so remarkable, and to have combined the action of the three arms with great skill and judgment, thus showing he was something more than a mere *beau sabreur*.

Lord Wellington, in his official dispatches, expresses himself in these terms:—

> The exertions and conduct of Lieutenant-General Sir S. Cotton, and of the officers and staff attached to him throughout this day, were highly meritorious; and although the charge made by the cavalry was not successful, I had the satisfaction of observing great steadiness in their movements.

Napier, with his usual injustice to the cavalry and Sir Stapleton Cotton, would lead the reader to believe that Lord Wellington, who came up in person towards the close of the affair, took the command out of Sir Stapleton's hands, and by his dispositions checked the progress of the enemy. Moreover, the latter's name is scarcely mentioned in the narrative. A slur is thrown on the commander of the rear-guard which is surely inconsistent with the tenor of Lord Wellington's dispatch, and it is notorious that the commander-in-chief was ever chary of commendation, and, to say the least, made no exception in favour of Sir Stapleton, During the remainder of the retreat, which ended on the 19th November, when the army, no longer molested by the French, took up cantonments round Ciudad Rodrigo, the retreat was covered by Cotton and his cavalry.

An anecdote connected with this period, and related by a distinguished officer of engineers, (Lieut.-General Sir Harry Jones, K.C.B.), to the writer of these pages, may not, perhaps, be deemed unworthy of insertion. The officer in question was, during the night of the 16th November, sitting beside a bivouac fire at the rear of the army, when a group of staff officers rode up. One of them, apparently a young *aide-de-camp*, gave some orders in an authoritative tone of command, and then galloped off.

"Who is that chap," said our informant to his chief, Sir Richard Fletcher, "who speaks in such an imperious manner?"

"Don't you know?" replied Sir Richard.

"No, I don't."

"Why, that is Sir Stapleton Cotton, commanding the cavalry."

In these times, our lieutenant-generals would scarcely be mistaken for young *aide-de-camps*, even by the most recently joined officers.

The same informant, speaking of the rich manner in which Sir Stapleton was, when on service, dressed and accoutred, says that it was remarked on the same occasion what a valuable prize Sir Stapleton would be to the enemy; for that, taking him and his horse as they stood, he could not be worth less than five hundred pounds.

During this retreat Sir Stapleton was, during three weeks, continually on horseback from daybreak to nightfall, and never changed his clothes once, on account of the loss of part, and the impossibility of getting at the remainder of his baggage. It may be imagined, under these circumstances, that he had little opportunity of indulging in the pleasures of the table. He contrived, however, an ingenious plan by means of which he occasionally obtained a hot meal. He procured a metal box with a partition running down the centre. On one side was a piece of meat, and by the other side a hot iron. This box was slung over his orderly's shoulder at the beginning of the day's march, and, the cooking going on as they rode along. Sir Stapleton was able to enjoy a warm dinner at the first convenient halt.

Towards the end of November, Sir Stapleton—the campaign being over for the year, and his state of health still continuing unsatisfactory, owing to his wound and the fatigue he had undergone—returned to England on leave. He left with the good wishes of Lord Wellington, who says, in a letter of the 27th November, that he soon hopes to have the benefit of his assistance again. A few days later, in a letter to Colonel Torrens, the military secretary at the Horse Guards, he expresses himself in still higher terms:—

> Sir Stapleton Cotton is gone home, and I sincerely hope will return. He commands our cavalry very well—indeed I am certain much better than many who might be sent to us, and who might be supposed cleverer than he is.

On arriving in England, Sir Stapleton Cotton became aware that his name was included in the vote of thanks by the two Houses of Parliament for the Salamanca campaign. Both he and his friends, however, considered that he had not been sufficiently rewarded for his services, and looked for a peerage. It is unnecessary here to discuss the propriety of the bestowal of such an honour; but considering Sir Stapleton was already a baronet, had served so, many campaigns in high command, had actually been in independent charge of two important and successful operations, namely, Llerena and Castrejon, had covered two retreats, and finally had led the cavalry in that attack which contributed so largely to the victory at Salamanca: considering all these circumstances, we say it could not have been asserted that to grant him a peerage was prostitution of the highest military reward. The Duke of Northumberland warmly urged on Lord Bathurst the bestowal of this honour, but in vain. Lord Wellington, writing to Lord Bathurst on the 7th September, mentions the matter in the following terms:—

> I always thought the Order of the Bath the mark of the King's favour which it was most desirable to an officer to receive; and I mentioned it to you as I thought it likely it would be agreeable to Sir Stapleton. It might be very proper to create him a peer; but I would not propose such an arrangement to Government.

On the 6th January, 1812, Lord Bathurst writes to Lord Wellington as follows:—

> With respect to Sir Stapleton Cotton, he is, I am sorry to hear, on his way home. I am afraid he is in pursuit of an object which cannot be granted to him. Of that I have already informed your Lordship. I am in hopes that a regiment of cavalry may become vacant very soon, and as he will have it given him, this may perhaps reconcile him to go back again to you.

On the 4th March, so slow was communication then with England, Sir Stapleton arrived in London, and on the 6th he called on Lord Bathurst, who was anxious to sound him as to the claims of Sir William Beresford, as marshal in the Portuguese service, to succeed to the temporary command of the allied armies, in case of anything happening to Lord Wellington, until a commander-in-chief could be sent out from England. The difficulty arose from the circumstance that Sir William was junior to Sir Stapleton in the British Army. Indeed, at Salamanca the latter had been—looking at it from that point of view—second senior officer in the English Army. Lord Bathurst sought to induce Sir Stapleton to waive his claim, which he, with some warmth, refused to do;

On the 9th March Sir Stapleton attended in his place in Parliament, and received the distinguished honour of the thanks of the House being there given him.

9th March, 1813.—

Lieutenant-General Sir Stapleton Cotton being come to the House, Mr. Speaker acquainted him that the House had, upon the 3rd day of December last, resolved that the thanks of the House be given to him for his distinguished exertions in the battle of Salamanca, upon the 22nd of July last, which terminated in a glorious and decisive victory over the enemy's army; and Mr. Speaker gave him the thanks of the House accordingly, as followeth:—

> Lieutenant-General Sir Stapleton Cotton,
> In this interval between the active seasons of war, your proper sphere of duty is within these walls, and we hail with pride and pleasure your return amongst us, bringing with you fresh marks of royal favour, the just reward of fresh services and triumphs.

Descended from a long line of ancestors, whose names are recorded in the earliest ages of our history, and characterized with those qualities of prudence, generosity, and valour which have laid the foundations of English greatness, your race has established many a model of that splendid worth which dignifies the gentlemen of England, always prompt to discharge the laborious duties of civil life, and never slow to take up arms at the call of their country. Such, in an eminent degree, was that venerated person from whom you have immediately derived your own hereditary honours, endeared by his active virtues to the public men of his own times, not unknown to some who still sit amongst us, and ever remembered by myself with the sincerest sentiments of respect and affection.

But, Sir, when the path of early life lay open to your choice, the then warlike state of the world called forth a congenial spirit, and your military ardour led you to encounter the toils and dangers of war in distant climates. Trained in the same camps, and animated by the same love of glory as the great captain who now commands our armies and fills the world with his renown, you have bravely followed in his brilliant career, and shared in his unexampled triumphs. Renouncing the charms of ease and the seat of your ancestors, you have gallantly gone forth to the tented fields of Portugal and Spain, and, having reaped the harvest of our thanks for your achievements in the Battle of Talavera, you now stand before us, crowned with the never-fading laurels of Salamanca; your squadrons, upon that memorable day, overthrowing the enemy's embattled ranks, laid open the road to victory; and the work which your gallantry had commenced your triumphant perseverance completed.

These heroic exploits have again entitled you to the public gratitude; and I do now, in the name and by the command of the Commons of Great Britain and Ireland in Parliament assembled, deliver to you their unanimous thanks for your distinguished exertions in the battle of Salamanca, on the 22nd of July last, which terminated in a glorious and decisive victory over the enemy's army.'

Upon which Lieutenant-General Sir Stapleton Cotton said:—
Mr. Speaker,

I cannot express how much I feel gratified and honoured by the vote of thanks which has been passed by
this House, and conveyed to me by you. Sir, in so flattering a manner. I am indebted to the discipline and bravery
of the troops I have the honour to command for this
most distinguished reward. In zeal for the service and
attachment to my king and country I yield to no man;
my feeble efforts shall ever be exerted to render myself
worthy of the great honour which has been conferred
upon me.

During his stay in England, which only lasted one month. Sir Stapleton, a remarkably handsome and comparatively young man—only
forty—coming also from the Peninsula with all his blushing honours thick upon him, secured the affections of Miss Greville, second
daughter of William Fulke Greville, Esq., and when he left London for
Spain he was an engaged man.

He would appear to have sailed for the seat of war about the beginning of April, and on his arrival at Lisbon received a long letter
from Lord Wellington, consulting him and asking his wishes regarding
a redistribution of the cavalry and the various officers to be placed in
command of brigades.

Following the army in its impetuous march to Vittoria, Sir Stapleton arrived at that place, unfortunately, just three days after the
battle. The annexed letter from Captain Owen, 16th Dragoons, to Sir
Corbet Corbet, shows the estimation in which he was held, and how
much his absence was felt:—

How bitterly I regret the absence of General Cotton! It gives
us, however, the opportunity of knowing the sentiments of the
army, who are loudly calling for their *Lion d'Or.* He is loved by
the soldiers and respected by the officers. I wish to God that
he was here.

During the remainder of the campaign of 1813 the cavalry, from
the nature of the ground, had no opportunity of distinguishing themselves. Cotton was, however, present at the series of actions termed the
Battle of the Pyrenees. During this period of comparative inaction. Sir
Stapleton wrote a letter to his aunt, strongly characteristic of the depth

of his feelings towards his family:—

Rintona, August 21st, 1813.

My Dear Aunt,—Your kindness to us upon all occasions has been very great, and nobody more grateful than I am for all your goodness, but particularly so for this late instance of your most affectionate anticipation of my mother's wishes. No place in England would have suited my mother so well as Audlem; and, thank God, she will be comfortably established near me, without your being obliged to leave our neighbourhood. I long very much for the time when I can join your society, with the comfortable reflection that our intercourse will not again be interrupted, and this I intend should happen when this campaign ends. I hope you will approve of the choice I have made, and I shall be glad to have your opinion of my intended should you see her in Cheshire before I go home. How very unfortunate I was in having a passage of *twenty-eight days!* I was *three* days too late for the Battle of Vittoria, which I shall ever regret. Our friend Leith has not joined the army yet.

Pray let me know what you think of the alterations—planting, painting, approach, &c. &c. &c.—at Combermere.

Believe me, my dear aunt,

Ever your most truly

Affectionate and obliged

Stapleton Cotton.

To Miss Stapleton.

In the autumn, he received a letter from the Commander-in-Chief, the Duke of York, notifying to him the grant of two clasps for Fuentes d'Onor and Salamanca.

Horse Guards, 21st September, 1813.

Sir,—His Royal Highness the Prince Regent having been graciously pleased to command, in the name and on the behalf of His Majesty that you should be permitted to bear additional marks of distinction in commemoration of the battles of Fuentes d'Onoro and Salamanca.

I have the satisfaction to transmit to you two gold clasps, which, by order of His Royal Highness, have been prepared for the occasion, and which it is His Royal Highness's command that you shall bear upon the ribbon to which the medal now in your possession is suspended.

14th Dragoons at Vittoria

I am, Sir, yours,

Frederick,
Commander-in-Chief.
To Lieut.-Gen. Sir Stapleton Cotton, Bart., &c.

In receipt of this he addressed a remonstrance to Lord Wellington, but did not succeed in obtaining his wish:—

22nd November, 1813.
My Lord,—In acknowledging the receipt of two clasps, which have been sent to me by the military secretary, by the command of His Royal Highness the Commander-in-Chief, I take the opportunity of humbly submitting to your Lordship my claim to a cross, which honour has been conferred on officers who have not served so long with the army nor have so frequently been engaged with the enemy.

Although the British cavalry could not be brought into action at Busaco, I trust that your Lordship will take into consideration the services rendered by that arm in covering the retreat of the army from Celerico to that position, and from thence to the lines in September and October, 1809, for which service your Lordship, in a letter to me from headquarters, near Cobral, was pleased to say that the army was much indebted to the cavalry for having made so good a retreat.

During the siege of Badajos, in 1812, the cavalry were actively employed with the covering army, and a few days after the fall of that place I had the good fortune, with part of the cavalry, to attack and defeat, with considerable loss to the enemy, a very superior body of his cavalry, near Llerena, in presence of the corps commanded by Comte D'Erlon.

In the same year your Lordship was pleased to express your approbation of my conduct before the enemy at Castrejon, and in covering the retreat of the army into position upon the Tormes. The cavalry which served in the north of Spain under the late Sir John Moore not having been in the action before Corunna, medals were granted to general officers and others commanding regiments for 'cavalry service' in Spain, 1808. I trust, therefore, that your Lordship will take my claims, and those of the other cavalry officers concerned, into your favourable consideration, and that your Lordship will be pleased to recommend that additional marks of distinction may be granted to us upon this occasion for the services of the cavalry.

I have the honour, &c.,

Stapleton Cotton,
Lieut.-Genl. Commanding the Cavalry.
Field-Marshal the Marquis of Wellington, &c.

After Lord Wellington had crossed the Bidassoa on the 7th of October, the headquarters of the cavalry were fixed at Hasparan, a town on the Nivelle, about two leagues from St. Jean, de Luz, where army headquarters were established. The different regiments of cavalry were cantoned in various villages along the river. As a watchful and enterprising enemy was in front of them, Cotton, who was as prudent as he was brave, always had the baggage packed and the horses saddled at sunset, in case of an attack. In this state of readiness, the force remained all night; and not until the picquets had reported at daybreak that all seemed clear was the baggage unloaded and the horses unsaddled.

While at Hasparan a Spanish priest used to bring General Cotton intelligence from the French camp. It soon transpired that this individual was in the habit of communicating the movements of the British army to the enemy. On being accused of this treachery he justified himself by saying that he should not have been able to obtain information from the French unless he gained their confidence by furnishing a report of what he heard in the English tents. This plea was accepted.

Passing rapidly over the events which preceded and accompanied the opening of the campaign of 1814 on the 14th of February—for the cavalry, though actively employed, on outpost duty and slight skirmishes, with great credit and success, undertook no operations of importance—we come to the Battle of Orthez, which was fought on the 27th February. In that well-contested fight, the cavalry were not engaged till the close of the day, when Sir Stapleton, at the head of Lord Edward Somerset's brigade and the 7th Hussars, charged in the pursuit three French battalions. These were broken, and three hundred of their number made prisoners. Two thousand more also threw down their arms in an enclosed field in the vicinity, but in the confusion, most of them managed to escape across the Luy de Bearn, a stream which was close at hand. Cotton, sent in pursuit next day with a part of Somerset's brigade, came up with the French rear-guard, and took some prisoners.

It was in this battle that Wellington was wounded by a spent ball

203

on the thigh. As he was stretched on the ground for a few minutes to recover, the bystanders, ignorant at first of the slight nature of his wound, broke out unanimously with the despairing remark, "Good God! who is to get the army out of the country?" A remarkable proof, were one needed, of the universal belief of his troops that in their commander was embodied the genius of victory.

The official dispatch of this victory speaks of Sir Stapleton Cotton:—

> Your Lordship will have observed with satisfaction the able assistance which I have received in these operations from Marshal Sir W. Beresford, Lieutenant-Generals Sir E. Hill, Sir J. Hope, and Sir S. Cotton; and from all the general officers, officers, and troops acting under their orders respectively. It is impossible for me sufficiently to express my sense of their merits, or of the degree in which the country is indebted to their zeal and ability for the situation in which the army now finds itself.

Beyond a few successful and brilliant skirmishes the cavalry had little to do in the interval between the battles of Orthez and Toulouse. Neither did they take an important part in the latter victory, the nature of the ground not admitting of their doing so.

The following day Sir Stapleton was sent in pursuit of Soult, with two brigades of cavalry. On the evening of the second, as Sir Stapleton was sitting down to dinner, the Quartermaster-General, Sir George Murray, suddenly arrived, bringing the intelligence of Napoleon's abdication. After sharing Sir Stapleton's dinner, Sir George rode on with a flag of truce to the enemy's camp and had an interview with Soult, who very properly affected to disbelieve the intelligence, as he had received no official intimation to that effect from his own government. On this. Lord Wellington informed the Marshal that, if the latter did not remain passive till the receipt of official information, he would pursue and attack him. In a short time, however, the expected notification arrived, and the war in which he had borne so distinguished a part having come to an end, Sir Stapleton proceeded to Toulouse, where he addressed the following farewell order to the cavalry, which had ever so devotedly followed where their brilliant chief had so gallantly led:—

Toulouse, April, 1814.
Lieut.-General Sir Stapleton Cotton congratulates the cavalry on the glorious termination of the war. It is the Lieut.-Gener-

al's wish to review every regiment previous to his departure for England; but finding that, from the dispersion of the cavalry, this will be impossible, he expresses in writing the gratification and pride which he feels in having had the honour of commanding the British cavalry with this army during the last four years.

The Lieut.-General requests the generals and other officers commanding brigades to accept his warm thanks for the cordial support they have at all times afforded him, and for the zeal and gallantry which they have displayed at the heads of their respective brigades.

To commanding-officers of regiments. Sir Stapleton's best thanks are due for the unremitting care with which they have attended to their men and horses when in quarters, as well as for their spirited and exemplary conduct in the field.

The Lieut.-General has to acknowledge the merits of officers commanding squadrons and troops, and he requests those, as well as the officers, non-commissioned officers, and privates, to be assured that he will never be unmindful of their services; and he begs to thank them for the prompt manner in which general and cavalry orders have been attended to.

The Lieut.-General is proud to say that the British cavalry have ever, when opportunities offered, distinguished themselves, so as to receive the strongest marks of approbation from the commander of the forces.

The Lieut.-General now takes leave of the generals and other officers commanding brigades, officers, non-commissioned officers, and privates, comprising the cavalry, assuring them of his best wishes for their collective success and individual happiness, and trusting that should they or any portion of them be again employed in the service of their country he may have the honour of being placed at their head.

Lieut.-General Sir Stapleton Cotton cannot sufficiently express his gratitude to Colonel Elley for the able manner in which he has effected the duties of the adjutant-general's department; the zeal which that officer has displayed for the service, and his indefatigable attention to the welfare of the cavalry, claim the Lieut.-General's warmest thanks.

Sir Stapleton has every reason to be satisfied with the services of Lieut.-Colonel Dixon, during the short time he has been attached to the cavalry; and the Lieut.-General thanks him, and

Captain Shakespeare, and the rest of his staff for their services.

Sir Stapleton then proceeded to Bayonne, where he embarked on board a man-of-war for England.

CHAPTER 11

Escape of Napoleon from Elba and Renewal of the War

On the 17th of May, this year Sir Stapleton Cotton was, for his distinguished services during the Peninsular war, raised to the peerage, by the style of Baron Combermere. The patent declared that the title was to descend to the heirs male of his body, and to support the dignity an annuity of 2000*l*. was attached to it for two generations. At the same time. Sir Rowland Hill, Sir John Hope, Sir William Beresford, and Sir Thomas Graham likewise obtained peerages. At that period Lord Combermere also received the order of St. Ferdinand of Spain.

On the 18th of June following. Lord Combermere married his second wife, Caroline, youngest daughter of Captain William Fulke Greville, R.N., grandson of the fifth Lord Brooke. Although there was a difference of twenty years between their ages, he being forty-one, and she twenty-one, the disparity did not appear striking. The gallant hussar seemed much younger than he really was, and commanded those great specifics for continued youth, buoyancy of mind and equanimity of temper. As we have said before, the bride possessed something more than the conventional charms and accomplishments generally attributed to young ladies about to marry; while he, noble in birth, distinguished in character, chivalrous in disposition, and withal a very handsome man, was a bridegroom whom any one might have coveted.

Lady Combermere being amiable, and Lord Combermere adding to great firmness and a solid judgment the attraction of a respectful deference towards the sex, their marriage seemed to be wreathed with bright hopes of a happy future. That these hopes were, alas! to a certain extent fallacious.

Unfortunately Lord Combermere was engaged to a dinner as well as to be married on the 18th June, and the former was an appointment which even under such circumstances he scarcely liked to forego, being the banquet given by the City in honour of the Emperor of Russia, the King of Prussia, and Marshal , Blucher. With true hussar activity, he determined to feast and wed the same day. The civic entertainment was of the most splendid description; the Lord Mayor, followed by the aldermen, mounted on chargers which had been lent by officers of the Blues for the occasion, and which were decorated with crimson, proceeded to Temple Bar to meet the Prince Regent and his royal companions, while every effort was made to maintain the world-wide fame of the Guildhall for gastronomical magnificence.

Withdrawing from the dinner at an early hour. Lord Combermere hurried to Lambeth Palace, where, between eleven and twelve at night, he was married by the Archbishop of Canterbury. After the ceremony, the newly-wedded pair set off for Combermere Abbey, where they spent the honeymoon. The next few months passed happily away in visiting their different friends and relations in the neighbourhood, introducing Lady Combermere to those members of the Cotton family whose acquaintance she had not previously made, and dispensing hospitality at the abbey. Lady Combermere was a most attractive hostess, and her charms, both of mind and person, admirably qualified her for the position she occupied.

Amongst other resources for passing the first period of leisure which Lord Combermere had known for years, and an additional bond of union to his wife, was their common fondness for music. Lady Combermere was an admirable performer and sang with a rare charm; while her husband, a passionate lover of music, had only relinquished the violin when his Salamanca wound rendered all circular movements of the arm difficult. Under these circumstances he was obliged to content himself with joining his wife in singing glees and vocal duets.

No welcome can be conceived more gratifying to a young bride than that which Lady Combermere received from her Cheshire neighbours. The fame of her beauty and accomplishments had preceded her, and the reality was not found to disappoint the anticipations formed. Each one vied with his neighbour in showing attention to the choice of their honoured and distinguished friend, whom they proudly termed "the Cheshire hero." Eager to give some public mark of gratitude to him who had so illustrated their county annals, the inhabitants of Chester invited him and Lord Hill, an inhabitant of the adjoining county of Shropshire, to a grand *fête* given in their honour. The following is a description of the affair, extracted from the *History of Chester*:—

August 15th, 1814.—This day was rendered remarkable by the splendid reception given by the city to Lords Combermere and Hill, on their return from the Peninsular and French wars. At an early hour in the morning the bells of the different churches struck up merry peals, and about nine o'clock the great bells of the cathedral commenced ringing on the steeples of St. John's and St. Mary's. The houses in Hanelbridge, Bridge-street, Northgate-street, Eastgate-street, &c., were decorated with laurel shrubs, and the Bridge-gate was ornamented in the form of a triumphal arch, the sides and the centre of the arch bound round with laurels and flowers, and on the upper compartment, on the south side, was the inscription, in large letters, 'Brave warriors, welcome!' and on the north side, in small devices, 'Almarez.' 'Salamanca,'
On the north side of the gate, in large letters, 'Europe Liberated!' 'Salamanca,' 'Almarez,' festoons of laurels, &c., also ornamented the grand gateway of the castle; above was the inscription, 'Britannia triumphant!' At eleven o'clock, the different trades, companies, clubs, &c., began to muster at their respective houses, and at twelve marched up to the Abbey-square, where they were marshalled; and about one o'clock the whole moved in the following—

ORDER OF PROCESSION.
Four trumpeters on horseback,
The trumpets decorated with the arms of the heroes.
Two emblematical blue banners, with the inscriptions—
'Cheshire's Pride;'—'The Pride of Shropshire,'
carried by men on grey horses.
Naval flags and pendants, carried by ship carpenters.
Shipwrights, two and two, in blue jackets and trowsers.
The beneficial dabs, four abreast, in the following order:—
Colours.
Then follows a list of all the trades, companies, and societies that formed in the procession preceding.
The Corporation,
In scarlet and blue gowns, accompanied by the Sword and

Mace, Banners, inscribed,
'Through noble deeds to noble honours,' &c. &c.
The Car,
An open carriage drawn by six beautiful greys, decorated with
crimson and white ribbons, and was lined with crimson cloth,
and on each side, on banners, were the armorial bearings of
Lords Combermere and Hill, beautifully painted; on the pan-
els, a large baronial coronet. In the front, rising from wreaths
of laurel, the plume of the Earl of Chester.
At the four corners, inverted eagles in burnished gold. The
whole had a very good effect; the horses rode by postboys in
red liveries, &c. &c.

Owing to the inhabitants of Holywell and Halkin taking Lord
Combermere's horses from his carriage and drawing him
through those towns, he was unable to make his appearance till
nearly half-past three o'clock, in a carriage ornamented with
the family arms. He was escorted by the Hawarden troop of artillery, which was placed under the command of Lieut. Boydell.
He wore the uniform of a cavalry general. On their lordships
appearing in view of the advanced part of the procession, the
bands of music struck up 'See the conquering hero comes,'
'Combermere for ever,' 'Hill for ever.'
Their progress of course was very slow; and on entering the
city, each side of the street was lined by a strong detachment of
the 22nd Foot. As the procession passed the bridge, the guns of
the castle fired a salute, and when they approached the Bridge-
gate the military presented arms. The festivities of the day terminated with a grand banquet.

After spending some nine months in a dignified ease, which had
been well earned by his arduous services, the escape of Napoleon
from Elba once more diverted Lord Combermere's thoughts from
beauty's bower to the tented field. A vast army was being assembled
in the Netherlands to withstand the Phoenix of War, who seemed to
emerge from the ashes of his hopes more formidable than ever. Lord
Combermere naturally expected the command of the cavalry in the
approaching campaign; and he had good right for his expectations, for
no one in England at that moment possessed a greater reputation as a
cavalry general than Stapleton Cotton. The thanks of Parliament still
sounded in his ears, the applause of a grateful country had scarcely yet

died away, time had not caused his laurels to wither nor rendered his name the mere burden of an old song.

He was in all the vigour of manhood; he was still the same man who had checked the pursuit of Marmont to Torres Vedras, who had chased Soult's horsemen at Llerena, who had withstood the whole force of Marmont at Castrejon, who had scattered the French infantry at Salamanca like chaff before the wind. Surely no other could supply his place in Wellington's final struggle with the great French captain! Yes, it was to be so; a miserable piece of spite on the part of the prince regent denied Lord Combermere all share in the crowning triumph of the long struggle with Napoleon. The prince regent had never forgotten Lord Combermere's share in spreading about the story of the nocturnal visit to Mrs. Fitzherbert at Brighton, some score of years before, and avenged on Lieutenant-General Baron Combermere, K.B., the offence given by plain Colonel Cotton. He nominated his personal friend, Lord Uxbridge, who had seen no service since 1809, to the command which it may be fairly said was Lord Combermere's right.

Ignorant of the prince regent's persistent and unworthy animosity, Lord Combermere anxiously awaited an order to resume the command of that cavalry which, during five years of arduous campaigns, had been trained by him to war and which he had so often led to victory. Week after week, however, passed away, and still the expected summons came not. At last he wrote to offer that famous sword which had never been dimmed save by the blood of a foe. He also communicated his wishes to his old commander, who, duly appreciating the value of so able a lieutenant, exerted himself strongly in his favour.

Extract from a letter, dated 1st April, 1815, (*Supplementary Dispatches*), written by Major-General Sir H. Torrens, Military Secretary at the Horse Guards, to the Duke of Wellington:—

> There appears to be a very general wish, on his own part as well as that of others, that Lord Uxbridge should be appointed to your cavalry. Will you have the goodness to let me know your confidential wishes and opinion on this subject?

Two days later Lord Combermere, who had come up to London to press his claims, wrote as follows to his old commander, (Gurwood's *Dispatches*), in which he refers to a previous letter, which, however, we have not been able to obtain.

15, Savile Row, 3rd April, 1815
My Dear Lord Duke,—I take the liberty of writing again to

request you will not forget me in the arrangements about to be made, and I hope my application will not be too late. Of course, it will be convenient to me knowing soon whether I am to be employed or not; but I shall, at all events, make my arrangements for joining you in as short a time as possible after I am appointed to the command of the British cavalry.

> I am, my dear Lord Duke,
> Your very sincere and faithful
>> Combermere.

To this the duke returned the annexed kind answer, (Gurwood's *Dispatches*):—

> Brussels, April 7
> My Dear Lord Combermere,—I received both your letters when Torrens was here, and I immediately spoke to him about you; as I assure you that I am most anxious to have the assistance of all those to whom, upon former occasions, I have been so much indebted. We shall have, I hope, an enormous body of cavalry of different nations; and I trust that Torrens will be able to make arrangements which will be satisfactory to you.
> Ever yours most sincerely,
>> Wellington.

On the 8th April Major-General Sir H. Torrens thus writes to Lord Bathurst:—

> I shall communicate fully with the Commander-in-Chief upon the Duke of Wellington's wishes respecting his staff. I am in hopes that an arrangement may eventually be made for the employment both of Lords Uxbridge and Combermere. Upon this point the duke has been perfectly fair and reasonable, but I shall reserve the details of what he proposes until I can personally communicate with His Royal Highness. (*Supplementary Dispatches*).

Again on the 16th April, Sir H. Torrens, in a letter from the Horse Guards to the Duke of Wellington, thus alludes to the matter:—

> I have given to Lord Combermere a full explanation of the circumstances attending the appointment of Lord Uxbridge, and I have no reason to think that he is dissatisfied with it. (*Supplementary Dispatches*).

Rather a cool and gratuitous assumption, this!

That the duke was not well satisfied with the arrangements, may fairly be inferred from the following passage in a letter written by him to Lord Bathurst on the 4th May:—

> To tell you the truth, I am not very well pleased either with the manner in which the Horse Guards have conducted themselves towards me. It will be admitted that the army is not a very good one; and being composed as it is, I might have expected that the generals and staff formed by me in the last war, would have been allowed to come to me again; but instead of that, I am overloaded with people I have never seen before; and it appears to be purposely intended to keep those out of my way whom I wished to have. However, I'll do the best I can with the instruments which have been sent to assist me. (*Supplementary Dispatches*).

The following letter belongs to this period:—

> Horse Guards, 1st July, 1815.
>
> My Lord,—The prince regent having been graciously pleased to command, in the name and on the behalf of His Majesty, that your Lordship should be permitted to bear additional marks of distinction in commemoration of the battles of Orthez and Toulouse, I have the satisfaction to transmit herewith a cross to which you are entitled, in consequence of the latter being the fifth occasion on which His Royal Highness has been pleased thus to mark his approbation of your military services.
>
> This cross and the clasp already in your possession for the Battle of Salamanca, are to be worn in substitution of the badges with which you have been previously presented.
>
> I am, my Lord, yours,
>
> Frederick, Commander-in-Chief,
>
> Lieut.-Gen. Lord Combermere, G.C.B., &c.

All was of no avail. Both, his personal claims and the representations of the Duke of Wellington failed to induce the prince regent to forego his revenge or partiality for the sake of the public service, and at Waterloo Stapleton Cotton's sword flashed not in the van as it was wont to do.

The disappointment was grievous, and to the end of his days he never could bear to speak on the subject of the Battle of Waterloo. So well-known was this feeling, that his friends made a point of carefully avoiding the topic.

When Lord Uxbridge's wound compelled him to resign the command of the cavalry, the vacant office was offered to Lord Combermere, who, in spite of the treatment he had experienced, possessed too much common sense, as well as too great a feeling of duty, to decline it.

The very day after the Battle of Waterloo, the Duke of Wellington, (*Supplementary Dispatches*), wrote to Lord Bathurst—

We must have Lord Combermere also, if he will come.

Lord Combermere did come, and arriving in Paris on the 18th July, was, with his wife and staff, quartered for two days at the Palais Beauharnais. The two following letters belong to this period:—

Paris, July 15th, 1815.

My Dear Mother,—I arrived here yesterday, just in time to see the king make his public entry. It was very gratifying, but would have been more so had one felt certain that the people were really glad to see him; but they have so often rung the changes upon '*Vive l'Empereur!*' and '*Vive le Roi!*' that I cannot give them credit for sincerity on the present occasion. The king is established at the Tuileries, and Paris seems as quiet as London.

The British and Prussians occupy the gates and some Prussians are quartered in the town, but the British Army is a league from hence and the rest of the Prussians are at St. Cloud. I am going to Malmaison, near which the cavalry are quartered. It is a delightful house, fitted up in the most comfortable and costly manner by Napoleon for Josephine. We shall be delighted to settle there; for it is in the country, with a park and grounds of five hundred acres. The gardens, I hear, are magnificent, with beautiful hot-houses, green-houses, &c. &c.

I will write to you in a day or two. You will be as glad as Caroline is that all is over. I regret more than ever not having been at the famous battle which decided the fate of Europe. Caroline unites in duty and love with, dear mother,

Your affectionate and very dutiful son,

S. Cotton.

Malmaison, July 22, 1815.

My Dear Aunt,—We have been established at this delightful villa about ten days. Our host, Eugene Beauharnais, is at Munich, but his *maître d'hotel*, cook, and housekeeper are here, and do the honours as well as the prince was he at home.

The housekeeper is a good, jolly, red-faced Tarporly lady, who lived seventeen years with Josephine, and before that with Lord Cholmondeley. It is very fortunate to have an English servant here, for none of ours speak French. The cavalry will, I believe, soon be moved into Normandy, and I shall have my headquarters at Rouen. When the army goes home Caroline and I think of going to Lyons, Marseilles, and Toulouse, in the winter to Italy, and returning home next summer via Switzerland. Any hints you can give us, or letters to your friends in Italy, will be thankfully received. We shall probably winter at Naples.

I shall never recover the disappointment and mortification which I feel at not having been at the famous Battle of Waterloo.

My mother writes in very good spirits. I suppose she has left you for Peover by this time.

Pray give my love to Sir Corbet, and Believe me, my dear aunt,

Your very affectionate and obliged

Combermere.

To Lady Corbet, Adderley Hall, Salop.

During the remainder of the summer Lord Combermere remained at Malmaison, formerly the country residence of the ill-fated Josephine. The housekeeper was a Cheshire woman, who some years previously had come to Paris as a servant to the Marchioness of Cholmondeley, and had afterwards married Josephine's *intendant*. She was deeply attached to the memory of her unfortunate mistress, never could speak of her without tears, and seized every opportunity of bearing testimony to her virtues. So far, indeed, did she carry this veneration, that when, on the Duchess of Rutland paying Lord Combermere a visit at Malmaison, he proposed to assign Josephine's private rooms to her Grace, the housekeeper evinced so much repugnance to the arrangement that out of deference to her feelings the idea was given up and other apartments selected.

During his stay at Malmaison his eldest daughter, Caroline, later the Marchioness of Downshire, was born.

The English received little favour or attention from either the Royal Family or the returned emigrants, to the tablets of whose minds a return of good fortune had served as a sponge to wipe out the recollection of the great hospitality received by them during their exile. Lord Combermere's unwilling host, however, displayed a feeling which stands out in bright contrast to those of his royalist fellow-countrymen. On Lord Combermere's departure from Malmaison, Eugene presented him with an alabaster vase, which had been the gift of Pope Pius VII. to Josephine, and gave Lady Combermere a work-table and frame, which had likewise belonged to his mother. Lord Combermere also asked for and obtained a posting-book, once used by Napoleon, as well as several works which had formed part of his library.

At the grand review of all the allied troops, held in the Champ de Mars this year Lord Combermere commanded the cavalry. After remaining some months at Malmaison Lord Combermere proceeded with the cavalry first to Cassel, and afterwards to Boulogne and Calais. While in this part of France he was quartered for some time at Pont de Brique, in a *château* belonging to a French noble.

The following letter belongs to this period, and though it has already been published in Gurwood's Dispatches of the Duke of Wellington, still, from the special nature of the subject, we think it may with propriety be reproduced here.

London, August 4th, 1816.

My dear Lord Combermere,—I have received your letter of the 28th August. I don't propose to encamp the cavalry at all. I may probably get them all together in closer cantonments, and in the neighbourhood of the camp of the infantry, when I shall assemble the latter.

I want very much that you would turn your mind to the order of the formation of the cavalry. My opinion is that the files of our cavalry are too loose. "We must adhere to the regulation, which I believe allows of a more loose formation than the cavalry of other armies; but we must adhere to it strictly, and not allow our order to become more extended than it is. Then, all our movements are too quick for large bodies of cavalry, and the consequence of this system, and of the looseness of our lines, is that in all great movements of our cavalry, they get into confusion. The horses are jaded before the moment of exertion arrives, and it becomes impossible for any man to produce the great effect with the cavalry of which it is capable.

Our horse, though I believe him to be the best in the world, becomes unmanageable in proportion as his rate of going is increased, and this is another reason for shortening the pace in all movements excepting the last and decisive charge.

I wish you would turn your mind to these objects:—

1st. To keep invariably as close order as the regulation will admit.

2nd. To draw the attention of the generals and commanding officers to the regulating the closeness and exactness of all their movements, and the preservation of strict order in all their parts, rather than to their celerity.

3rd. To prevent the repetition of commands by those not authorised by the regulation to give them when in line or squadron.

4th. To keep the charge, as well as all other movements, at the pace with which the middling goers, if not the slowest, must keep up.

5th. To notice particularly all officers or soldiers whose horses break the ranks or general line without orders, whether in a charge or any other movement.

I gave Ponsonby leave to come to London, but omitted to write to Barnes upon it. The fact is, that I had much to do at the moment, and was going to Cheltenham at the time I forgot it. The fault is mine.

Remember me most kindly to Lady Combermere, and believe me ever yours,

Most sincerely,

Wellington.

In the autumn of 1816, the army of occupation having been reduced. Lord Combermere lost his command, and returning to England proceeded to Combermere Abbey, where he remained till his appointment in the spring of 1817, as Governor of Barbadoes, and Commander-in-Chief of the Leeward Islands. In accordance with custom, he received, together with his appointment, two full-length pictures of George III. and his consort, copied by Gainsborough from the originals of Sir Joshua Reynolds. (These pictures are now—1866—at Combermere Abbey). It is related of Gainsborough, that George III. entertained such a dislike to him, on account of his private character, that when the former was appointed sergeant painter the king never could be induced to sit to him for the picture which in virtue of his office he was bound to paint. The only resource, therefore, left to Gainsborough was to sketch an outline of the king's face when he attended the theatre, and to trust to memory to fill in the details.

Immediately on receiving the intimation of his appointment to the Government of Barbadoes, Lord Combermere, accompanied by his wife and infant daughter, hastened to London, where he established himself at Thomas's Hotel, in Berkeley Square. He commenced at once to make preparations for his departure, and to take the necessary directions from military and civil authorities.

Berths were engaged in a West Indian ship for himself, his family, his military secretary, the Hon. Captain Finch, and their immediate attendants. Government placed at his disposal a brig of 800 tons, for the conveyance of baggage, horses, carriages, and the remainder of his servants. In this vessel were to sail two *aides-de-camp*, Lieutenant Rowland Cotton and Captain Boyd.

The latter was a young man of great accomplishments, who had latterly been studying at the Staff College, Farnham, and had previously acted as *aide-de-camp* to Sir Charles Wade in the West Indies. Captain Boyd, a few years later, was appointed equerry to the Duke of Gloucester, by whom he was as much prized as by his earlier chief. Lord Combermere, for the ready courtesy with which he performed his duties. He is one of the few *aides-de-camp* who survived their old commander.

In May, Lord Combermere embarked for his destination, and about the same time his two *aides-de-camp* sailed with the luggage from Portsmouth in another ship. Proceeding along the coast of Portugal, they arrived off the mouth of the Tagus, without accident or impediment. Here, from between the Berling Rocks, stood out two large frigates, without colours, which bore down on the brig and fired, to bring her to. She immediately obeyed the signal, the captain believing that the nearing vessels were British, until undeceived by seeing the Algerine flag hoisted at their mast heads. At the same time a boat appeared alongside the brig, and on her deck jumped an officer, who, by his brogue, was at once recognised to be an Irishman. "You are my prisoners," said this person to the captain, "and, with these gentlemen, must go with me. The boat's crew will remain in possession of the brig."

Here was a disagreeable position for two young officers on their way to assume pleasant staff appointments. Their imaginations carried them rapidly from cocked hats to chains, while they glanced at the ruffianly appearance of their new acquaintance, by whom they fancied themselves viewed with an appraising stare. Their next thought was for Lord Combermere's property, which would be equally sacrificed to the rapacity of these miscreants.

The two young officers dressed themselves in uniform, and with the master of the brig got into the privateer's boat, under the direction of an interpreter. When they came alongside the frigate this individual politely handed them on to the deck, and there desired them to sit down in view of the captain, who eyed them silently, smoking stolidly all the time. The prisoners were not, however, treated uncivilly; pipes were handed to them, and towards night a carpet was presented for the accommodation of each. Till eleven next morning they lay on deck, in a state of great suspense, anxiously watching the silent corsair. They then requested the interpreter to inform the captain that their ship was not a merchantman, but one dispatched by government for the transport of property belonging to the English commander-in-chief of the Leeward Islands, adding that they were his *aides-de-camp.*

The young men were still left to themselves till four p.m., when the interpreter appeared and required them to sign a paper which stated that the brig belonged to the British Government, and its cargo to a British general.

Immediately after this proceeding the captives were conveyed on board their own vessel, which soon got under way, and in four days reached Funchal. There they learnt that Lord Combermere and his party had landed five days previously, and were stopping at the hospitable house of Mr. McBean, one of the merchant princes of the island. Thither the *aides-de-camp* proceeded, and were at once invited to take up their abode there. Great was the amusement of all present when the adventures of Boyd and Cotton were related to a party assembled at dinner the evening of their arrival.

After staying three days longer at Madeira, and laying in a store of Mr. McBean's best wine, the whole party re-embarked together and left the harbour, saluted by all the coast batteries and by a Portuguese man-of-war at anchor in the bay. Directing their course for Carlisle Bay, Barbadoes, they arrived there after a pleasant run of ten days, without the occurrence of any particular incident.

Lord Combermere: A Short Military Biography

1

To the left of Lord Lynedoch's portrait in the "Senior" hangs that of Lord Combermere. There is striking contrast between the men. Lynedoch's portly figure is the sturdy Scot, with strong good sense predominating over an air of martial resolution. Combermere is a soldier of very different type: the light cavalry leader *par excellence*, the *beau sabreur*, disputing with Anglesey the *sobriquet* of the Murat of the army, delighting in the pomp and the trappings of war. He made the most of his rare chances of distinction, and though scarcely mentioned half-a-dozen times in the pages of Napier, like the Pagets he did good service on more than one battlefield, and more especially in protecting retreats.

But the cavalry were rather out of the running in the Peninsular campaigns, and had frequently to look on as spectators at combats they would gladly have shared. The cavalry was Wellington's weaker arm; he nursed it, and it may be said that he carried it in a sling; yet on occasion it could strike strong and sharp. The actions were often fought in the mountains or on broken ground; the passes in the sierras were steep and rugged; forced marches were frequent, forage was scarce, and the strain upon horseflesh was severe.

Stapleton Cotton came of a hunting family and was brought up in the saddle. He was the second son of Sir Robert Salusbury Cotton, member for Cheshire, and was born in 1778 at Llewenny Hall in Denbighshire. When Sir Robert succeeded to the title, on the death of his father, he had removed to Combermere Abbey, the chief family seat. Both he and his predecessor had done their best to dilapidate extensive estates. Unlike many of their aristocratic contemporaries,

221

they were neither courtiers, *roués*, nor gamblers; but they never condescended to business details, and kept open house for all comers. The stables were filled with horses; there was welcome for the horses of any number of guests, and the very servants were encouraged to entertain their friends as they pleased.

Stapleton, though free-handed like his forebears, had enforced opportunities of economising in Spain, when the death of his elder brother had made him heir to the estates. At the age of eight he went to a private school and thence to Westminster. He was not a bookish boy; he must have been a thorn in the side of his teachers; but if his high spirits were always landing him in scrapes, his pleasant manners made him a general favourite.

After four years at Westminster, his father reluctantly consented to his entering the army, but would not hear of his going to one of the French military schools. For his misfortune, the boy missed the opportunity of studying the science of war and acquiring foreign languages; he was put in charge of a dull-witted Shropshire major who cared for nothing beyond buttons and pipeclay. But if he had slight advantages of education, he had nothing to complain of in the way of promotion, for on attaining his majority the fortunate youth was colonel of a crack light cavalry corps.

In 1791, he had been gazetted to the Royal Welsh Fusiliers at Dublin, and thence he was transferred to a troop in the Carabineers. The Carabineers were an Irish regiment—such a regiment as might have suggested the most rollicking scenes in *Charles O'Malley* or *Jack Hinton*. They were notorious as a hard-living and deep-drinking set—backing each other's bills with generous recklessness, and ready to "blaze" on the slightest provocation. Naturally the young captain's friends were anxious; with his buoyant spirits and careless temperament, there was cause enough for anxiety. But he showed unusual strength of will, with discretion and moral resolution that carried him safely through the ordeal. He could take occasional liberties with an iron constitution, but in that convivial age he was remarkable for sobriety.

Yet his jovial colonel, who took a great fancy to the lad, set him the worst possible example; and when the Carabineers were ordered to the Low Countries most of them modelled themselves on the general in command of the forces, who made a point of getting drunk after an early dinner. While in Flanders, in a single week Cotton figured twice in the *Gazette*. He was promoted first to a majority in a line regiment, and immediately afterwards to the lieutenant-colonelcy of the 25th

LORD COMBERMERE

Light Dragoons. He had actually left the camp for England on the morning of the 25th May 1794, when dropping shots were heard in the distance. He turned bridle and galloped back to place himself at the head of his still vacant troop and play a distinguished part in the Battle of Cateau. (*Guns at Le Cateau* by A. F. Becke & C. de Sausmarez is also published by Leonaur.)

The 25th was quartered at Weymouth and the young colonel, who frequently attended the king on his rides, was a special favourite. George III. liked him for his joyous humour and pleasant manners. Gay, rather handsome, and with brilliant prospects, Colonel Cotton was naturally in favour with the fair sex, but he never seems to have been much of a ladies' man, though he could love very seriously and was thrice married. At any rate, he never cared for a Capua at home when honour was to be won abroad. In 1796 his regiment was under orders for India. His mother and sisters besought him to exchange, but he declared he would rather throw up his commission than forego the opportunity for distinction in foreign service. He had no opposition to fear from his father, for old Sir Robert, though he seems to have been a henpecked husband, sympathised with his son's military ardour. The transport touched at the Cape when the Dutch were threatening a descent to recover their lost colony. Cotton landed his smart dragoons and mounted them on ragged little Boer horses, but their services were not called into requisition. They looked on, disappointed spectators, when the tables were turned at the surrender of the Dutch fleet to the future Lord Keith.

He was disappointed, too, at being disembarked at Madras instead of proceeding to Calcutta, as he had expected, for the pay and allowances in the premier presidency were higher. But he consoled himself with the hope of seeing some fighting, and his wishes were soon gratified. Tippoo Saib was preparing to make his last stand, and it must be owned that Lord Mornington's suave and provocative diplomacy had been pushing the fiery Sultan hard. Malavelly was almost a bloodless action on the British side, but the *Nizam's* soldiers and two regiments of Floyd's cavalry, commanded by Cotton, bore the brunt of the engagement, such as it was. Tippoo, with his own wild horsemen, had attempted a turning movement, when they found themselves faced by Cotton's dragoons and a native cavalry regiment. The enemy drew bridle and turned before Cotton could charge, though the fugitives were followed in hot pursuit Tippoo rallied his broken host in the fortress he deemed impregnable to any assault.

But a breach was made, and in open day Seringapatam was stormed. Tippoo died fighting gallantly at the northern gate, and there in a gloomy archway, with eyes unclosed and a scowl on his haughty features, the body of the fallen autocrat was found by the captive he had chained in his dungeons a few years before. It was a strange freak of fortune when Tippoo and Baird were brought face to face for the second time. During the campaign Cotton made the acquaintance of Colonel Wellesley, who was seven years his senior. No mutual attraction ever drew the men together, and though Lord Wellington appreciated Sir Stapleton's services in the Peninsula, he was never over liberal of praise.

In 1800 Cotton came home, to be gazetted full colonel. A matter that concerned him more nearly was his marriage. It was at once a marriage of love and of *convenance*. His wife was a very beautiful girl, but she was also the daughter of the Duchess of Newcastle, and the stepdaughter of General Craufurd's elder brother. So, Cotton added to his own family influence that of the powerful house of Newcastle with its plurality of parliamentary votes. If he made friends by the match, he was soon to make a formidable enemy. Quartered at Brighton, he was a frequent guest at the Pavilion, and honoured with the intimacy of the Regent. A foolish indiscretion as to the prince's somewhat mysterious relations with Mrs. Fitzherbert cost him the royal favour, for the Regent was vindictive over mere trivial offences.

He left the luxuries of Brighton for quarters in the Irish bogs, when the country was seething with the spirit of sedition, and he was in command of the cavalry in Dublin when Emmet's rebellion broke out. That amiable enthusiast could not control the demon of anarchy he had evoked. The venerable Lord Kilwarden was brutally murdered in his daughter's arms—a repetition of the tragedy of Magus Moor—and a colonel riding through the streets in uniform and unattended was shot down in cold blood.

For that afternoon, alarmed by the popular excitement, the Lord-lieutenant had called the colonels of regiments to a council at Kilmainham. Cotton rode thither from his distant barracks and returned in safety, but he had the intelligence to skirt the sounds of the shouting and avoid the streets where the rioters were committing all manner of excesses. He had seen and heard enough to make him urge General Fox (the brother of Charles Fox) to call out the military and fire on the mob, and so the *émeute* was suppressed before the conflagration spread to the provinces.

The Regent might be unfriendly, but Fortune was still his friend. In 1805, at the age of twenty-seven, he was a major-general. Next year saw him seated as member for Newark, one of the Newcastle boroughs. The *amari aliquid* was then to come. The young wife to whom he seems to have been warmly attached sickened of consumption and died at Clifton. Like Graham, he sought relief in action. As it happened, he was ordered to Portugal in charge of the 14th and 16th Dragoons, brigaded together. He landed too late to take part with Moore in the advance to Sahagun. When Soult was descending on Oporto through the Tras-os-Montes, his brigade was dispersed on outpost duty, and he pushed his patrols to the Vouga.

When the conditions had changed and Wellesley dared what Cradock would not have been justified in attempting, he was with the cavalry division under Payne on the march to the Douro. On the 9th May 1809 he found himself facing Franceschi and his horse, from the southern bank of the Vouga. Hill had turned one flank of the enemy, Beresford the other, and Wellesley had devised a scheme of combination which was to surround Franceschi and crush the French centre. Napier does not mention that Cotton in the afternoon had ridden to headquarters to urge Sir Arthur to let him anticipate the hour fixed for his crossing the river, that he might surprise Franceschi with a night attack. Wellington always disliked nocturnal operations, and moreover he probably objected to any disturbance of his arrangements.

Be that as it may, when Cotton passed at midnight as prearranged, Franceschi had got wind of the allied movements. Gun carriages were breaking down in narrow defiles, and the difficult passages were obstructed. Cotton's guides misled him; when he came upon the French it was broad daylight, and they were formidably posted in superior numbers. To his mortification he could only look on while they retired, for his orders forbade him to hazard an encounter. So, the cavalry had but the role of onlookers at the passage of the Douro, only two of the squadrons being sent across. Yet it seems that, had they been passed over at Avintas, they might have done good service, when Murray let the rabble of fugitives go by without firing a shot.

At Talavera, the cavalry were in three brigades, and one of them was commanded by Cotton. Recalled from outpost duty, he had ridden on to the battlefield on the evening of the 26th July, anticipating Craufurd's arrival by several hours. His post was in reserve behind the great field redoubt which marked the left of the Spanish line and the right of the British. The nerves of our redoubtable allies were so highly strung that, though they knew the French were massed in front, they greeted Cotton's dragoons with a scattering volley. In the morning, on the plain below, the French brought off the surprise at Salinas; when Wellington himself was well-nigh captured, Cotton was hastily called forward to help in covering the retreat. On the day of the battle he was in rear of Campbell's division, the rest of the cavalry being held in reserve on the extreme left. The battle had begun in the intense heat of a sultry noon, and through the afternoon it was raging fiercely. Hill still held to the height on the right, the key of the position, and Campbell was standing firm on the other flank.

It was then that Lapisse flung his serried columns on the allied centre. Received with a deadly discharge, shrinking from the shock of the bayonets, they were hurled back in a scattered rout. The Guards broke their ranks and rushed down in reckless pursuit. The flying masses met their supports, rallied on them, and returned. The Guards were broken, the Germans were in confusion, and the British centre was pierced. Cotton had no orders, but it was no time to wait for them, and he sounded the charge.

At that moment, the orders came from the hill whence Wellington had been looking down on the *mêlée*. As the 48th Foot fell upon the flank of the triumphant French, Cotton charged them in front. The centre battle was restored and the day was won. He was afterwards thanked by the House for his deeds at Talavera, but got little credit through the general, who seems always to have been chary in praising him. Wellington indeed had thanked him personally, but did not even name him in despatches. Yet a private letter to his sister shows that it was a desperate piece of service, and Cotton, though he wrote freely to please his family, was never the man to blow his own trumpet.

I have before experienced an equally hot fire, but never one of such duration. From ten in the forenoon of the 27th to the close of the day on the 28th (with the exception of a few hours at midnight) I was exposed to the enemy's shot. . . . The charge of cavalry, so much talked of in your newspapers, was led by your humble servant, at the head of two squadrons of the 23rd Light Dragoons, and so desperate was the undertaking, out of the two squadrons consisting of 160 men, all were either killed or wounded, with the exception of myself and six or seven dragoons.

The close of the day was unsatisfactory. He came back, hoping for supper and a change of clothes, to find his baggage had been pillaged by the flying Spaniards. The actual pecuniary loss must have been serious, for no general officer carried about a more costly kit When the British withdrew from the valley of the Tagus, he covered the passage at Arzobispo. When the army was in cantonments on the Guadiana, being made a local lieutenant-general, he became ineligible for the command of a brigade, but Sir Arthur gave him a lieutenant-general's command at Merida, attaching some artillery to his cavalry. He was fortunate in escaping the fever which sent many of his men into hospital; he always said that he had been saved by sobriety and his habit of taking early exercise on horseback. In the winter, having heard of his father's death, he went home on furlough.

In possession of the estates, devoted to his family, delighting in the life at Combermere, though by no means averse to the gaieties of the fashionable world, he nevertheless was not to be tempted to retire, and rejoined the army in the summer of 1810. He was given command of the whole cavalry, for now the cavalry was a separate division. But it was only occasionally, in general actions or when protecting a retreat, that the leader was personally engaged, and Cotton, although notorious for intrepidity, is said never to have crossed swords in single combat. Even as a veteran in retreat, he was not garrulous, and was seldom to be drawn as to his personal actions. Detachments of his division were in skirmishes on the Coa and Agueda.

In Craufurd's unfortunate affair of the 11th July, two squadrons of his old regiment, the 16th Light Dragoons, were very unjustly reproached with misconduct. In reality, they had behaved with surpassing courage, and their gallant colonel, when charging home, had actually fallen on the enemy's bayonets. Cotton took up the matter with characteristic zeal; the mendacious calumnies were conclusively refuted, and Wellington wrote in express terms that the 16th had merited high commendation. But when mud is flung some will always cling, and the calumny has been revived in many popular histories.

Masséna descended on Portugal and Wellington withdrew to the lines. Throughout the long and harassing march, broken only by the interlude of Busaco, Cotton protected the retreating forces, nor did he lose a single baggage waggon. It is another example of how wild rumours are accepted credulously by conscientious historians, that Southey tells in his *Peninsular War* of Cotton losing six guns at Quinta del Torre. In reality, his conduct of the retreat may compare with that of Ney when the tables had been turned, and he showed himself equally skilful as strategist and tactician. There were daily and nightly skirmishes between the hostile pickets and patrols. His system was to throw out light lines of skirmishers, to lure the enemy forward into traps and ambushes, where stronger reserves and supports were concealed.

Then came the counter-charge, the flight and the pursuit, for though the allied cavalry were inferior in numbers, they were much the better mounted. For himself, he was continually in the saddle, and often reconnoitring with the leader of his rear-guard. A hot-tempered man, he was not to be trifled with, but on calm reflection he was inexorably just. He was a strict disciplinarian as to essentials, but, military dandy as he was, he never worried his men needlessly over details of ornamental equipment They had a rough time enough as it was, for in one of his officers' journals is the regular entry:

Rained heavily all night.

The skirmishes, in which they were almost invariably successful, gave his men a confidence which stood them in good stead, and the chief set an example of personal coolness which sometimes looked like *fanfaronade*. On one occasion, he was with his rear-guard, and riding with Captain Brotherton, one of the *paladins* of the army. While the feeble guard was holding the enemy in check, a deep ravine dividing it from the main body, some squadrons were seen descending into the chasm to intercept it. Cotton was surveying the foe through his field-glasses, when Brotherton hinted it was high time to be off. The answer was worthy of the Iron Duke: "Why, Brotherton, what a fuss you're in!" and he "bluffed" the enemy for a little longer before wheeling round to gallop away. Brotherton (afterwards Sir Thomas) owned he was stung, "for I was one of Sir Ralph Abercromby's soldiers, and had seen some service before the Peninsula."

There was no place for horsemen on the precipitous steeps of Busaco. They held the plain behind the ridge, to the extreme left of the positions, a single heavy regiment being in reserve on the sierra. But there had been sharp fighting before that at the fords of the Mondego, and they were heavily engaged afterwards at Alcoentre and Quinta del Torre. Tompkinson, then a captain in the 16th Dragoons, gives a soldier-like but very graphic account of the affair at Alcoentre, and we take it as a representative sketch of what happened at many other places.

A narrow, hog-backed bridge spanned a yawning torrent bed, and beyond was the main street on a steep ascent, turning sharply off at right angles. The enemy brought up two regiments of cavalry, and the English picket was withdrawn behind the bridge. The supports were hurried into the village from the upper side, and were ready to charge down the street. "Colonel Elley" (the assistant adjutant-general) "was standing shaving at a window, as we came in. The confusion was complete; the street was blocked with gun carriages and ammunition waggons, with mules and oxen." The enemy sent two squadrons into the village; when they turned the sharp corner, they found themselves in face of the English; then the front ranks turned to fly, but those in the rear, knowing nothing of what was passing in front, were still pressing forward.

> They got so close that it was impossible to get at them, but we took twelve and killed six, driving them over the bridge again, and by this means allowing what remained in the town to get away. The enemy dismounted their dragoons and we retired through the town, forming on the heights on the other side.

When the army was safe within the lines of Torres Vedras, the cavalry was sent to the rear. Wellington wrote in a despatch to Lord Liverpool:

> Since the end of July, they have done the duty of the outposts and the enemy has never been out of sight of them; and on every occasion their superiority has been so great that the enemy does not use his cavalry except when supported and protected by his infantry.

Again, Sir Stapleton was in England, and again in April he was back with his division. Actively engaged in outpost duty and patrol work, constantly employed in keeping open communications, for a year he was necessarily kept in the background, and he did little more than look on at Fuentes d'Onore. In the end of February 1812, he had left the Agueda for the neighbourhood of Badajoz. On the 16th March that fortress was invested, and Graham was despatched towards Llerena to cover the siege operations. Cotton accompanied him in command of two cavalry brigades. Trusting in the tenacity of Philippon's defence, hoping against experience for a junction with Marmont, Soult was bringing up the army of Andalusia to the relief.

On the 8th April, he learned simultaneously that Badajoz was taken and that Marmont had failed him; then he withdrew his headquarters from Llerena. Cotton was following with his cavalry, and Peyremont's horse were protecting the retreat. Then Cotton planned a daring operation, devised with remarkable skill, to surround and capture Peyremont's brigade. He had orders from Graham to make a demonstration. Mounting a church steeple, he made his survey. He could see that Usagre, a perilous advanced post, alternately held by the French and the allies, was still occupied, while in an intervening wood were the bivouacs of Peyremont's cavalry. Behind that wood was a line of low heights upon their left. Immediately he took his measures. His light dragoons under Anson marched at midnight; the officers were called away from a ball they had been giving to the Spanish ladies.

While Anson amused Peyremont from the front, Le Marchant with the heavies was circling round to cut the road to Llerena. But Anson began his attack too soon, and the French, seeing nothing of Le Marchant, who was screened by the heights, fell back to form again in order of battle. Anson still kept the enemy in play, till Le Marchant came up to charge them in flank. There was a fierce encounter; the French horse broke and fled; in the hot pursuit many were cut down, and a considerable number of prisoners were taken. For that, as for the more important affair of Castrejon, Cotton got but cold commendation. In the despatches, he was merely bracketed with Le Marchant and the soldiers under his command.

Castrejon came off in this wise. In July, the warfare had shifted from the Guadiana to the Douro. Wellington was watching the river, passable by various fords and bridges. On the 17th, Marmont, after sundry feints and manoeuvres, had concentrated at Nava del Rey, to the south of it, and driven in the allied pickets on its tributary, the Trabancos. Wellington was much in the dark as to the strength and positions of his enemy. On the night of the 17th, Cotton with the right wing, composed of the 4th and Light Divisions, with Anson's cavalry, was guarding the Trabancos. His position was weak, and though he did not know it, he was opposed to the whole French army. Wellington learned at midnight that Cotton was in touch with the French— Cotton had sent the tidings by three separate messengers—and immediately threw himself into the saddle, ordering the other cavalry brigades to follow.

At daybreak Cotton's pickets were again driven back. He drew up his infantry behind the village, but the divisions were separated by a ravine. Before them his horse were posted with a troop of horse artillery, but the country in front was so broken that the enemy and their movements were effectually concealed. Cotton, seeing nothing but horse patrols, advanced his own cavalry by his right towards the river. The movement was answered by a heavy fire from musketeers and masked batteries. He sent forward a foot regiment to the support of his horse, and skirmishing went on till, at seven o'clock, Wellington and Beresford galloped on to the ground.

It was then Wellington had a more narrow escape than at Salinas before Talavera, when the incident occurred that has been described elsewhere, and when the course of European history might have been changed, had the Commander of the allies gone a prisoner to Paris. Then Cotton, by his able handling of his force, kept the enemy at bay till supports came up, and with equal skill covered the retreat to the Guarena. Wellington paid him with only verbal thanks, but Soult gave warmer praise. He wrote in despatches, that had it not been for the stand of General Cotton, Marmont would have surprised and defeated the British before Wellington could have rallied them in a defensible position.

The 21st July was the eve of Salamanca, the battle that shook Napoleon's hold on Spain and went far to win the Borodino. Yet Wellington was never in greater anxiety than when back in his old positions on San Christoval; be had been out-marched and out-manoeuvred in the race for the Tormes. He had to choose between seeing his communications with Portugal cut and abandoning Salamanca, or adopting the third alternative of risking a battle at disadvantage. He could not foresee that next day he would be vouchsafed such a crowning mercy as Cromwell at Dunbar, and that his watchful and sagacious enemy would deliver himself into his hand. Marmont had passed the fords on the Upper Tormes and was extending his left under cover down the left bank. Wellington had also passed by fords and bridges lower down, but he still kept the 3rd Division and D'Urban's cavalry on the right bank.

The darkness had deepened as Anson's brigade of horse, following the Light Division, descended the heights. It was the prelude to the bursting of one of those terrific storms which heralded so many of the Peninsular battles. The peals were deafening: the lightning was flashed back from the points of the bayonets as the columns waded the Tormes shoulder high. Anson's brigade had hardly bivouacked when the horses tore up the picket pins and stampeded. Colonel Dalbiac of the 4th Dragoons was seated with his wife in front of the brigade. "We had barely time," wrote Captain Tompkinson, "to hurry the lady for safety under a gun."

The day broke, and Wellington from the heights was watching the development of operations. The initiative was with Marmont, for he could not even continue a retreat without exposing both flank and rear. Then ensued the fighting from the twin heights of the Arapiles; but, as the day went on and operations dragged, Wellington personally withdrew from what was called the English Arapiles and waited. At three o'clock news was brought which roused him to activity. He galloped forward to a commanding headland, and saw that Marmont had given the unhoped-for opportunity.

Weary of waiting, seeing no considerable force on the right bank of the river, circling round behind the wooded screen of a forest, the French marshal had sent General Thomières forward to throw himself across the Rodrigo road. "Now I have him," was Wellington's exclamation, for the continuity of the hostile line was broken by a broad and inviting gap. The order was given, the signals were passed, and the troops massed on the English Arapiles were launched like an avalanche on the plain beneath.

It was at five according to Napier, an hour earlier according to other authorities, that Pakenham struck his tremendous blow at Thomières. The French general, emerging from the woods and gaining an isolated hill which terminated the southern heights, in place of seeing the British in full retreat, found himself faced by Pakenham and his solid columns. His own line had straggled in threading the woodlands; the irresistible shock of his adversary rolled it up. He was driven back on a host already in confusion, though desperately disputing each inch of ground. Marmont had gone down, two other generals of division had fallen, and Clausel was left in command. While Pakenham was fiercely pressing upon Thomières, Cotton with his heavy and light brigades, and Ball's troop of horse artillery, were following along the higher ground on his left rear.

Cotton had ridden forward to reconnoitre. What he saw was Thomières closing up on Clausel, Pakenham fast closing in upon the flanks of both, and the 5th Division assailing the front through a storm of ball and cannon shot Immediately beneath the hill where he stood was a division of French infantry. Riding back, he formed his men in three lines: the heavies under Le Marchant first, Anson behind, and Victor Alten in the last. When he brought them to the summit he saw that the division below had weakened, a part having been drawn off to the right battle of the French. He gave the order to charge; it is said that Le Marchant asked in what direction; that Cotton answered briefly, "To the enemy," and that high words ensued.

Naturally both those hot spirits were fired to fever heat, but it is hardly within the range of possibility that Le Marchant can have suspected that any impeachment of his courage was intended. Be that as it may, Cotton had cause to lament the outburst of temper, for those were the last words Le Marchant ever uttered. The tempest gathering on the hill burst on the French below. Le Marchant's heavies came thundering down, flanked emulously by Anson with his light cavalry. Twelve hundred Frenchmen were literally trampled down; the survivors, awed by the suddenness of the catastrophe, sought refuge in their panic in British squares.

Le Marchant had soon lost his saddle, but then Cotton and Anson took the lead. The tremendous onset was furiously continued, a second column of infantry was ridden down, and five cannon were captured. Wellington had as usual turned up where the battle was hottest and most critical. He may not have loved Cotton, but for once his feelings found vent. "By God, Cotton," he exclaimed, "I never saw anything more beautiful in my life! The day is yours!" That burst of feeling, on the spur of the moment, was worth more than any formal praise in despatches.

Le Marchant's dragoons, wearied with striking and slaughtering, were relieved by D'Urban's brigade. Anson's light cavalry still led, Cotton riding with the brigadier; D'Urban followed, and the rear was brought up by Alten's Germans. As Clausel was driven back towards Alba de Tormes, which in Wellington's belief was held by Carlos d'España, the cavalry, keeping between the retiring foe and the Tormes, made many prisoners. But Wellington had missed the full cast of the net, for the Spanish garrison had evacuated Alba and the broken battalions of the French were streaming unmolested across the river.

Cotton had escaped in the battle by a miracle, though his magnificent dress and the gorgeous trappings of the superb charger he rode made him a conspicuous mark. He had been posting his pickets towards Alba and was returning to camp, when he was fired at by a handful of Portuguese soldiers, who mistook his party for a French patrol. A bullet shattered his arm; the consequences were serious, nor did he ever altogether recover the injury. But those Peninsular heroes were men of iron, priding themselves, from the highest to the lowest, on the stoicism with which they supported pain. Recalling the experiences of the wounded commander of the cavalry, we can realise the sufferings of the subalterns and the rank and file.

Mastering his agony. Cotton rode on to the nearest village. There he found shelter in a hovel, and they made him as comfortable as possible in a pig trough. Wellington, on hearing the news, galloped thither to inquire, having picked up. a surgeon on the way. The surgeon would have amputated, but Cotton refused till the sentence was confirmed by the chief medical officer. The result was that the arm was saved, though the recovery was painful and tedious. Wellington wrote, in recommending him to Lord Bathurst for the red ribbon of the Bath:

> No cavalry could have done better than ours in the action, and I must say for Stapleton that I don't know where we could find an officer who could command our cavalry in this country as well as he does.

Sir Corbet Corbet, his uncle, was a constant correspondent, and now, when Cotton was incapacitated from writing, Sir Corbet had a letter from a lieutenant in the 16th Dragoons.

> Do not be alarmed—slightly is Sir Stapleton wounded in the arm. It could not be otherwise; he is so desperate in exposing his life. It is perhaps a fortunate thing for his family and friends that he is impeded in his glorious but too dangerous career. He never goes into action but in the richest of dresses, puts himself at the head of everything, and courts danger like a soldier of fortune whose future welfare depends upon a single dash. But Sir Stapleton's conduct is admirable, and the lowest soldier reveres him. If we lose him, the British cavalry will be in a wretched plight.

His wound laid him up for many weeks. It was fortunate that his staff surgeon was at his side to curb his impatience, but there was a tragic incident when Dr. Littledale fainted on his shoulder in their carriage, and was carried away to his deathbed. Spanish *grandees* vied in their attentions; one offered a palace at Salamanca, and another lent a coach with the team of mules. He rejoined on the retreat from Burgos, and headed some hard fighting on the 29th October. When the army withdrew to winter quarters he went home on sick leave, and Lord Wellington expressed his regrets in a letter to the military secretary at the Horse Guards. At the same time the praise was in more modified terms than the despatch sent off in the excitement of victory.

He commands our cavalry very well—indeed I am certain much better than many who might be sent to us, and who might be supposed cleverer than he is.

The congratulations that greeted his return were not unmixed with mortifications. His services had been considerable, his position was high, and his connections were powerful. He seems confidently to have counted on a peerage, but the honour was as yet denied him. There and towards another object of his aspirations it was Beresford who blocked the way. Wellington represented that a peerage for Cotton would be a tacit slur upon the marshal, nor was he prepared to press either claim on the ministry.

Moreover, two days after his arrival Cotton was invited to an interview with the Minister at War. His hopes were high, but if he expected that it would pass off pleasantly, he was disappointed. Beresford was Cotton's junior in the service, and in point of fact the minister wished to persuade him to waive his claims to succeeding by seniority as temporary second-in-command of the allies in the event of anything happening to Wellington. It was very natural that Cotton should refuse; it was still more natural that, in the interests of the country, ministers should hesitate as to giving the supreme command to a cavalryman.

Returning to Portugal, he hurried after the army, arriving at Vittoria, as an Irishman might say, barely in time to miss the battle. The cavalry quartered in the plains could only hear of the mountain warfare which succeeded, and even after the invasion of France there were few laurels for the horsemen to gather. After the passage of the Bidassoa they were on constant outpost duty before a vigilant and daring enemy; and then, like Craufurd on the Coa, each evening Cotton had his baggage packed and his horses saddled.

Nothing of consequence happened to him before Orthez; then when Hill was hanging over the French communications, and their retreat had degenerated into a race, Cotton charged through some covering companies, sabred several hundreds of the fugitives, and made 2000 prisoners. His work would have even been more effective had it not been for a rugged torrent bed, beyond which the bulk of the fugitives saved themselves. Nor did he do more than look on at the battle of Toulouse, though with two brigades he had followed the retreat of Soult, watching the roads by which the army of Arragon might have answered Soult's summons to the rescue.

Napoleon had abdicated; Soult had recognised the armistice; and

Cotton, coming back to Toulouse, issued his farewell "order" to the cavalry. Remembering the course of events in the following year, there is pathos in the passage where he expresses a hope—it was really confident assurance—that, should they again be employed in the service of their country, he looked forward to the honour of being again at their head.

He was in England in May; this time he had his peerage, nor had he any reason to complain of the delay. It would be difficult as invidious to draw distinctions, but those associated with him in the honours were Hill and Hope, Graham and Beresford. Cotton had passed through the fires of the war, and come off with an arm slightly maimed; he was not yet forty, and had half his life before him; he was rich, handsome, and a lion in society. He had engaged himself on his previous visit, and now he was married to Miss Greville. The marriage proved ultimately unfortunate, though the causes of the disagreement have never been cleared up, but meantime he was passionately in love.

One taste the betrothed couple had in common, for both were devoted to music, and before the Portuguese bullet had splintered his arm bone. Cotton had been no mean performer on the violin. A man of middle age, he looked young for his years. With regard to that. Sir Harry Jones of the Engineers had a good story to tell. He was in a group of staff officers sitting round a bivouac fire, when apparently a young *aide-de-camp* galloped up to give some peremptory orders.

"Who is that chap?" asked Jones of the distinguished engineer, Sir Richard Fletcher.

"Don't you know?" was the answer; "why, that is Sir Stapleton."

Lord Combermere celebrated his wedding with characteristic dash. It seems to have been fixed for a particular day, when an imperative engagement clashed with it, for the city was giving the great banquet to the allied sovereigns. Lord Combermere duly dined at the Guildhall; he slipped away early, and drove to Lambeth Palace, where he was married by the primate just before midnight.

For nine months the honeymoon was prolonged, and then Napoleon had broken out of Elba. Europe was again shaking to the tread of armed hosts, and Lord Combermere was confident he could redeem the pledge he had given in orders at Toulouse. A great army was assembling in the Netherlands and Wellington was in command. Impatiently he waited for the expected summons, but no summons came. Then he lost patience and wrote the duke to place his services at his disposal. It would appear that Wellington really wanted him, and had made application for his appointment.

It may be plausibly assumed that a grumble of the duke to Lord Bathurst had special reference to the case of Lord Combermere. He wrote that, as he had consented to take command of a raw army, he might have been permitted to choose his own instruments. But it has been suggested that the powerful influence of the Prince Regent was thrown into the opposite scale. He had never forgotten or forgiven the indiscretion of Colonel Cotton at Brighton, so Lord Uxbridge received the coveted command, when he won some glory and lost an arm.

Lord Uxbridge had lost his arm and was invalided; the very day after Waterloo, Wellington wrote to Lord Bathurst: "We must have Lord Combermere if he will come." Covetous of fame, it was a cause of never-ceasing regret that he had missed the crowning battle of the closing campaign. With many similar passages, there is this one in a letter to an aunt: "I shall never recover the mortification and disappointment which I feel at not having been at the famous battle." But he accepted the proffered command and joined the army in Paris, to be quartered in Josephine's favourite Malmaison.

Oddly enough, the caretaker left in charge by Eugènie Beauharnais was a Cheshire woman, to whom the memory of her divorced mistress was sacred. Lord Combermere's consideration for the old lady's feelings is an engaging trait in his character. When the Duchess of Rutland was coming on a visit, he had arranged that her Grace should occupy the private apartments of the empress. But the old housekeeper looked glum, and consequently the order was countermanded.

3

With the withdrawal of the army of occupation came a break in Cotton's career. Napoleon was an exile in the Atlantic, and there was the promise of a long European peace. It might have been supposed that he would have settled on the patrimonial estates, kept open house at Combermere, and given occasional attendance in the Lords. His income must have been ample, and moreover an annuity had just been voted him. We are puzzled to surmise why he should have accepted such an exile as had been forced upon the fallen emperor. But in 1817 he sailed for Barbadoes as governor of that colony and commander-in-chief of the Leeward Islands.

There he remained for four years, practising hospitality in Government House, in place of his own old Abbey, oiling the wheels of diplomacy with our French neighbours by his gracious manners in an interchange of courtesies, and reducing the heavy mortality in the garrisons by attending to the sanitation of their quarters. In 1822, he was again in Ireland as commander-in-chief, after an absence of fourteen years. The country at that time was comparatively quiet, and Lord Combermere gave a lead to the gaieties of the capital, making many Irish friends. One of his cronies, and a congenial spirit, was Lord Norbury of duelling fame—the Toler who was said to have shot himself into practice—and who, had their *rôles* been interchanged, would have revelled in heading a cavalry charge. But he was summoned of a sudden to very different scenes, and for the first time he was to have an opportunity of handling an army of all arms in the field.

There was war in Burmah, there was trouble brewing in India, and the strong fortress of Bhurtpore—the fortress which had given the name to Colonel Newcome's favourite hack—was in the hands of a daring usurper, who was bidding defiance to the British flag. It seemed likely that another expedition must be undertaken against the formidable place which had baffled Lord Lake of Laswaree. At that juncture the health of Sir Edward Paget, who was in chief command, had given way, and he expressed a wish to resign. The juncture was critical. Many of the native princes were disaffected, and if Doorjam Sal, the usurper at Bhurtpore, could hold his own, there were not a few who were ready to throw in their lot with him.

Moreover Runjeet, the old lion of the Punjaub, was not to be trusted. Professing friendship, he was waiting on events. A deputation from the directors of the company sought counsel of the Duke of Wellington, asking him to suggest a successor to Paget. He seems to have thought more highly of Lord Combermere than formerly, for he answered unhesitatingly:

You can't do better than have Combermere: he is the man to take Bhurtpore.

The deputation objected, in language which was the echo of the duke's Peninsular despatches:

We don't consider him a man of any great genius.

"I don't care a damn about his genius," said His Grace, "I tell you he is the man to take Bhurtpore."

The deputation withdrew, and Lord Combermere had the appointment

Everything happened as had been feared and foreseen: the usurper remained recalcitrant, gaining increasing confidence from the assurances he received. All the surrounding states were seething with excitement, and the eyes of their restless rulers were turned upon him. And, indeed, it appeared probable enough that the English would recoil from risking a second check. The garrison the *rajah* had gathered was largely composed of fighting Rajputs and Pathans: they were encouraged by the prestige of the former success, and, as it proved, they were men to die at their posts. Although the *rajah* had won his position by poison and the dagger, they could not have found a more gallant leader. In numbers, they were scarcely inferior to the besieging force, which consisted of natives, stiffened by four English regiments and one or two batteries of artillery. With his 25,000 men Combermere was to invest a city with an *enceinte* of eight miles.

Enclosed in formidable ramparts, with many bastions which enfiladed the intervening curtains with flanking fire, those defences might be battered but could scarcely be breached. For they were built on a peculiar system of Oriental architecture, of clay and cow dung mixed with straw, and supported by balks of timbers, each layer having been baked hard in the sun-blaze before the next was laid on. The *enceinte* was encircled by a deep and broad ditch, in many places a natural torrent bed, and (the low lands beyond could be flooded by a cutting from an adjacent lake.

In the centre of the city was the citadel, commanding everything and tremendous in its strength, with wall rising over perpendicular wall, each of them flanked with semi-circular towers and bastions. Lake had made a rush on the place from the west side and failed. Combermere, impetuous as he was by nature, realised the gravity of the crisis, and made his preparations with extreme deliberation. Nine days were devoted to a survey: then he decided on conducting operations from the east, and began by cutting the lake channel, so as to be free from the danger of flooding. The trenches, once opened, were pushed steadily forward, under heavy fire. It became comparatively harmless as the parallels were advanced, for the guns riveted on the ramparts could not be depressed, but then the sorties became more frequent.

Combermere had no little trouble with the *coolies*, who naturally objected to deadly exposure for small pay, and with the *sepoys*, who had taken it into their superstitious heads that they were made the subjects of experiments in hospital. In dealing with them he showed exemplary tact and patience. In many respects, it was a remarkable siege, and it dragged slowly. The line of investment was weak, and at one place a body of horsemen broke through. It might be well for the *rajah* to get rid of his horse, but the rest of the garrison were staunch to his standard. The fire of the besiegers was heavy and sustained; in a single day, and scarcely an exceptional one, 1600 shot and shell were expended. Latterly, while the batteries were cannonading the ramparts, the mortars were showering shell upon the city. "A disagreeable necessity," but the end must be attained quickly, or there would infallibly be a second failure.

The reserve arsenals at Agra were nearly emptied, and no wonder. For, as the works defied ordinary breaching, the attack was carried on chiefly by mine and sap, and the consumption of powder was enormous.

The parallels were thrust forward, nearly to the foot of the ramparts; galleries were being driven under the ditch, and beyond scarp and counterscarp. Small mules were frequently exploded under the bastions to aid the guns in the breaching. There were exciting scenes in that subterranean warfare, when mine was met with countermine. Once, when there was but a thin partition of earth, the British sappers heard voices and the clink of iron. They quietly deposited some powder casks at the end of their passage, laid a sausage, lighted the train, and blew the counter-miners into eternity. The guns were directed upon four points; explosives and shot had broken the ramparts, but these breaches were rather rough landslips than practicable slopes.

Moreover, the besiegers learned by their spies that, wherever there was an earth-slip, the crown had been retrenched. It was of the last importance to learn how far the access was practicable, and some of the ventures made to obtain information read like episodes from an extravagant romance of knight-errantry. Once a single *havildar* crawled up in broad daylight, the mark for a thousand matchlocks. On another occasion, a party led by two English officers went on a forlorn hope as desperate: they actually gained the summit and pelted the soldiers of the *rajah* with stones. Yet, in both cases, the daring adventurers came back almost unscathed. Their reports of the obstructions convinced Combermere that if the place was to be taken, it must be taken by mines.

The day was fixed for the assault. Everything had been done to keep the matter secret, but an intensified cannonade seems to have given the enemy some warning, and they were not taken altogether by surprise. Combermere had adapted his dispositions to the difficulties to be surmounted and the defence to be overpowered. The explosions were to create confusion and clear the way. There were to be no forlorn hopes as at Badajoz or San Sebastian; the attack was to be delivered by companies, and as far as possible by regiments. So, every man fought shoulder to shoulder with his comrades, and under the leading of his own officers.

It was to be delivered in two columns, subdivided into six sections, and for the last time in the story of British warfare there were "grenadiers" actually handling grenades. In reality, it was a confession of impotence which reminds one of the tactics of the Chinese, for, though the *fusees* were lighted, the grenades were not charged. The general directing the attack counted on the moral effect on the enemy, but declared that loaded grenades were most destructive to the men who carried them.

At eight o'clock in the morning the signal was given to fire the mines. There were two minor mines, and a third near the chief breach, which contained the almost unprecedented quantity of 10,000 pounds of powder. The smaller mines were sprung with deadly effect, followed by a brief interval of breathless suspense. Then came a roar and rush like the outburst of a volcano; it was succeeded by an earthquake, and the air was darkened with such clouds of dust and *débris* as overwhelmed Pompeii and Herculaneum. The troops had been prudently kept back in the third parallel, where they crouched in comparative safety. Combermere, eagerly watching, stood more exposed, and was enveloped in the falling showers of brick and timber.

One of his brigadiers had been struck down at his side, and two of his orderlies were killed behind him. But the besiegers were prepared for the shock and the beleaguered were not. Before the clouds had lifted or thinned, the heads of the attacking columns were at the foot of the works and scrambling up the landslips. They were aided by light bamboo ladders, lined with stout canvas, in the manner of fire-escapes. They gained the ramparts barely in time, turning to right and left, for the gallant defenders were already rallying. On that narrow roadway, rent across occasionally by mines discharged by the retreating garrison, and with an abyss on either side, the combat raged, the bayonets clashing with the sabres and *tulwars*. At one point, there was a singularly tragical episode.

Two hundred of the enemy, forced to the verge of the rampart, were taken simultaneously in front and rear. There was no asking for quarter or thought of surrender. The strength of the onset was irresistible, and to a man they were hurled down into the ditch. To add to the horrors of the scene, muskets flashed off at close quarters had set fire to the armour of quilted cotton, and those who had fallen unhurt on the bodies of their comrades were suffering the agonies of slow cremation. Combermere, when the great mine went off, had been with difficulty restrained from heading the stormers; he had hurried forward with the supports, when the enemy, recovered from their alarm, were pouring in a deadly fire. He came up with his staff, when some of those miserables were still alive and piteously shrieking for succour. Giving assistance was a work of extreme peril, for matchlocks and ammunition pouches were still exploding. Some scorched and blackened victims were extricated, but the rest had to be left to their fate.

The carnage was well-nigh over and the town was won when Combermere emerged from the narrow streets on the glacis of the citadel It had already hung out the white flag, and the gates were reluctantly opened, though not before guns had been ordered up to blow them in. The easy surrender was probably owing to the flight of the *rajah*. At the head of a troop of horse, heavily girdled with gold *mohurs*, he had forced a picket and ridden forth into the jungle. But the skirts of the wood were guarded by our cavalry.

After lurking in hiding for two hours, the *rajah* broke out prematurely: had he had the patience to wait a little longer, he might have effected his escape, for the brigadier, believing that all was over, had already ordered his men to dismiss. The stubborn resistance of Bhurtpore may be gauged by the fact that half the garrison were killed or wounded. The treasure taken was nearly half a million, and these were golden days, for the commander-in-chief for his share got £60,000, and the shower even reached the privates, who had £4 per man.

The campaign had justified Wellington's penetration and greatly raised Combermere's reputation. He had admirably handled a force of all arms, and showed himself possessed of qualities of which he bad scarcely been suspected. He had adapted himself to trying circumstances, gone to work circumspectly, and mastered his own impetuous temperament. In his strategy, he had displayed both initiative and decision; and, unlike Lynedoch at San Sebastian, where conscious of ignorance he had let himself be guided by the counsels of the professional engineers. He received the thanks of the governor general and of both Houses of Parliament, and besides the pecuniary reward, he gained a step in the peerage.

For nine months, while Lord Amherst was invalided in the hills,

Combermere was acting governor-general. The double work was severe, but he was indefatigable in the discharge of his duties. Calcutta in the hot season might have tried any constitution, but he kept his health by early exercise, regular habits, and extreme sobriety. He breakfasted lightly and dined at four, when the *aide-de-camp* on duty was victimised to keep his chief in countenance over an ascetic meal.

But seven was the regular dinner hour, when the staff assembled, and at great entertainments guests of many classes and conditions had hospitable welcome.

The host merely trifled with a little rice and some weak wine and water. Always energetic and delighting in change of scene, he made many progresses through the expanding empire. There were still a Great Mogul, with the shadow of power though the substance had departed, and a King of Oude, with feudatories of various degrees, but all with exorbitant pretensions. The progresses, being political, were pompous as the ceremonial receptions, and Combermere's letters and journals are full of picturesque description. His camps, with the attendants and interminable baggage trains, often contained 5000 souls. At the entry into Lucknow, like Marmion scattering angels on the drawbridge at Norham, the king, the commander-in-chief, and the resident were tossing handfuls of gold *mohurs* to the crowds.

At the close of the festivities the city was blazing with lights and the Jumna was illuminated with showers of fireworks. At the interview with the Mogul, though the resident, as was customary, removed his shoes, Combermere insisted that he and his staff should approach the presence in boots and spurs. But he could not escape the dress of honour, and to his disgust was invested over his uniform with a flowing robe of spangled muslin.

At Sirdanha he renewed acquaintance with that very remarkable woman, the Begum Sumroo. She had come to him in his camp before Bhurtpore, begging to be permitted to assist in the attack. The offer, which was courteously declined, was probably prompted with a view to sharing the spoils; for, although the treasure actually taken was great, there was a belief, and apparently a credible one, that fabulous riches were buried about the place. The *begum* was a famous Amazon who headed her armies in the field, and extended effective protection to the feeble descendant of Akbar when menaced in Delhi by his warlike feudatories.

Combermere and the lady were kindred spirits; regard and admiration seem to have been mutual She promised solemnly to remember him in her will—a promise she failed to keep—and persuaded him to pledge himself to act as guardian to her stepson, with whom he was to share her wealth. For the *begum* had been twice wedded, and both times to European adventurers. Her stepson and heir was the once well-known Dyce Sombre. When the youth came to England many years afterwards, plunging headlong into a career of folly, Combermere did his best) to redeem an embarrassing pledge which caused him infinite trouble and anxiety.

Possibly the missionaries and chaplains might have objected to one part of his policy. He made a point, of conciliating the Hindoo priests and falling in with, their superstitions; if he did not actually worship at their shrines, he offered sacrifices to their idols. The customary victim was a sheep: the head was severed at a blow, and it was diplomatically arranged that the gods should graciously accept the offering. So all the omens were invariably favourable when the progress moved forward on the next stage.

Then, as before, it was the familiar story; as Macaulay has put it tersely in the essay on Hastings: "Govern leniently and send more money," was the invariable refrain of the Board in Leadenhall Street. On one point Combermere gratified them, and at some sacrifice of popularity: addicted to personal display as he was, he suppressed the costly bodyguard, kept up for show. But in a more serious matter he crossed their wishes, and he protested earnestly against an edict of Lord William Bentinck, who had succeeded Lord Amherst as Governor-General. The field allowance granted to officers of the native army was to be arbitrarily reduced It was a paltry piece of false economy, for the saving was barely £20,000 a year.

The officers were thrown into a ferment of discontent, and they had the sympathy of the *sepoys*, who feared that their own pay might be cut down. Combermere laid stress on the danger of a discontented army, but the directors declined to recede from their decision, and he anticipated dismissal by handing in; his resignation.

4

After all his service in India did not help him pecuniarily, and, as his hospitalities had been profuse, he doubtless returned a poorer man. He had placed his Bhurtpore prize-money with a firm of Calcutta bankers. There were whispers as to their credit: he repeatedly desired to withdraw his funds, and was as often persuaded to delay on representations that the firm was perfectly solvent, but that the withdrawal of the commander-in-chief's confidence would be their death-blow. He had come back to England and gone down to Combermere Abbey when the news reached him that Alexanders' had failed. He and his family had been getting up a little dramatic performance: the host played his part with his accustomed serenity, and all went merry as a marriage bell. Not till the next morning at breakfast did he mention that he found himself poorer by £60,000.

In the preceding year, he had been gazetted colonel of the 1st Life Guards; consequently and *ex officio* he was one of the gold-sticks in waiting. As the gold-sticks were in personal attendance on the sovereign, it had been customary to swear them in as members of the Privy Council. Lord Combermere vainly expected an intimation which did not come. He had always been on cordial terms with the Duke of Clarence, and the explanation of the delay came from the outspoken sailor-king. His Majesty said that the Duke of Wellington had objected, and that the objection had only been overcome by his own imperative order.

More than that, it had been intended to create him an earl, and in the circumstances, nothing could have seemed more natural, but there again the duke stood in the way. In fact, the attitude of Wellington towards his lieutenant is almost as inexplicable as Combermere's sudden separation from his wife. The duke was straightforward to a fault, and his actions were governed by the strictest sense of honour and duly. Yet with Cotton he seems always to be blowing hot and cold; sometimes he ignores him in despatches; sometimes he gives him moderate, and at other times unstinted praise. He created a special command for him on the Guadiana, that he might retain his services; yet in a private letter he damned him with the faintest praise, after his splendid behaviour at Castrejon and Salamanca.

In later life, some of the letters were almost affectionate; and on his side, when the duke was to be laid to rest in St. Paul's, Combermere's letter to Hardinge, begging for an invitation to assist at the funeral, is that of a bereaved friend and sincere mourner, mindful of old times and grateful for many kindnesses.

Like his Grace of Richmond—the Lord March of the Peninsula— who, as he used to say at agricultural dinners, had taken to breeding South Downs when he sheathed his sword, Combermere betook himself to rearing cattle. His herd of Ayrshires was famous; he kept his bailiffs up to the mark, and looked carefully to his farming accounts. The balance was always on the wrong side, but that was inevitable. The best of landlords and a great builder of ornamental cottages, there was an annual gathering in an adjacent village, when tenants and neighbours met to celebrate his birthday. He seldom went to town when he could help it, and his old comrade, Lord Hill, who was tied to the Horse Guards by his duties, was always ready to relieve him as gold-stick in waiting.

But he had a special summons to take leave of King William on his deathbed, and as gold-stick he attended at the young queen's coronation. The wife from whom he was separated had died, and in 1838 he married for the third time. That proved a happy union, and, though already sixty-five, he had still a long period of matrimonial felicity to look forward to. The years immediately succeeding his marriage were passed between the abbey and travel on the Continent.

In 1852, he was somewhat mortified by being passed over for the master-generalship of the ordnance when Lord Hardinge received the appointment, but on the death of Wellington he was consoled with the constableship of the Tower. As constable and colonel of the 1st Life Guards, the veteran of eighty found ample occupation. He had commanded the regiment for thirty-five years; he had been careful in the selection of candidates for commissions; and he took a paternal interest in the officers, who had, one and all, been chosen by himself. When the Crimean War broke out, like an old war-horse he scented the battle from afar, and would gladly have taken the field again had there been a chance of his services being accepted.

After sixty-five years on the army lists, with the distinction he had gained, he felt it as a grievance that the baton of field-marshal had not been bestowed. The coveted honour came at last in the summer of 1855, when he was agreeably surprised by a graceful letter from Lord Hardinge. Men of exceptional strength and vigour are inclined to become morbidly sensitive to any indications of old age. Lord Combermere met with a mortifying contretemps at the grand volunteer review, when, ignoring his years, he appeared on horseback in the heavy uniform of the Life Guards and carrying the gold stick of office. His friends fancied they had found him a safe charger warranted to stand firing and shouting, but the horse got restive, took to plunging violently, and finally had to be led by one of the pages.

On the return of the procession he became altogether unmanageable, when His Lordship was persuaded to condescend to take a seat in one of the royal carriages. Nor was his annoyance lessened by comments in the papers next morning, with sympathetic condolences on his years and infirmities. His last public appearance was at the wedding of the Prince of Wales, when he was one of the witnesses to sign the register. For many seasons, as his friend Lord Londonderry said, he had been in the habit of "boiling himself" at Buxton, latterly passing his winters in the milder climate of Bath or Clifton.

It was at Clifton he died in 1865 in his ninety-second year: till he lay on his deathbed he had kept his faculties unimpaired, though his strength and vitality had been gradually decaying. He had outlived all his distinguished contemporaries, and when he passed away he was the last of Wellington's lieutenants. His resting-place might well have been in Westminster Abbey or St Paul's, but he was buried in the family vault in his own parish of Wrenbury.

www.ingramcontent.com/pod-product-compliance
Lightning Source LLC
Chambersburg PA
CBHW032042080426
42733CB00006B/168